Miscarriage

Other titles edited by Roy G Farquharson published by Quay Books,
Mark Allen Publishing Limited

Vignettes for the MRCOG, volume one
Vignettes for the MRCOG, volume two
Vignettes for the MRCOG, volume three

Miscarriage

edited by
Roy G Farquharson

Quay Books

Mark Allen
Publishing Ltd

Quay Books Division, Mark Allen Publishing Limited,
Jesses Farm, Snow Hill, Dinton, Wiltshire, SP3 5HN

British Library Cataloguing-in-Publication Data
A catalogue record is available for this book

© Mark Allen Publishing Ltd 2002
ISBN 1 85642 203 8

Printed in the UK by Cromwell Press, Trowbridge, Wiltshire

Contents

List of Contributors

Dr Paul Adinkra, Clinical Research Fellow, Department of Obstetrics and Gynaecology, Northwick Park Hospital, Watford Road, Harrow, Middlesex HA1 3UJ, UK

Dr Arvind Arumainathan, House Physician, Liverpool University, PO Box 147, Liverpool L69 7TF, UK

Ruth Bender Atik, National Director, Miscarriage Association, Clayton Hospital, Northgate, Wakefield WF1 3US, UK

Ware Branch, Professor and Vice-Chairman, HA and Edna Benning Chair, Department of Obstetrics and Gynaecology, Room 2B200 Medical Center, University of Utah, 50 North Medical Drive, Salt Lake City, Utah 84132, USA

Dr Leanne Bricker, Lecturer, Department of Obstetrics and Gynaecology, University of Liverpool, Liverpool Women's Hospital, Crown Street, Liverpool L8 7SS, UK

Dr Sara Brigham, Specialist Registrar, Department of Obstetrics and Gynaecology, Liverpool Women's Hospital, Crown Street, Liverpool L8 7SS, UK

Dr Andrew Carlin, Specialist Registrar in Obstetrics and Gynaecology, Liverpool Women's Hospital, Crown Street, Liverpool L8 7SS, UK

Dr Larry Chamley, Scientist, Department of Obstetrics and Gynaecology, National Women's Hospital, Auckland 3, New Zealand

Dr Andrew Drakeley, Specialist Registrar, Department of Obstetrics and Gynaecology, Liverpool Women's Hospital, Crown Street, Liverpool L8 7SS,UK

Sean Esplin MD, Department of Obstetrics and Gynecology,University of Utah Health Sciences Center, 50 North Medical Drive, Salt Lake City, Utah 84132, USA

William Fraser, Professor, Department of Clinical Chemistry, Royal Liverpool University Hospital, Prescot Street, Liverpool, UK

Michael Greaves, Professor, Department of Medicine and Therapeutics, Aberdeen University Medical School, Foresterhill, Aberdeen, AB25 2ZD, UK

Ann-Maria Hughes, Nurse, Miscarriage Clinic, Liverpool Women's Hospital, Crown Street, Liverpool L8 7SS, UK

John Jacobs, Senior Lecturer, Centre for Social Policy and Social Work, Essex House, University of Sussex, Falmer, Brighton BN1 9RQ, UK

Dr Ronnie F Lamont, Consultant in Obstetrics and Gynaecology, Northwick Park Hospital, Harrow, Middlesex HA1 3UJ, UK

Dr Hilary Liddell, Consultant in Obstetrics and Gynaecology, National Women's Hospital, Claude Road, Epsom, Auckland 3, New Zealand

Christine Moulder, Research Fellow, Centre for Social Policy and Social Work, Essex House, University of Sussex, Falmer, Brighton BN1 9RQ, UK

Neil Pattison, Professor, Department of Obstetrics and Gynaecology, Middlemore Hospital, Auckland 6, New Zealand

Dr Siobhan Quenby, Senior Lecturer, Department of Obstetrics and Gynaecology, University of Liverpool, Liverpool Women's Hospital, Crown Street, Liverpool L8 7SS, UK

Dr Jayne Shillito, Lecturer in Obstetrics and Gynaecology, St James's University Hospital, Leeds LS9 7TF, UK

Dr Cheng Hok Toh, Senior Lecturer in Haematology, Royal Liverpool University Hospital, Prescot Street, Liverpool, UK

Dr Joanne Topping, Consultant, Department of Obstetrics and Gynaecology, Liverpool Women's Hospital, Crown Street, Liverpool L8 7SS, UK

James J Walker, Professor, Department of Obstetrics and Gynaecology, St James's University Hospital, Leeds LS9 7TF, UK

Introduction

There are events in the womb of time as yet, undeliver'd.

William Shakespeare, *Othello*, i. iii. 369

Understanding miscarriage is as perplexing now, as it has been, since Malpas wrote his seminal paper in 1938 on 'A study of abortion sequences' from Liverpool Women's Hospital. There are many adverse events in the womb during pregnancy for which an explanation remains 'undelivered'. This lack of insight reflects our meagre understanding of normal early pregnancy development, let alone the occurrence of miscarriage, an event with untold consequences for individuals and couples alike.

The mystery of miscarriage continues to deepen when trying to explain to couples why all the maternal signals may be right yet an ultrasound scan shows a complete absence of a developing fetus when there have been no abnormal symptoms. The so-called afetal sac or embryo loss remains a virtually inexplicable paradox to the mother who rightly thinks that the absence of fetal development should automatically mean immediate miscarriage and expulsion of a non-viable process. This is one enigma among many that reveals more about the complexity of early pregnancy formation than explanation. The interaction between endometrial receptivity, genomic transmission and fetal development requires careful elucidation before any reasonable explanation can be formed about incomplete or incorrect processes that may cause miscarriage. A single over-arching and all encompassing explanation is no longer tenable.

Coping with miscarriage has been significantly improved by the supportive efforts of the Miscarriage Association who have done much to bring help to sufferers and spread the word of women's needs at a vulnerable time.

This book has been largely based on our experience at the Miscarriage Clinic. More importantly, it reflects the enormous influence that others have brought into this burgeoning area of frontline investigation and clinical need, that could be termed a Cinderella area for funded research. What started out as an enthusiastic group dealing with the commonest pregnancy complication has spread out over many areas to adopt a multidisciplinary approach, as well as overseas to colleagues with the same interest and focus. To pay adequate tribute to these friends and colleagues would be impossible. Their excellent contributions reflect the genuine interest and tremendous commitment that they have shown towards the appearance of this text.

Finally, this book may show evidence of repetition but this is strength of consensus in an area of controversy, rather than a weakness of content. All authors agree that if classification of pregnancy loss were adopted by clinicians world-wide then this book will have served good purpose.

Roy G Farquharson
Liverpool Women's Hospital
October, 2001

Section I:
Women-centred approach

I

Miscarriage and ectopic pregnancy: patients' experiences, professional help

Ruth Bender Atik

Miscarriage[1] is a common occurrence. It is estimated that one in four pregnancies ends in miscarriage (Smith, 1988), but from a clinical point of view it is generally regarded as a minor medical event. It is not usually life threatening and requires only brief medical or surgical intervention, if any. From the woman's perspective, and from that of her partner, it is rarely an insignificant event. At the very least it is a crisis, physically unpleasant and disruptive. For many, it is the loss of a much-wanted baby.

Women often perceive their miscarriage differently from the people around them. For example, comments made to women by family, friends and professionals include:

> *It's nature's way*
> *You're young — you can always have another one*
> *At least it happened early on*
> *It was only a bunch of cells*
> *It wasn't really a baby yet*
> *You should try to forget you were ever pregnant*

Women talking about their experience may say:

> *To my husband and me it was a baby and it was going to be*
> *our son or daughter*
> *This was my first baby, I wanted it so badly*
> *It seems like all my dreams and hopes have been shattered*

Despite improvements in medical care and an increase in public and media recognition of the misery which miscarriage can cause, there is still resistance on the part of both health professionals and the public to accept the emotional dimension of miscarriage. Clinicians may refer to implantation failure, anembryonic pregnancy, or

---

1 The term miscarriage can be taken generally to include ectopic and molar pregnancy, unless these conditions are specified in the text. The generic term 'pregnancy loss' is also used occasionally

embryonic or fetal demise. The professional support or even acknowledgement routinely provided for miscarrying women is limited. Family, friends and colleagues may attempt to minimise distress with comments which deny the reality of the pregnancy. Some couples will find this helpful and reassuring. For others such comments, however well meant, will only exacerbate their distress.

Individuality of response

There is no single emotional response to the experience of miscarriage and it is difficult to predict how women will respond or for how long. Some will be devastated, their distress persisting for some months, others will adapt to the miscarriage quite quickly and carry on with their lives. Contrary to conventional wisdom, the degree of distress is not necessarily proportionate to the length of gestation nor the length of time a woman has known of her pregnancy. A miscarriage at eight weeks may be as distressing to one woman as a sixteen-week loss is to another, however different the physical experience. A woman with an ectopic pregnancy may find out that she is pregnant only at diagnosis, yet still experience intense feelings of grief.

Studies show that miscarriage can have a significant impact on many women's lives (Slade, 1994; Robinson *et al*, 1994) and that for a minority the consequences may be severe and prolonged (Cordle and Prettyman, 1994). Many factors have been suggested in the research literature as determining women's reactions to a miscarriage, although no firm conclusions can be drawn (Friedman and Gath, 1989; Lasker and Toedter, 1991; Slade 1994).

As with any illness or medical condition, patients with an identical diagnosis will display different reactions (Moulder, 1998, 2001). Each pregnancy has a meaning and physical process of its own which will influence the way the miscarriage is experienced. Women who miscarry more than once may react differently to each loss. A miscarriage is unique to that particular woman at that particular time.

Women's accounts of their experiences suggest that feelings about the pregnancy, reproductive history, personal circumstances, personality, culture and personal style are some of the factors to take into account in considering how they react to a miscarriage.

Pregnancy history: Previous pregnancy loss may make miscarriage harder to bear, particularly if some form of treatment had been tried on this occasion. A history of recurrent miscarriage will rarely make the experience easier to cope with, even if it means that the miscarriage is half expected. Similarly, if a miscarriage occurred at a later gestation than a previous loss, raised hopes that this pregnancy was going to be successful will have been shattered. Feelings, long buried, about a previous termination of pregnancy may resurface when a woman miscarries. Whatever the reason for the termination, women may feel guilt and self-blame when miscarriage occurs.

Fertility problems: Difficulties in conceiving can make miscarriage extremely distressing. Women's feelings about the miscarriage may be affected by whether the pregnancy was achieved naturally or by assisted conception. The swing from the elation of a confirmed pregnancy to the shock of its loss is likely to be felt keenly. Barriers to trying again, emotional and/or financial, can exacerbate the problem. For some women, this may have been their last chance of a pregnancy.

Current pregnancy: A long period of uncertainty as to the viability of the pregnancy, with continuing symptoms and inconclusive scans, may mean that the final diagnosis that the pregnancy has ended brings elements of relief. There may also be a sense of relief if the pregnancy was unwanted and especially if the woman had contemplated termination. Equally, however, it may cause feelings of guilt and a belief that negative thoughts caused the miscarriage.

Ectopic and molar pregnancy: Ectopic pregnancy is likely to compromise future fertility, whether because of a decreased chance of pregnancy or because of a higher risk of another ectopic pregnancy, or both. A woman may feel that she has lost not only her baby, but also some of the hope of ever having a baby. Women with the diagnosis of molar pregnancy may have an even more complex reaction. Not only are they warned not to conceive until completion of several months' follow-up, but they also have to deal with real anxieties about their future health.

Social and personal factors: Older women are likely to be concerned about the chances of conception and the increasing risk of miscarriage or fetal abnormalities. Women whose social, cultural or religious background holds childbearing as being of great importance may be devastated by the experience of miscarriage, and particularly by recurrent loss. Miscarriage may come as a considerable blow if the birth of a baby was crucial to the relationship. Personality and personal style are very likely to affect the way in which women and their partners react to miscarriage. While some may take the view that the pregnancy 'was not meant to be', others may experience profound distress. Women will bring with them to the miscarriage their past life experience and their hopes for the future.

Common themes in pregnancy loss

While it is important to guard against making assumptions, there are common themes which emerge in couples' accounts of pregnancy loss.

Loss

> *I feel so empty and lost, I wonder if I'm going mad.*
>
> *I feel like I'm running and looking and never finding anything. I feel like I'm broken and I can't fix it.*

For many, if not most women, miscarriage represents the loss of a baby. This may be at odds with the clinical definition of what has been lost, but it does reflect common language and beliefs. The announcement of a pregnancy usually prompts questions and calculations as to when the baby is due. Forward planning is often baby-centred. When the pregnancy ends abruptly, it represents a multiple loss — of the baby and of the hopes and plans that accompanied it as well as loss of the parental role. Women who suffer an ectopic pregnancy are, in addition, likely to lose some degree of fertility, perhaps all.

Grief

> *I can't stop crying, and its been weeks now...*
>
> *Everyone thinks I should be over it now, that I should just have another baby.*

Feelings of grief may be intense and persist over time. For some this is an instant reaction, whereas others may experience a wave of grief some time after the event. Calls to the Miscarriage Association helpline suggest that critical times are the first period after a miscarriage, the due date and the first anniversary of the loss — often long after the woman feels she has recovered. Such feelings are not necessarily erased by the birth of a subsequent baby — indeed, this may bring previously repressed feelings to the surface. Feelings of grief may be complicated in multiple pregnancy, when one (or more) sibling dies, but one (or more) survives. Here, grief is likely to be tempered with, but not obliterated by, relief.

Anxiety and fear

I'm so frightened of getting pregnant again — what if it's another ectopic?

Bleeding and pain in pregnancy create anxiety; about what is happening, what it means for the baby and for the mother, and about what might happen next. A study of women who were scanned because of bleeding in early pregnancy showed that anxiety levels remained high even among women whose pregnancy was shown to be continuing (Grant, 1997). In addition, miscarriage often arouses fear of a similar outcome in any future pregnancies (Statham and Green, 1994).

Ectopic pregnancy is often diagnosed and managed in an atmosphere of high tension. The woman may herself have suspected that something was wrong but there may have been some delay before diagnosis. The speed of events can be dramatic, especially if the woman is at the point of collapse and this can be very frightening for both the woman and her partner.

Molar pregnancy can also cause considerable anxiety, especially since most women will be told of the diagnosis some time after the miscarriage. Just as they begin to come to terms with their loss, they are given a diagnosis which they and even their GP may not understand. The headed notepaper on their follow-up letter immediately creates fear that they have been diagnosed as having cancer and lack of clear information and explanation will increase fears for the future.

Shock and numbness

I had no idea anything was wrong.

I don't seem to feel anything.

Some women who appear to cope well at the time of miscarriage (or of its diagnosis, which may be later) may be in a state of emotional shock. This may be particularly true for women who did not know they were pregnant — particularly if the diagnosis is ectopic pregnancy —

and for those where a routine scan picks up anembryonic pregnancy or missed miscarriage.

Anger, guilt and self-blame

Why should it happen to me? I did everything by the book.

I feel a failure as a mother, I feel a failure as a wife, and I feel a failure as a woman.

Anger is a common component of bereavement and is no less common in miscarriage. It may be directed at one's partner, at medical or nursing staff, at other visibly pregnant women or mothers with babies, or at God or fate. It is very often directed inwards, especially in the absence of other explanations, with either partner assuming that something they did caused the miscarriage. Feelings of failure, particularly in comparison with friends and family, may also be present.

Powerlessness and confusion

I felt like I was on a conveyor belt and couldn't get off.

Women and their partners expect to be able to control their fertility. They are often shocked to find that there is nothing which they or anyone else can do to stop a miscarriage and this can create a sense of powerlessness. This can be exacerbated by being in a hospital system in which their control of what takes place is even more diminished, as they are passed from department to department or from person to person, often with little explanation.

The need for explanations

I feel I need some factual information on why miscarriage happens.

Why won't they do some tests and tell me why it happened?

Probably the two most common questions asked of doctors are; Why did it happen? and, Will it happen again? The first question aims to find an explanation, preferably one which can be used to reduce the risk next time. In the absence of a clear answer — and there rarely is one — women (and sometimes their partners) will assume that the miscarriage was their fault. A guide to the risks of a further miscarriage, or another ectopic or molar pregnancy, can help in deciding whether to try again. If the decision is yes, it can provide a way of managing anxiety.

Good practice

One of the nurses sat with me while I cried and they answered every question I asked.

We weren't told what to expect or given any written information. I felt as if I was on a conveyor belt. Some situation to be dealt with, not a person with emotions and feelings.

The doctor seemed to think I should be grateful that something imperfect had been taken away.

My GP has been very good and concerned [although] other than saying give it a couple of months before trying again, she has not offered me any information or advice.

The management of pregnancy loss in hospital and in the community health setting can have a major impact on patients' perceptions and memories of this event. Anecdotal evidence (Miscarriage Association, 1998) suggests that while women generally feel physically well cared for during and immediately after miscarriage, they are very often unhappy at what they perceive as insensitive management. The research literature confirms women's dissatisfaction with medical care when they miscarry (Lee and Slade, 1996; Conway, 1995). Lack of information and staff attitudes are often identified as the basis of women's criticisms of their care (Moohan *et al*, 1994) along with the insensitive use of language and lack of follow-up care. Health professionals are identified as persistently failing to appreciate the personal significance of early miscarriage (Cecil, 1994).

While thoughtless practice can make a negative experience even worse, care around the following key issues can help patients.

Acknowledgement of the event

It might be commonplace for them, but it wasn't for me.

In the pressured environment of A&E or even a designated early pregnancy unit, it is easy to forget that miscarriage is likely to be a significant event for the woman or couple involved. There may be anxiety about what to say and how to say it, or concern about opening the floodgates for an already distressed patient. Members of the healthcare team with personal experience of pregnancy loss may find that they too become distressed when caring for patients in this situation.

While saying nothing may feel the safest bet, it is a missed opportunity. Comments intended to minimise distress, ie. 'It's only a group of cells at this stage' or, 'Never mind, you can always have another one', may well exacerbate it. A simple acknowledgement, 'I'm sorry you've lost your baby', is likely to be perceived and remembered as caring and compassionate.

Explanations and information

Why do I have to have another scan next week? Why did I miscarry? Was it something I did? What's a D&C? How long will I bleed? When can I try again?

I have noted above that miscarriage is often a frightening experience. The questions above are some of those most frequently asked on the Miscarriage Association's helpline and it seems clear that answers, however general, can help reduce anxiety and confusion. Our experience strongly suggests that women want information and explanations about their pregnancy, the miscarriage, hospital procedures and the implications for the future, both short and long-term.

Information needs to be clear, direct and free from jargon. If there is no obvious explanation for a miscarriage or statistic on future risks, it is better to say so than to suggest that this is not a reasonable question. Providing more general information and explanations is even better.

Ensuring sensitive language and practice

This time, they called it a missed miscarriage, not a missed abortion like the first time. What a difference that made.

Information should be not only clear and jargon-free, it also needs to be patient-sensitive. Terms such as missed abortion or recurrent abortion are no longer acceptable (RCOG, 2000), and even a term such as incompetent cervix can appear to patients to have a rather accusatory ring.

In our experience, most women going through pregnancy loss would prefer their carers to refer to the baby rather than to the foetus, the pregnancy or the products. This may not be equally true for women undergoing elective terminations (though it might) and health professionals might be best advised to take their cue from the language their patient uses.

Sensitive practice allows enough flexibility to take account of patients' needs and preferences. Even if a specialised early pregnancy assessment unit can offer scan, diagnosis and ERPC within a day, some women may prefer to be given the option of coming back for the ERPC another day, or indeed, the choice of surgical, medical or expectant management. In a situation where events are moving very quickly and where they may well feel powerless, most women will appreciate being given options and time to choose between them, though some may prefer the medical team to make a recommendation. Situations where patients cannot be offered time to think (such as a ruptured ectopic) will be relatively rare.

The setting for care is also important. Not all hospitals will be able to offer a designated miscarriage unit, but many women will be particularly distressed by being placed next to someone who is heavily pregnant or someone who is waiting for a termination of pregnancy. Even if the setting is not ideal, staff can make the woman feel expected and cared for, rather than someone who does not fit in and is best avoided.

Staff need to be aware of hospital policy and practice on the disposal of fetal remains and be prepared to answer questions honestly and sensitively. If hospital policy is to incinerate fetal tissue, then it is not appropriate to refer to this as cremation, however kind the intention. If parents request further details, this 'white lie' is likely to increase distress. Doctors, nurses and midwives all have a part to play in promoting sensitive disposal (SANDS, 1992; Kohner and Leftwich, 1995; Royal College of Nursing, 2001) and while some parents will not wish to discuss this, the views and wishes of those who do should be treated with respect.

Support and information

> *The hospital gave me a leaflet with this number. I've had it for months.*

Support may be given in hospital at the time of diagnosis or management or it might be better offered after the woman has gone home. Given the brief nature of hospital care, there may not be time to offer anything other than an acknowledgement of the loss, and information about support services available may not be remembered. Providing written details for patients to take home gives them the opportunity to consider these in their own time.

Written information about miscarriage, ectopic or molar pregnancy is also important. Some hospitals provide a series of leaflets which are suitable for patients attending for scanning; one excellent example offers information on bleeding in pregnancy, the scanning procedure, possible outcomes and management, and follow-up (Leeds Teaching Hospitals NHS Trust, 2000). A number of hospitals simply provide a brief information sheet on self-care after ERPC and others provide one or several of the Miscarriage Association's leaflets. In all cases, a contact point for queries and concerns is crucial, whether this is the hospital, the GP, community midwife or patient organisation.

We have noted that while requests for information are most common in the days following pregnancy loss, requests for support are more likely to come several weeks or months down the line. Critical times are the first menstrual period, the beginning of the next pregnancy, the due date and the anniversary of the miscarriage.

Follow-up

> *I really thought they'd tell me why it had gone wrong, but the doctor hadn't even read my notes and seemed to think I was there for a postnatal check.*

There is considerable variation in the provision of follow-up after pregnancy loss, with some hospitals offering an outpatient appointment six weeks later, some referring this to the GP and many making no mention of follow-up at all. It is important to be aware that where a follow-up appointment is offered, women and their partners tend to invest much hope in it. They anticipate being told more about the cause of the loss and being given advice for the next pregnancy in order to avoid a recurrence.

Clarity and honesty are the key words here. Information about the purpose and nature of the follow-up appointment will help both patient and clinician as will reading the case-notes before talking to the patient.

The next pregnancy

I've had two miscarriages, at eight and eleven weeks. I'm fourteen weeks now but I just can't relax — I feel like I'm just waiting for things to go wrong again.

Pregnancy after miscarriage or ectopic pregnancy is very often filled with a mixture of hope and anxiety. The anxiety may diminish considerably after the date of the previous loss/es or it may continue and even transfer to a potential hazard later in the pregnancy. The support and reassurance of the medical team can be crucial. There is evidence to suggest that 'tender loving care' alone is a potent factor in pregnancy success after idiopathic recurrent miscarriage (Stray Pederson and Stray-Pederson, 1983; Liddell *et al*, 1991).

Women often feel guilty about being anxious and 'troubling the doctor'. They worry too that anxiety will itself increase the risk of miscarriage, as one women neatly put it: 'It's bad enough feeling anxious without being anxious about it'. It can be helpful to rephrase the expression 'over-anxious' into 'understandably anxious' and to note that there is no evidence that anxiety is harmful to pregnancy. Support organisations may be particularly helpful at this time.

Early scans may offer such reassurance, but equally they may not, especially if an early scan is inconclusive and needs repeating. Ideally, doctor and patient should discuss the relative benefits and disadvantages of early scanning and make a joint plan for care.

Summary

The loss of a baby in pregnancy is generally a significant and distressing life event. The care provided by the healthcare team can make a considerable difference to the way this experience is perceived and worked through. Health professionals have a responsibility to be sensitive to individual needs, to provide clear information where this is wanted, to give women choice where that is possible, to be prepared to discuss sensitive and difficult issues and to make best use of other sources of help.

The Miscarriage Association is a national charity which works to complement professional care. We offer a staffed helpline, co-ordinate a UK-wide network of telephone contacts and support groups and provide information on pregnancy loss, some in Asian languages and on tape. For further details, contact: The Miscarriage Association, c/o Clayton Hospital, Northgate, Wakefield WF1 3JS.
Tel: 01924 200799; e-mail: miscarriage association@care4free.net; www.miscarriageassociation.org.uk

References

Cecil R (1994) Women's views of care. *J Reproductive Infant Psychol* **12**(1)

Conway K (1995) Miscarriage experience and the role of support systems: A pilot study. *Br J Med Psychol* **68**: 259–67

Cordle CJ, Prettyman RJ (1994) A two-year follow-up of women who have experienced early miscarriage. *J Reproductive Infant Psychol* **12**(1)

Friedman T, Gath D (1989) The psychiatric consequences of spontaneous abortion. *Br J Psychiatry* **155**: 810–13

Grant A (1997) *A study of the psychological responses of women immediately after spontaneous and threatened miscarriage.* Leeds University Hospital, St James's, unpublished dissertation

Lasker JM, Toedter LJ (1991) Acute venous chronic grief: the case of pregnancy loss. *Am J Orthopsychiatry* **61**: 510–22

Lee C, Slade P (1996) Miscarriage as a traumatic event: A review of the literature and new implications for intervention. *J Psychosom Res* **40**: 235–44

Leeds Teaching Hospitals NHS Trust (2000) *What happens next: a guide*

Moohan J, Ashe RG, Cecil R (1994) The management of miscarriage: results from a survey at one hospital. *J Reproductive Infant Psychol* **12**(1)

Moulder C (2001) *Miscarriage: women's experiences and needs.* Revised edn. Routledge, London

Moulder C (1998) *Understanding pregnancy loss: perspectives and issues in care.* Macmillan Press, London

Miscarriage Association (1998) *Survey of 300 women, self-selected through questionnaire in popular women's magazine.* Unpublished

Oakley A, McPherson A, Roberts H (1990) *Miscarriage.* Penguin, London

Robinson ER, Stirzinger R, Stewart D, Ralevski E (1994) Psychological reactions in women followed for one year after miscarriage. *J Reproductive Infant Psychol* **12**(1)

Royal College of Nursing (2001) *Sensitive disposal of all fetal remains: guidance for nurses and midwives*. RCN, London

Royal College of Obstetricians and Gynaecologists (2000) *The management of early pregnancy loss, Guideline No. 25*. RCOG, London

Slade P (1994) Predicting the psychological impact of miscarriage. *J Reproductive Infant Psychol* **12**(1)

Smith NC (1988) Epidemiology of spontaneous abortion. *Contemp Rev Obstet Gynaecol* **1**: 43–8

Statham H, Green JM (1994) The effects of miscarriage and other 'unsuccessful' pregnancies on feelings early in a subsequent pregnancy. *J Reproductive Infant Psychol* **12**(1)

Further reading

Kohner N, Leftwich A (1995) *Pregnancy loss and the death of a baby: a training pack for professionals*. National Extension College Trust Ltd, 18 Brooklands Avenue, Cambridge, CB2 2HN, 1995
Training pack aimed at those working with people experiencing pregnancy loss.

Leon IG (1990) *When a baby dies. Psychotherapy for pregnancy and newborn loss*. Yale University Press
A sensitive book about the psychodynamics of pregnancy loss and issues in providing therapeutic help.

Mander R (1994) *Loss and bereavement in childbearing*. Blackwell, Oxford
A source book for midwives, research based and personal accounts from midwives.

Moulder C (1999) Miscarriage: preparing SHO's for their role in hospital care. *J Obstet Gynaecol* **19**(1)

Moulder C (1990) *Miscarriage: Guidelines for Good Practice*. Miscarriage Association, Wakefield

Stillbirth and Neonatal Death Society (1995) *Pregnancy loss and the death of a baby: Guidelines for Professionals*. SANDS, London
A guide for professionals to the needs of women and families experiencing miscarriage, stillbirth, neonatal death and the termination of pregnancy. Covers all aspects of care.

Stillbirth and Neonatal Death Society (1992) *A dignified ending*. SANDS, London
Report of small qualitative research study into disposal of the body or remains of a pregnancy before twenty-eight weeks' gestation; recommendations for good practice.

Schott J, Henley A (1996) *Culture, Religion and Childbearing in a Multi-racial Society*. Butterworths, London
An excellent resource for professionals providing care in pregnancy loss; includes information about different cultures and religions, attitudes to grieving and funerals.

2

Researching pregnancy loss: the case for qualitative research

Christine Moulder, John Jacobs

Aim

Good quality care in the field of pregnancy loss must be based in part on women's and health professionals' experiences of care. We must enable both groups to talk about matters which are often highly charged with feelings of loss, grief, guilt, anger and fear. Despite the lip service paid to this point of view in NHS policy documents,[1] the reality remains that research based on the statistical analyses of large samples is more highly valued and more easily attracts research funding than do smaller qualitative studies which explore in greater depth the complexities of individual experience. In this chapter we argue the case for qualitative research in the development of good practice.

We illustrate our argument with examples of the experience and management of pregnancy loss drawn from a case study in one hospital (Moulder, 1998). The purpose of the research was to identify ways of improving professional practice. The experiences of twenty women were documented over a six-month period together with those of their health professionals. The research set out to understand women's experiences of pregnancy loss and the health care that was provided and the health professionals' experiences of providing that care.

Part I: Qualitative research; a poor relation?

Whereas quantitative research focuses on the relationship between

---

1 Department of Health (1993) *Changing Childbirth: part I.* Report of the Expert Maternity Group, HMSO, London
National Health Executive (1996) *Patient partnership: building a collaborative strategy.* Department of Health, London

variables and the testing of hypotheses, qualitative research aims to give a better understanding of social phenomena by focusing on how people experience their world. The aim of qualitative research is succinctly put by Mays and Pope (1996: 4) as, 'the development of concepts which help us to understand social phenomena in natural (rather than experimental) settings, giving due emphasis to the meanings, experiences, and views of all the participants.'

We do not claim that qualitative research is superior to quantitative but rather that it reaches parts that quantitative methods cannot reach.

> *Because health care deals with people and people are, on the whole, more complex than the subjects of the natural sciences, there is a whole set of questions about human interaction, and how people interpret interaction, which health professionals may need answers to. Experimental and quantitative methods are less well suited to answer these questions.*
>
> Mays and Pope, 1996: 5

A qualitative approach:

- enables access to areas of social life that lie beyond the scope of quantitative research
- offers unique insights into processes and feelings
- is about generating rather than testing hypotheses
- is about different ways of making sense of the world, discovering the views and meanings of those being researched
- is about diverse interpretations and is about explanation.

Its hallmark is its focus on the social meanings for the participants.

Why is qualitative research considered problematic?

Qualitative research has a long and reputable history in the social sciences and is becoming increasingly acceptable in health research (eg. Coffey and Atkinson, 1996; Mason, 1996; Lofland and Lofland, 1995; Woolcott, 1994.) Nevertheless, a qualitative approach continues to arouse criticism, particularly among those from a more traditional scientific background. The culture of the health service is one in which a quantitative approach predominates. Cost effectiveness, measuring outcomes, evaluation and evidence-based practice are the preoccupations of the current climate. Evidence-based practice assumes that if research is sufficiently rigorous the 'truth' will be revealed, which will form the basis for professional practice. (Trinder, 1996.) What counts as evidence is usually what can be easily measured rather than the more complex process or the feelings that may underlie the indicators of the outcome. In this culture, understanding individual experience, taking feelings and process into account may be undervalued.

The criteria used in judging qualitative research often appear to be more suited to quantitative projects. Application forms for research funding are geared to quantitative research and ask questions about the statistical basis for the sample and details of statistical analysis that will be used. The demands for academic rigour often seem to be equated with forcing qualitative research into a quantitative mould with pressure to put numbers to experiences that ultimately cannot be quantified. Publication of qualitative research in medical journals takes a poor second place.

The interpretative nature of qualitative research poses problems and attempts have been made to address this issue (Mays and Pope, 1996; Bluff, 1997; Britten *et al*, 1995). All researchers bring with them their own conceptual framework based on personal experience. This may colour the decisions made about the way the research is conceived, the methods adopted and the analysis of the data. The integrity, judgement and interpretation of the researcher are integral to qualitative research. Different researchers may give aspects of the findings different emphases if not different interpretations. Those who believe that evidence must lead to the one revealed truth will see this as problematic. Those who think that the value of qualitative research lies in its ability to uncover complexities, probe relationships between perspectives and suggest new possibilities arising from the data will not.

Analysis

Another problematic aspect of qualitative research is the sheer wealth of data it can generate. This poses problems of analysis which invariably involve the researcher imposing some sort of order on the raw data (Coffey and Atkinson, 1996; Dey, 1993). This is often presented as a possible source of bias which may vitiate the results.

However, order has to be imposed on raw data at some stage, whatever method is being used, and in this respect qualitative research is no different from quantitative.

The analysis will depend on the purpose of the research. The same data can be used for generating new hypotheses, providing evidence of the links between policy and practice, describing the social relations between different groups, as evidence of the cultural norms of particular groups and so on. There is no right way to analyse the data, only ways that are appropriate to the purpose. This again may make those schooled in the rigours of scientific analysis feel sceptical about what such different interpretations have to offer. If the analysis is able to transform and interpret the data to capture the complexity of the social world we seek to understand and lead on to better practice, this will justify the approach taken.

The research findings

Qualitative research often addresses complex issues where the nature of the topic militates against the concise summary of neat conclusions. The results are more likely to open up complexity and diversity and point to conflicting perspectives. One feature of qualitative research is that the results may make life more difficult. The health service needs research with clear answers to difficult questions; qualitative research may not do this in the straightforward way that is required. For example, the pregnancy loss study revealed the diversity of women's experiences and the problems this posed for managers and for professionals in providing care appropriate to individual women. By confirming that good care takes account of the needs, views, and personalities of the individual women and is not amenable to a formulaic approach it complicated what could have been a simpler, though misguided, approach. But, in doing so, it demonstrated those respects where the perspectives of the health professionals were broadly congruent with those of the women and those where they were not; thereby confirming them in some of their judgements and offering the opportunity to rethink others.

Learning from the conclusions

The validity of findings drawn from what is often a small sample is perhaps the most damning criticism levelled at qualitative research. The time-consuming nature of such research and the shortage of funding to undertake work on the grand scale mean that case studies are often based on small samples in one location. Concern is therefore expressed that the research is not applicable to other locations. This criticism stems from a misunderstanding about the nature of qualitative research and from the misguided attempt to fit it into the mould of quantitative research. One may find from talking to only one woman that she found that no-one gave her the time to discuss why she had miscarried. The issues this raises may generate a number of questions about the process of care she has been through. The more women one talks to the clearer the answers to these questions may become, or, more probably, the more variations on the theme will emerge. Looking at one case will illuminate important factors that need further investigation and, together with the points that emerge from the other women studied, will contribute to a better understanding of the process of care.

Part 2: The value of qualitative research in health care

Having suggested reasons why qualitative research has to struggle to gain acceptability in the hard-nosed world of medical science we argue that the insights it provides offer valuable guides to improving practice.

The pregnancy loss study is used as one example. A full account of the research is provided elsewhere (Moulder, 1998). The purpose here is to draw on certain aspects of the research to illustrate the following issues about qualitative research:

- the appropriateness of the choice of method
- the nature of the research interviews
- the role of the researcher and the need for consultation and supervision
- the nature of the research findings
- the value of the findings.

The pregnancy loss project

The research, funded by the Department of Health, was designed to underpin *Pregnancy loss and the death of a baby: Guidelines for Professionals* published by the Stillbirth and Neonatal Death Society (SANDS, 1995).

The study consisted of semi-structured interviews with twenty women selected from one large urban hospital to represent the different categories of pregnancy loss together with the ninety-six health professionals whom they identified as significant in their care. The work on the SANDS Guidelines had identified the elements of health care that were important and defined the boundaries of the research. The overriding factor in determining the approach was the need to take into account the sensitive nature of the topic.

Choice of method: a sensitive topic

Many aspects of pregnancy loss are frequently unacknowledged and even taboo. We do not like to think about what a preterm, malformed baby may look like, the method of disposal for the products of conception after a first-trimester miscarriage or how we feel about the difficult issues that pregnancy loss raises. They are issues we do not normally discuss and may actively protect ourselves from, whether as a woman going through the experience or as a health professional participating in the care. When we do think about them they may arouse strong feelings of revulsion or fear.

As well as responding to their patients' distress, staff providing the care will be faced with the feelings aroused in themselves by the distressing nature of the experience. For example, they may fear that they have contributed to their patient's distress by something they did or didn't do. However, the opportunity to discuss and explore these feelings is often limited. The research may be perceived as additionally threatening to staff, who find their professional practice under scrutiny and may raise anxieties about management's views of their work.

For all these reasons pregnancy loss is a sensitive subject to research. Choosing a research method that took into account the emotional nature of the experience as well as the political and ethical sensitivities that surround it was vital. It was essential that the method adopted enabled the researcher to access the information required and allowed for the meaning of the experience and the feelings it engendered to be expressed and explored in a safe and constructive way that protected the interviewees. This pointed to the use of semi-structured interviews.

The nature of the research interviews

Nicky Britten succinctly summarises the purpose of the research interview in a study such as this:

> *In a qualitative research interview the aim is to discover the interviewee's own framework of meanings and the research task is to avoid imposing the researcher's structures and assumptions as far as possible. The researcher needs to remain open to the possibility that the concepts and variables that emerge may be very different from those that might have been predicted at the outset.*

Britten, 1996: 29

Interviews for this purpose are different from clinical interviews or more structured research interviews and place demands on the interviewer. A balance had to be achieved between creating the optimum environment and gaining the necessary information.

Based on areas of care identified in the SANDS guidelines, a review of the literature and issues identified in discussions with key informants, interview schedules were prepared. There were specific topics that needed to be covered but open-ended questions were asked. Prompts were used to ensure that the different aspects of care that they were likely to have encountered were covered.

For some, the act of telling their story became an exploration which they used to re-evaluate their experience. For example, one senior registrar reflected on his ignorance of certain aspects of the healthcare system and the inadequacy of his explanations for some women. He did not simply tell his story but found himself forced to rethink his practice. For him the interview was a learning experience.

A qualitative approach emphasises the role of the researcher as one who engages with the people being studied. Ann Oakley arguing for a feminist methodology, which has parallels with qualitative research in general, illustrates this point:

> *It requires, further, that the mythology of 'hygienic research' with its accompanying mystification of the researcher and the researched as objective instruments of data production be replaced by the recognition that personal involvement is more than dangerous bias — it is the condition under which people come to know each other and to admit others into their lives.*

> Oakley, 1981: 3

The quality of the relationship established with the interviewees was central to the research (Cannon, 1989). The interviewers aimed to create a climate of trust where people felt able to tell their story and share their experience; they had to be approachable and exude a sense of comfort with the subject matter and confidence that difficult subjects could be talked about and anxieties contained. The interviews were often more anxiety provoking for the professionals, who may have felt that their professional practice and expertise were being judged, than for the women, who usually welcomed the opportunity to talk about their experience.

The need for consultation and supervision

Supervision and consultation for the researchers in this study were provided by colleagues and by an independent psychotherapist. The researchers needed the opportunity to talk about the impact of the interviews on them, and also to explore the nuances of individual cases and alternative ways of making sense of emerging themes. It was useful to be able to discuss issues that were in direct conflict with the research literature or received wisdom, for example, women wanting to get pregnant again quickly and appearing to be both mourning their dead baby and simultaneously investing in their next pregnancy.

The research findings: the richness of the material

The themes that emerged from over a hundred interviews provided insights into the process of care from both patient and professional perspectives. They showed how women experienced the different stages of their care from the awareness that something had gone wrong with the pregnancy through to their discharge from hospital and the follow-up care that they may or may not have had. They showed what was important to the women; what they valued in the staff and what made them feel uncared for. The following are some of the examples of the issues it was possible to explore, drawing on the interview material:

❖ The match and mismatch between the women's perceptions and those of the staff.

❖ The fit between what the women wanted and the way health care was organised.

❖ The lack of opportunity for women to talk about the emotional aspects of early miscarriage despite health professionals' beliefs to the contrary.

❖ The different meanings women gave to early pregnancy and the ways in which this was largely unrecognised by professionals.

❖ Women's needs for information about the remains of an early pregnancy and the difficulty in asking for and getting this information.

❖ The difficulty for women in making informed choices when in distress.

❖ The implications of the nature of the relationship between a woman and the midwife caring for her during the labour and delivery of a dead or malformed baby.

❖ The difficulty some women have in accepting the help that is offered.

Similarly, the data showed what the staff experienced dealing with women in distress; how they handled giving information; how they felt about offering comfort and what the difficulties and satisfactions were for them in providing care. The interviews built up a picture of the problems identified and enabled us to explore the different cultures of the professional groups and the effects that these had on aspects of their professional behaviour. It was possible to explore the following:

❖ How staff coped with their own feelings about pain, disfigurement, death and loss.

❖ How staff prepared parents for seeing their dead and possibly deformed baby and facilitated the grieving process.

❖ How staff helped women to make choices (about, for example, whether to see their dead baby, what level of pain relief to have).

❖ The complexity of adequately preparing women for the labour and delivery of a dead and/or malformed baby.

❖ How staff felt about the ever present possibility of disaster and the fear of litigation.

To illustrate in more detail the kinds of issues the research was able to elucidate and the richness of the material, we focus on three topics:

1. The nature of professional support.
2. Communication between staff and the women.
3. An overview of the process of care.

Professional support

The following brief extract from an interview with a senior house officer illustrates how the health professionals described their need for support.

> *It's either sink or swim right from medical school, all the way through and the people who can't handle it are the ones who drop out. ... you just learn your own defences And in medicine.., there's not much support goes on really, it's quite sort of hierarchical. ... it's like admitting defeat or weakness and you don't want to do that to your colleagues. ... it's not really team work a lot of the time. ... you are almost in competition with people sometimes which I know that you shouldn't be but in reality that's what it's like.*

Here we begin to glimpse the kind of world this junior doctor inhabits, a world where 'you either sink or swim' and where to ask for support is a sign of weakness. He inhabits a 'hierarchical world' where colleagues are seen not as sources of potential help but as competitors. At the same time, there is a recognition that it 'shouldn't be' like that. This begins to raise questions about how junior doctors cope with the heavy emotional load so that they aren't the ones who 'drop out'.

Other hospital doctors spoke in a similar vein. Comments such as, 'you're expected to get on with the next bit of work', 'there is very little support really', 'when something dreadful happens you are just meant to get on with it' were mentioned by doctors at all levels of seniority. A junior doctor would not ask for support because to do so would be seen as a sign of weakness which may impede his way up the career ladder; a consultant was reluctant to ask for it because consultants are supposed to know what they're doing and to ask for emotional support would 'reflect on your professional manner'. What might seem to be one obvious way of coping with the emotional load, looking for support from colleagues, appeared to be blocked because of the possible repercussions on the doctors' professional standing.

At the same time most doctors said how hard it could be dealing with women in distress and working with dead and deformed babies. They talked of feeling 'overwhelmed by the amount of trauma and distress', of feeling at times that they 'can't cope', that things can be 'dreadful', and of the fear of 'going to pieces'. Some recognised that the lack of support available to them was a problem and they envied the nurses and midwives who seemed better able to look after each other. Others felt that such support smacked of 'indulging our emotions' which was not only unnecessary but possibly even counter-productive.

These examples are only a small glimpse into the world of the hospital doctors dealing with pregnancy loss in this particular hospital. Nevertheless, they open up lines of enquiry about the cultural context within which medical care was practised in this hospital. Why was the culture of self-sufficiency so strong and the idea of seeking support so difficult? Was it brought into the hospital by the doctors, who had learned from their training that doctors just 'get on with the next bit of work'? Was it sustained by the culture in this particular hospital and, if so, how?

Health professionals working with pregnancy loss routinely encounter many situations that may leave them feeling upset. One might expect them to have systems of giving each other emotional support either routinely or at times of particular crises. However, the health professionals in this study reported that such support was never offered in any planned way, and was available at times of crisis in an informal way more for some professional groups than for others. Whether it was available was related more to the ethos of the particular professional group than to whether it was likely to be needed.

What it shows and what it doesn't show

What is the value of this kind of research? It does not claim to provide the 'truth' about support in this hospital. The questions being addressed are not how much support is available, but of what kind and to whom. It would not be possible from the findings to compare the actual level of support and its effectiveness between the doctors in this hospital and other professional groups in the same hospital; still less, between this hospital and others. What this kind of research does is explore the meanings that concepts such as support have for those involved and their perceptions about it.

The research shows the diversity of views within one professional group and between all the professional groups on such matters as; what support means, whether it is desirable, whether it is available, what the obstacles are in asking for it, and so forth. Talking about support enables the respondents to think about it as an issue for themselves personally and for the organisation they work in and, in so doing, to possibly transform the way that they view it and what they do about it. It gives the organisation information on which to base possible changes in the way it supports those doing potentially distressing work.

The fact that the research is concerned with the subjective experiences of those in this particular hospital does not mean that it is irrelevant to other hospitals. Focusing on the concept of support makes it possible for anyone in any hospital to reflect on their own experiences of dealing with distressing situations; on the culture they work in; and on the effects on their personal and professional lives of the way that they deal with these issues. This may lead them to think about how to deal with them more effectively.

Communication between health professionals and women

Usually I say, 'How do you feel about things?' and quite often they say, 'I'm alright' ... you can't really probe more than that.

Emergency ward nurse

From the interviews with both sets of respondents it became clear that communication around pregnancy loss is fraught with difficulties. The women experienced difficulties in asking questions about things they wanted to know about, or felt that they were left to cope with feelings of distress when they would have welcomed a friendly overture from a nurse; conversely, some felt that they were being asked to talk about their feelings when they would have preferred to be left alone. Some health professionals talked about how difficult they found it to know when and when not to comfort women, whether to talk about potentially painful matters or to say nothing, what to say when they did feel it was necessary to say something, whether to volunteer information or to wait until asked.

Some of the problems arose because pregnancy loss usually involves distress for the women and staff might want to protect the women as much as they could. They would, for example, talk down the impending problems of induced labour and reassure women that everything would be done to make it painless. Those women who then experienced a high level of physical pain, plus the emotional pain of giving birth to a dead baby, felt misled by the reassurance, however well intentioned.

Sometimes the professionals were protecting themselves as well as the women from the unpleasantness of dealing with a dead and/or deformed baby. Most of the staff were uncomfortable talking about the disposal of the remains of the dead baby or fetus. They often did not know what happened to the remains and would have felt uneasy if questioned. This meant that they did not welcome such questions and did not make it easy for women to ask them, and when they were asked often resorted to little white lies to spare the women's feelings. None would routinely volunteer such information. They said that there was no need to know about such things because the women seldom wanted to know. While some women said that they did not want to know, others clearly did want to know but had felt inhibited from asking. The assumption that women were not interested in the remains of their baby or fetus, especially from an early miscarriage, owed more to protecting the feelings of the staff than it did to the wishes of many of the women.

A common difficulty for some staff was knowing when and how to respond to women in distress. Their own feelings of discomfort at seeing women in so much emotional pain hindered them from being able to respond as they would have liked. The following words of one nurse were echoed by others:

> *Most of the time she was on the verge of tears. She avoided eye contact and didn't speak very much and it made me feel awkward because I didn't really know.... I could see she was really upset but I didn't know what to say to make it any better because there wasn't anything I could say.*

Even when staff wanted to comfort women there was often a problem finding the right words. For example, how did one refer to what had died? Some staff had difficulty in knowing when to call it a baby. Some believed that a baby began at conception, others when it was visible on the scan; one thought it was a baby only once it was born, another when it moved in the womb; one thought it was a baby after twenty-four weeks' gestation, another after twelve weeks; some thought a baby could only be defined in terms of how it seemed to the mother. The problem was put succinctly by a staff nurse:

> *You have to choose your words carefully... because sometimes they don't want you to say it's a baby and they would prefer you to say it's a fetus. That's really difficult because you don't want to antagonise them in a very difficult situation.*

What made communication even more difficult was that women varied in their abilities to express their feelings and to be receptive to being comforted. While some wanted to be asked about their feelings, others found such questions intrusive. Staff were generally well aware of this, complicating still further what was already problematic. And all of these problems had to be dealt with in a busy ward, often on the basis of a short-term relationship with the women. Midwives, who were able to build up a more significant relationship with the women, claimed to have far fewer problems in communicating appropriately with the women they cared for.

How does this help practice?

The value of this investigation into the nature of communication between staff and the women depends on the reason for doing the research. The focus here was on helping professionals to understand better how women experienced their care so that the quality of care might be improved. The important points were those that contributed to an understanding of the women's experiences and those that staff referred to as problematic. These included the clash of perspectives between the women and staff on matters such as the need for information and the ways in which women interpreted negatively a perceived lack of concern by some staff for their distress. The views expressed by the women either confirmed or challenged the assumptions of the staff. On the one hand, this helped to confirm those aspects of care which the women valued and, on the other hand, prompted staff to reconsider those aspects where the women felt neglected.

Similarly, drawing attention to the issues that the staff said they found difficult enabled suggestions to be made about how staff could be helped to cope. Sometimes it would be enough just to show that some of their assumptions were not supported by the views of the women; sometimes the difficulties would arise from factors less amenable to change, such as the inherent difficulty of dealing with so much pain and distress, when longer term remedies, for example, more effective support systems or training, may be indicated.

Again, the issues raised here will almost certainly be easily recognised by staff in other hospitals grappling with similar issues, even if the details of their organisation, culture and approach are different.

An overview of the process of care

Tracking women through the system of care over a period of time meant a picture could be built up of the system of care from the woman's point of view. For example, in this study the health care for women who miscarried early in pregnancy is compartmentalised. The chain of care includes; consultation with the GP; referral to hospital for assessment in the early pregnancy assessment clinic located in the Accident and Emergency department; ultrasound; admission to the emergency ward; an ERPC under general anaesthetic in theatre; return to the emergency ward; discharge home; and finally follow-up with the GP. This system was described by the women as 'passing from pillar to post' and by the professionals as 'being processed'.

This overview of the system of care revealed that there was little opportunity for women to talk about the emotional aspects of miscarriage and that the professionals often thought that they had already had it or would have the opportunity at the next stage of the process. For example, the SHO in A&E thought that the nurses on the emergency ward were very good at talking. The nurses said that they were very busy and the emergency ward was the wrong place for the women, but the local support groups were very good and all women were referred to their health visitor. However, none of the women in the study who miscarried early in pregnancy saw a health visitor or approached a self-help group.

Taking the hospital as a whole allows a particular aspect of care to be looked at from different angles; for example, in this study the disposal of the baby or remains of the pregnancy. This aroused strong feelings in staff and women and was universally experienced as difficult to talk about. Staff at all but the most senior levels were ignorant of the procedures and the hospital policy. A picture is built up drawing evidence from different personnel of the complexity of the issue and the lack of openness about it. It seems clear that little progress will be made until staff are better informed and better able to deal with the issue.

Conclusion: the value of qualitative research

We conclude by quoting from Mays and Pope. The final chapter in their apologia for the value of qualitative research in the health services is by Keen and Packwood and ends with the following statement:

> *The complexity of the issues that health professionals have to deal with and the increasing recognition by policy makers, academics, and practitioners of the value of case studies in evaluating health service interventions suggest that the use of such studies is likely to increase in the future. Qualitative methods can be used within case study designs to address many practical and policy questions that impinge on the lives of professionals, particularly where those questions are concerned with how or why events take a particular course.*

Mays and Pope, 1996: 66

The strength of a case study lies in the wealth of material it is able to gather. In the pregnancy loss study it was possible to draw conclusions about the constituents of good care and how staff can best be equipped to provide it. The discrepancies in the different definitions of experience (the women's, the health professionals' and the organisation's) became clear and showed that the women were more likely to feel positive about their care if the organisational definition of their needs fitted with their own. The research also gave insights into the complexity of providing high quality care when women's needs are so diverse, and pointed to the importance of the relationship between women and the professionals, of negotiating about aspects of care and of attending to the emotional nature of the experience. Providing care in this way puts pressure on health professionals and suggestions could be made about how this could best be handled, and the importance of effective training and professional support.

The value of qualitative research like this lies in giving a better understanding of how an organisation and those within it function, make sense of their experiences, cope with events, and deal with the daily issues that arise in the provision of health care. This better understanding can suggest improvements to policies and practice resulting in care which is more responsive to women's needs and, in a working environment, more sensitive to the needs of staff. Patients who feel their emotional needs have been taken seriously may be less likely to displace the hurt and anger that can so often accompany the loss of a pregnancy on to staff and be less likely to look to formal complaints or litigation. The women, the health professionals and the hospital all stand to benefit from the better understanding that comes from giving proper weight to the emotional worlds of patients and staff.

References

Bluff R (1997) Evaluating qualitative research. *Br J Midwifery* **5**(4): 232–5

Britten N (1996) Qualitative interviews in medical research. In: Mays N, Pope C (eds) (1996) *Qualitative Research in Health Care*. BMA Books, London

Britten N, Jones R, Murphy E, Stacy R (1995) Qualitative research methods in general practice and primary care. *Fam Pract* **12**(1): 104–14.

Cannon S (1989) Social research in stressful settings: difficulties for the sociologist studying the treatment of breast cancer. *Sociology Health Illness* **11**(1): 62–77

Coffey A, Atkinson P (1996) *Making sense of qualitative data: complementary research strategies*. Sage Publications Ltd, London

Department of Health (1993) *Changing Childbirth: Part 1. Report of the Expert Maternity Group*. HMSO, London

Lofland J, Lofland L (1995) *Analysing Social Settings: a guide to qualitative observation and analysis*. Wadsworth Publishing, Belmont CA

Mason J (1996) *Qualitative Researching*. Sage Publications Ltd, London

Mays N, Pope C (eds) (1996) *Qualitative Research in Health Care*. BMA Books, London

Moulder C (1998) *Understanding Pregnancy Loss: Perspectives and Issues in Care*. Macmillan Press, London

National Health Executive (1996) *Patient Partnership: building a collaborative strategy*. Department of Health, London

Oakley A (1981) Interviewing women: a contradiction in terms. In: Roberts H, ed. *Doing Feminist Research*. Routledge and Kegan Paul, London: chap 4

Stillbirth and Neonatal Death Society (1995) *Pregnancy loss and the death of a baby: Guidelines for Professionals*. SANDS, London

Trinder L (1996) Social work research: the state of the art (or science). *Child Fam Social Work* **1**: 233–42

Woolcott H (1994) *Transforming Qualitative Data: description, analysis and interpretation.* Sage Publications Ltd, London

Further reading

Chapple A, Rogers A (1998) Explicit guidelines for qualitative research: a step in the right direction, a defence of the 'soft' option, or a form of sociological imperialism? *Fam Pract* **15**(6): 556–61

Devers KJ (1999) How will we know 'good' qualitative research when we see it? Beginning the dialogue in health services research. *Health Services Res* **34**(5) 1153–88

Lee R (1993) *Doing Research on Sensitive Topics.* Sage Publications Ltd, London

Roberts H (ed) (1992) *Women's Health Matters.* Routledge, London

Woodfield R (2000) *Women, Work and Computing.* Cambridge University Press, Cambridge: chap 4

3

Recurring miscarriage — investigation and classification

Roy G Farquharson

Introduction

Spontaneous miscarriage occurs in approximately 15%–20% of all pregnancies, as recorded by hospital episode statistics. The actual figure, from community-based assessment, may be up to 30%, as many cases remain unreported to hospital (Everett, 1997). Between 1% and 2% of fertile women will experience recurring pregnancy loss and, despite a wide range of investigations, no apparent cause can be found in approximately 50% of cases (Stirrat, 1990).

Miscarriage is the commonest pregnancy complication. The great majority occur early, before twelve weeks' gestation, while mid-trimester loss, between twelve and twenty-four weeks, occurs less frequently and constitutes <5% of all pregnancy losses. Clinical assessment of pregnancy loss history demands clarification of pregnancy loss type and accurate classification, whenever possible (*Table 3.1*). The traditional grouping of all pregnancy losses prior to twenty-four weeks as 'abortion' may have had pragmatic origins, but it is poor in terms of definition and makes little sense. Increasing knowledge about early pregnancy development, with the more widespread availability of serum Beta HCG measurement, the advent of high resolution ultrasound and a clearer description of gestation at pregnancy loss, makes for a more sophisticated assessment of miscarriage history. Modern day investigators should attempt to assign each pregnancy loss into pre-embryonic, embryonic or fetal. The introduction of this classification addresses the largely different nature of biological events occurring during each of the development periods and provides a sensible, although limited approach to the modern study of pregnancy loss. In addition, it should be remembered that the term 'missed abortion' should be replaced by 'delayed miscarriage' (Hutchon and Cooper, 1997).

Table 3.1: Pregnancy loss classification

Type of loss	Typical gestation (weeks)	Fetal heart activity	Principal diagnostic group	Beta HCG level
Pre-embryo	<6	Never	Idiopathic	Low then fall
Embryo	6–8	Never	Oligomenorrhoea/ idiopathic	Initial rise then fall
Fetal	>8	Lost	Antiphospholipid syndrome	Rise then static or fall

Ultrasound criteria

With the introduction of transvaginal ultrasound, longitudinal assessment of early pregnancy development can be made, in terms of viability and growth. Ultrasound plays a major role in maternal reassurance, where fetal cardiac activity is seen and is pivotal in the assessment of early pregnancy complications, such as vaginal bleeding (Jauniaux *et al*, 1999). However, there are limits to ultrasound resolution of normal early pregnancy development. Recent advice concludes that a diagnosis of an afetal gestation sac (embryo loss) should not be made if the visible crown rump length is less than 5mm, as only 65% of normal embryos will display cardiac activity (Royal College of Obstetricians and Gynaecologists, 1995). Repeat transvaginal ultrasound examination after at least a week showing identical features and/or the presence of fetal bradycardia are strongly suggestive of impending miscarriage. The possibility of incorrect dates should always be remembered by the alert clinician.

Conservative management, further ultrasound and the avoidance of unnecessary surgical evacuation are worthy of implementation and consideration.

Diagnostic groups

A wide array of diagnostic investigations is necessary to provide a comprehensive screen in couples suffering from recurring pregnancy loss (Li, 1998).

A list of relevant investigations include the following:

Early Antiphospholipid syndrome
~ Dilute Russell Viper Venom Time (DRVVT) for lupus anticoagulant
~ Anticardiolipin antibody (IgG/IgM)
Parental chromosome anomaly
Oligomenorrhoea
~ FSH/LH/Prolactin/Testosterone

Late Cervical weakness or uterine anomaly
~ Hysteroscopy
Bacterial vaginosis
~ Vaginal swabs
Thyroid function
Thrombophilia
Activated protein C resistance, hyperhomocystenaemia

Many authors have discontinued some historical favourites, such as anti-paternal cytotoxin antibody, HLA typing, endometrial swabs for Chlamydia, virology study, including TORCH screen, random blood glucose, blood group and renal function test.

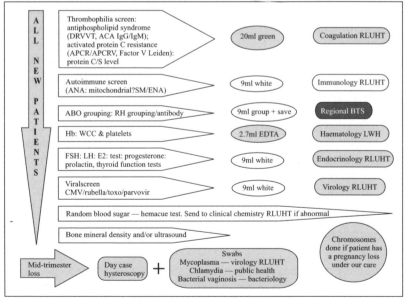

Figure 3.1: Miscarriage clinic list of investigations, 2001

Recurring miscarriage is a heterogeneous condition, which has many possible underlying causes and associations (*Table 3.2*) (Gleicher, 1997; Stirrat, 1990). Clinicians are already aware that 'association is not causation' and this dictum applies equally to assigning a specific cause to recurring miscarriage. For example, the continuing debate about the relevance of polycystic ovarian disease and recurring pregnancy loss continues. It must also be remembered that the underlying causes of mid trimester loss are rather different to those responsible for first-trimester loss. Structural uterine anomaly, cervical incompetence, bacterial vaginosis are recognised causes and associations of mid-trimester loss, but these are rarely associated with first-trimester miscarriage. Antiphospholipid syndrome, on the other hand, may be seen with either first-trimester loss (15%) or second-trimester loss (30%). In addition, the presence of dual pathology, comprising two diagnostic factors operating concurrently, should be remembered and is present in approximately 10% of mid-trimester loss cases (Drakeley *et al*, 1998).

Table 3.2: Pathogenesis and antiphospholipid syndrome
⌘ Thrombosis and end stage placental infarction
⌘ Direct inhibition of trophoblast cell proliferation and differentiation
⌘ B2-glycoprotein I is antigen for ACL
⌘ Interference with spiral artery remodelling in second wave trophoblast invasion

Idiopathic group

The diagnosis of idiopathic recurring miscarriage is by a process of exclusion. This group is the largest and comprises at least 50% of a study group (Clifford *et al*, 1994; Brigham *et al*, 1999).

Antiphospholipid syndrome

The association of recurring miscarriage with antiphospholipid syndrome (APS) has become increasingly accepted since the first description of successful immuno-suppression treatment in 1983 (Lubbe *et al*, 1983). Consensus discussion over diagnosis and laboratory quality control is largely resolved. At present, two separate measurements, at least six weeks apart, of a prolonged phospholipid dependent Dilute Russell Viper Venom clotting Time (DRVVT) and/ or raised anticardiolipin antibody (IgG/IgM) is diagnostic laboratory proof. These criteria, however, must be seen in conjunction with:

1. Three or more consecutive spontaneous losses before the tenth week of gestation, with maternal anatomic, hormonal abnormalities and paternal and maternal chromosome causes excluded.
2. One or more premature births of a morphologically normal neonate at or before the thirty-fourth week because of severe pre-eclampsia or placental insufficiency
3. One or more unexplained intrauterine death of a morphologically normal fetus at or beyond the tenth week of gestation (Wilson *et al*, 1999).

In addition to pre-pregnancy testing, recent evidence suggests that a first-trimester test is beneficial in excluding APS, as evidence of APS activity is most prominent within the first twelve weeks of pregnancy (Topping *et al*, 1999).

Historically, the pathogenesis focused on placental thrombosis and end stage infarction, associated with the known pro-coagulant state, causing fetal demise (*Table 3.3*). Initial studies (*in vitro*) show decreased prostacyclin production from vascular endothelial cells incubated with affected patient serum (Carreras *et al*, 1981). Recent work casts doubt on this attractive hypothesis (Chamley *et al*, 1998), by suggesting direct inhibition of trophoblast cell proliferation. A reproducible *in vitro* assay reflecting the pathogenic behaviour of APS activity remains elusive, but high quality research continues in several centres.

The presence of antiphospholipid syndrome is significantly more common in those women who suffer recurrent fetal death, severe pregnancy induced hypertension, fetal growth restriction, preterm delivery, placental abruption, as well as maternal thrombosis (Lockshin *et al*, 1985; Branch *et al*, 1992) (*Table 3.3*).

Table 3.3: Obstetric complication and APS
⌘ Fetal growth restriction
⌘ Pregnancy-induced hypertension
⌘ Preterm delivery
⌘ Abruption

Oligomenorrhoea

A hormonal aetiology for recurring miscarriage is an attractive concept for several reasons. Progesterone is known to be essential for the maintenance of early pregnancy (Csapo *et al*, 1973). Progesterone is secreted by the corpus luteum initially, but, by fourteen weeks' gestation, this function is replaced by the fetal placental unit. The change in site of production coincides with the majority of clinically recognised miscarriages, thereby casting doubt on the sufficiency of steroid production and hormonal support of pregnancy at a crucial phase.

Until very recently, it was thought that polycystic ovarian disease (PCOS) predisposed to recurrent miscarriage and that hyper-secretion of lutenising hormone (LH) was the main factor. As a result of continuing studies by several authors, this seemingly inseparable relationship has been breached. Examination of PCOS groups by hormonal evaluation and ultrasound criteria found no detectable effect of PCOS on parity or miscarriage (Farquhar *et al*, 1994; Quenby and Farquharson, 1983; Li *et al*, 1993; Rai *et al*, 2000).

Oligomenorrhoea, defined as the presence of menstruation more than thirty-five days apart on a consecutive basis, carries the highest risk load for a subsequent miscarriage (Quenby and Farquharson, 1993). Oligomenorrhoea is over represented in the recurring mis-carriage population (between 10% and 15%), which is in sharp contrast to the incidence in the general population of 1%. The presence of oligomenorrhoea has also been shown to have a higher chance of a normal karyotype miscarriage (Hasegawa *et al*, 1996), which, again, strongly supports the concept that oligomenorrhoea is a loading risk factor for recurring miscarriage, rather than a repeated and random abnormal chromosomal karyotype.

Mid-trimester loss

Mid-trimester loss is defined as pregnancy loss between twelve and twenty-four weeks' gestation. In 1938, Malpas wrote that;

> *Repeated miscarriage may be caused by some condition inimical to the growth of the fetus recurring in each pregnancy.*

Historically, analysis of cause revealed infrequent explanations for these losses. In modern practice, conditions and diseases are known to contribute to second-trimester miscarriage, either in isolation or in combination with other disease processes. Antiphospholipid syndrome is far more frequently found in the mid-trimester loss population, up to 30% (Drakeley *et al*, 1998). For instance, cervical weakness is a well established cause of mid-trimester loss, but may coexist alongside antiphospholipid syndrome to create a double pathology. The presence of cervical weakness (8%) and other less frequent, but important, causes, include uterine anomaly (<5%), bacterial vaginosis (between 5% and 10%) and hypothyroidism (2%).

Bacterial vaginosis

In women with bacterial vaginosis found in early pregnancy, a five-fold increase in late miscarriage, as well as preterm labour, has been reported. Bacterial vaginosis was found far more commonly in second-trimester miscarriage than recurrent early miscarriage (Llahi-Camp *et al*, 1996). Bacterial vaginosis is an important poly-microbial imbalance of vaginal flora. It is increasingly associated with adverse sequelae in both obstetrics and gynaecology, especially preterm labour, preterm delivery and premature rupture of membranes (Lamont, 1997; Drug and Therapeutic Bulletin, 1998).

Chromosome abnormality

It is generally accepted that a significant percentage of all early spontaneous miscarriages at less than twelve weeks' gestation in the general population are due to fetal chromosome abnormalities (Guerneri *et al*, 1987; Bessho *et al*, 1995). In the recurrent miscarriage population, it is recently reported that the frequency of normal embryonic karyotypes linearly increases with the number of previous miscarriages when the subsequent pregnancy fails (Ogasawara, 2000) (*Table 3.4*).

Uterine anomalies

Anatomic uterine anomaly occurs in probably less than 5% of a recurring miscarriage population. It is, however, important to exclude, by diagnostic hysteroscopy in the presence of a mid-trimester loss, such common abnormalities as bicornuate uterus, unicornuate uterus with rudimentary horn or marked subseptate uterus. In addition, this will allow assessment of cervical length and patency to exclude cervical weakness. Explanation for late miscarriage includes limited uterine space available and inability to expand (Strassman, 1966) or implantation into an avascular septum (Decherney *et al*, 1986).

Abnormal endometrial morphology

Recent reports of abnormal endometrial morphology (Lim *et al*, 1998; Quenby *et al*, 1999) suggest that there is some maladaptive endometrial pathology. These studies suggest that a different population of leucocytes is found in the pre-implantation endometrium from recurrent miscarriage patients, as compared to those from a fertile control. These differences were accentuated in women who had a miscarriage subsequent to the biopsy, compared to those who subsequently had a live birth, indicating some maladaptive change in the endometrium.

Emerging causes

Recent consideration of a thrombophilia state, such as protein C deficiency and protein S deficiency, as well as hyperhomocystenaemia, has brought considerable attention to the possibility that these pro-coagulant states predispose women to recurring pregnancy loss, as well as intrauterine death and stillbirth in later pregnancy (Preston *et al*, 1996). More recently, activated protein C resistance (APCR) has been discovered to be associated with recurring pregnancy loss in a small number of women. Genetic testing for the Factor V Leiden mutation, which constitutes 95% of an APCR population, has aroused considerable interest and results of prospective population studies are awaited (Dahlback *et al*, 1993; Meinardi *et al*, 1999). Recent controversy over selective testing for inherited thrombophilia and adverse pregnancy outcome, will require further evaluation before a consensus can be reached on whether routine testing for Factor V Leiden should be made in a recurring miscarriage population (Nelson-Piercy, 1999), as some authorities have suggested that Factor V Leiden screening in the first trimester in repeated miscarriage is not warranted (Balasch *et al*, 1997).

Table 3.4: Results from recent studies comparing sample size, maternal age and frequency of chromosome abnormalities

Study	Number of patients	Unsuccessful karyotype	Mean maternal age	Abnormal karyotype %	Monosomy	Chromosomal trisomy	Abnormalities* triploidy	Tetrapoidy	Other**
Stern et al	224	0	36	57.2	6(4.7)	100(78.7)	15(11.8)	7(5.5)	0
Sanchez et al, 1999	109	7.3	31.7	62.8	4(7.5)	34(64.2)	14(26.4)	1(1.9)	15(28)
Ogaswara et al, 2000	1309	49	31.3	60	5(4.2)	63(52.5)	18(15)	N/A	27(22.5) Not specified
Carp et al, 2001	167	25.1	31	28.8	5(13.8)	24(66.7)	5(13.8)	0	2(5.6)
Awartani et al, 2001	285	0	34	47	16(8.1)	130(66)	37(19.3) Triploidy and Trisomy combined	N/A	0

*values are n(%)

**including structural abnormalities

Treatments for recurring miscarriage

This is a controversial area, as there is little evidence-based practice to support treatment interventions that satisfy the criteria for inclusion, in terms of rigorous study design, adequate laboratory quality control, method of randomisation and recruitment, data verification and analysis and, finally, substantive power calculation achievement. It should be understood that many reported treatments are not truly tested by modern discriminatory criteria .

Historically, couples with unexplained miscarriage were thought to have an allo-immune abnormality that prevented the mother from developing immune responses essential for the survival of the genetically different conceptus. Increasing evidence has cast doubt on this immunological aetiology (Christiansen, 1996). Recently, a randomised controlled trial, utilising immunisation with paternal mononuclear cells, did not improve pregnancy outcome in women with unexplained recurring miscarriage (Ober *et al*, 1999). Other immuno-modulation therapy has shown no statistically significant improvement above placebo (70% success) when randomised against intra-venous immuno-globulin (73%) (Jablonowska *et al*, 1999). As a consequence, there has been a swing away from immunotherapy and at present, in the UK, it should be seen only in an experimental research method and should not be seen as a mainstream therapy for clinical use.

Overview

The study of recurrent miscarriage has yielded a great deal of information, regarding clarity of classification, identification of underlying causes and associations and an increasing understanding of pathogenesis of unique and newly identified mechanisms. For the clinician, what is more important is to construct reproducible and verifiable treatments of proven benefit to help the couple through a subsequent pregnancy, following a history of recurrent pregnancy loss. Although in some areas of investigation we may not be wiser, it would seem, in the year 2001, that we are better informed.

References

Balasch J, Reverter JC, Fabrogues F *et al* (1997) First trimester repeated abortion is not associated with activated protein C resistance. *Hum Reprod* **12**: 1094–7

Bessho T, Sakamotoh H, Shiotani S *et al* (1995) Fetal loss in the first trimester after demonstration of cardiac activity: Relation of cytogenetic and ultrasound findings. *Hum Reprod* **10**: 2696–9

Branch DW, Silver RM, Blackwell JL *et al* (1992) Outcome of treated pregnancies in women with antiphospholipid syndrome: An update of the Utah experience. *Obstet Gynaecol* **80**: 614–20

Brigham SA, Conlon C, Farquharson RG (1999) A longitudinal study of pregnancy outcome following idiopathic recurrent miscarriage. *Hum Reprod* **14**: 2868–71

Carreras LO, Machin JJ, Deman R (1981) Arterial thrombosis, intra-uterine death and lupus anticoagulant detection of immunoglobulin interfering with prostacyclin production. *Lancet* **1**: 244–6.

Chamley LW, Duncalf AM, Mitchell MD, Johnson PM (1998) Action of anticardiolipin and antibodies to B2-glycoprotein-1 on trophoblast proliferation as a mechanism for fetal death. *Lancet* **352**: 1037–8

Christiansen OB (1996) A fresh look at the causes and treatment of recurrent miscarriage, especially its immunological aspects. *Hum Reprod* **2**: 271–93

Csapo AI, Pulkeinen MO, Wiest WG (1973) Effects of lutectomy and progesterone replacement therapy in early pregnancy patients. *Am J Obstet Gynecol* **115**: 759–65

Clifford K, Rai R, Watson H *et al* (1994) An informative protocol for the investigation of recurrent miscarriage: Preliminary experience of 500 consecutive cases. *Hum Reprod* **9**: 1328–32

Dahlback B, Carlsson M, Svensson PJ (1993) Familial thrombophilia due to previously unrecognised mechanism characterised by poor anticoagulant response to activated protein C. *Proc Natl Acad Sci* **90**: 1004–8

Decherney AH, Russell JB, Graebe RA, Polan ML (1986) Resectoscopic management of Mullerian fusion defects. *Fertil Steril* **45**: 726–8

Drakeley AJ, Quenby S, Farquharson RG (1998) Mid-trimester loss — Appraisal of screening protocol. *Hum Reprod* **13**: 101–6

Drug and Therapeutics Bulletin (1998) Management of bacterial vaginosis. *Drug Ther Bull* **36**: 33–5

Everett C (1997) Incidence and outcome of bleeding before the 20th week of pregnancy: Prospective study from general practice. *Br Med J* **315**: 32–4

Farquhar CM, Birdsall M, Manning P *et al* (1994) The prevalence of PCO on ultrasound scanning in a population of randomly selected women. *Aust N Z J Obstet Gynecol* **34**: 67–72

Gleicher N (1997) Antiphospholipid antibodies and reproductive failure: What do they do and what they do not do; How to and how not to treat! *Hum Reprod* **12**: 13–16

Guerneri S, Bettio D, Simoni G *et al* (1987) Prevalence and distribution of chromosome abnormalities in a sample of first trimester abortions. *Hum Reprod* **2**: 735–9

Hasegawa I, Takakawa K, Tanaka K (1996) The roles of oligomenorrhoea and fetal chromosomal abnormalities in spontaneous abortions. *Hum Reprod* **11**: 2304–05

Hutchon DJ, Cooper S (1997) Missed abortion versus delayed miscarriage. *Br J Obstet Gynaecol* **104**: 73

Jablonowska B, Selbing A, Palfi M *et al* (1999). Prevention of recurrent spontaneous abortion by intravenous immunoglobulin: A double-blind placebo controlled study. *Hum Reprod* **14**: 838–41

Jauniaux E, Kaminopetros P, El-Rafaey H (1999) Early pregnancy loss. In: Rodeck CH, Whittle M, eds. *Fetal Medicine*. Churchill Livingstone, Edinburgh: 835–47

Lamont RF (1997)The diagnosis and obstetrical implications of bacterial vaginosis. *Fetal Maternal Med Rev* **9**: 199–207

Liddell HS, Pattison NS, Zanderigo A (1991) Recurring miscarriage – – Outcome after supportive care in early pregnancy. *Aust N Z J Obstet Gynecol* **31**: 320–2

Li TC (1998) Guide for practitioners: Recurrent miscarriage principles of management. *Hum Reprod* **13**: 478–82

Li T Cm Serle E, Warren MA *et al* (1993) Is endometrial development in the peri-implantatic period influenced by high concentrations of luteinising hormone in the follicular phase? *Hum Reprod* **8**: 1021–4

Lim KJH, Odukoya OA, Ajjan RA *et al* (1998) Profile of cytokine MRNA expression in peri-implanatatic endometriums. *Mol Hum Reprod* **4**: 77–81

Llahi-Camp JM, Rai R, Ison C, Regan L, Taylor-Robinson D (1996) Association of bacterial vaginosis with a history of second trimester miscarriage. *Hum Reprod* **11**: 1575–8

Lockshin MD, Druzin ML, Goel S *et al* (1985) Antibody to cardiolipin as a predictor of fetal distress or death in pregnant patients with SLE. *N Engl J Med* **313**: 152–6

Lubbe WF, Palmer SJ, Butler WS, Liggins GC (1983) Fetal survival after prednisone suppression of material lupus anticoagulant. *Lancet* **1**: 1361–3

Meinardi JR, Middledorp S, de Kam PJ *et al* (1999) Increased risk for fetal loss in carriers of the Factor V Leiden mutation. *Am Intern Med* **130**: 736–9

Nelson-Piercy C (1999) Inherited thrombophilia and adverse pregnancy outcome: Has the time come for selective screening. *Br J Obstet Gynaecol* **106**: 513–15

Ober C, Karrison T, Odem RR *et al* (1999) Mononuclear-cell immunisation in the prevention of recurrent miscarriages: A randomised trial. *Lancet* **354**: 365–9

Ogasawara M, Aoki K, Okada S, Suzumori K (2000) Embryonic karyotype of abortices in relation to the number of previous miscarriages. *Fertil Steril* **73**: 300–4

Preston FE, Rosendaal FR, Walker ID (1996) Increased fetal loss in women with heritable thrombophilia. *Lancet* **348**: 913–6

Quenby S, Farquharson RG (1983) Predicting recurring miscarriage — What is important? *Obstet Gynaecol* **82**: 132–8

Quenby S, Bates M, Doig T *et al* (1999) Pre-implantation endometrial leucocytes in women with recurring miscarriage. *Hum Reprod* **14**: 2386–91

Rai R, Backos M, Rushworth F, Regan L (2000) Polycystic ovaries and recurrent miscarriage: A reappraisal. *Hum Reprod* **15**: 612–15

Royal College of Obstetricians and Gynaecologists (1995) *Guidance and Ultrasound Procedures in Early Pregnancy*. RCOG, London

Strassman EO (1966) Fertility and unification of double uterus. *Fertil Steril* **17**: 165–76

Stirrat GM (1990) Recurrent miscarriage 1: Definition and epidemiology. *Lancet* **336**: 673–5

Stray-Pederson B, Stray-Pederson S (1983) Etiological factors and subsequent reproductive performance in 195 couples with a prior history of habitual abortion. *Am J Obstet Gynecol* **148**: 140–6

Topping J, Quenby S, Farquharson RG, Malia R, Greaves M (1999) Marked variation in antiphospholipid antibodies during pregnancy: Relationships to pregnancy outcome. *Hum Reprod* **14**: 224–8

Wilson WA, Gharavi AE, Koike T, Lockshin MD, Branch DW, Piette JC (1999) International consensus statement on preliminary classification criteria for definite antiphospholipid syndrome: Report of an internal workshop. *Arthritis and Rheum* **42**: 1309–11

4

The role of the dedicated miscarriage nurse

Ann-Maria Hughes

The recurrent miscarriage clinic began at Liverpool Women's Hospital in the late 1980s and the patients that we saw were relatively uncomplicated. Patients were referred following three miscarriages and were investigated in the clinic. In those early days, the majority of the patients seen underwent a battery of tests without a cause for their recurrent miscarriages being found. In spite of this, the clinic was successful with the majority of patients achieving a full term pregnancy or pregnancies. Treatment at that time was mostly by providing fortnightly 're-assurance' ultrasound scans and the knowledge that there was someone on the end of the phone if something seemed to be going wrong. Patients, however, still did not know the cause of their previous traumatic losses and would often say that they wished that a cause had been found because they wanted to understand what had happened and why it happened.

In the ten years since I started working in the clinic there has been an increase in the amount of information that we are able to give to patients. Our knowledge of the causes and treatment of recurrent miscarriage has increased through improvements in the tests that we do and the research that we have been involved with over that time. In addition, the work that we do has received recognition in that the number of patients referred to the clinic has increased and many of our patients travel long distances to attend.

Four years ago I was asked to set up a nurse-led clinic in which I would see all new patients. This clinic provides the first point of contact between the patient and the team of staff who will be giving ongoing advice, support, information and treatment throughout future pregnancies. The clinic itself is very small as I usually only see three couples in each clinic, but this allows me the time to:

- take the blood samples for a range of screening tests
- take a full medical history from the couple
- discuss the way in which the clinic works and give the couple details on how to contact me
- arrange the first appointment to attend for results of tests taken that day.

Blood tests

All new patients will have the full range of screening tests done even though some of these tests might have been done in other hospitals. This might appear wasteful but there can be quite large variations in results from one laboratory to another and it is important that the information we give is as reliable as possible. Over the years the range of tests has changed as our knowledge of recurrent miscarriages has increased. At one time we routinely screened all couples for chromosome analysis but have found that this is only useful in those couples who have a subsequent pregnancy loss with us and is positive in less than 3% of tests.

The results from all these tests provide the information the doctors need to make an analysis of risk and a prediction of success in future pregnancies.

Medical history

Before I started this clinic I underwent further training so that I understood this important aspect of patient care. All patients, whether they attend for a hospital appointment or their GP's surgery, need to give a full history so that the doctor can make a diagnosis, prescribe treatment, etc. It is up to the doctor or, in my case, the nurse, to ask the right questions. For some years a specially devised history sheet has been used in the miscarriage clinic and I was trained to use this.

The history involves asking patients about previous pregnancies and is very detailed. The information about previous pregnancy is a diagnostic tool but it can be traumatic for the patient and her partner who have to re-live the trauma of pregnancy loss. I always encourage the partner to come in on this consultation because I think it is important that they are aware of what is going to happen too. We recognise that miscarriage is not something that only affects women. In some instances, this has been the first time that the man has been able to express how he feels about what has happened. It is often apparent that the woman has been unaware that her partner finds the experience of miscarriage as distressing as she does.

An explanation of all the tests is given before I take the blood samples. It is important for couples to know why samples are taken and to be reassured that all known risk factors for recurrent miscarriages will be explored. During the course of this consultation I also discuss the treatments that are available. This might seem a little early but I believe that it prepares couples for their first medical consultation. I also explain that, although we have made advances in this field, there is still a strong chance that the test results will fail to identify a cause for their recurrent miscarriages.

This clinic provides an ideal opportunity to discuss lifestyle changes and to talk about pre-conceptual care. I emphasise the need to limit alcohol intake and smoking cessation and the importance of folic acid. I also take this opportunity to talk about the work of the Miscarriage Association and its very supportive role. We have a Miscarriage Support Group in the hospital and I make sure that couples are given details of the monthly meetings and the name of the nurse who is the link to the group.

I arrange for a six-week follow-up appointment for the couple to see the consultant. I advise each couple that they are welcome to contact me at any time before their appointment; particularly if they should achieve a pregnancy.

I have gained a great deal of satisfaction from the nurse-led clinic. I feel that it enables me to develop a closer relationship with patients and their partners. This makes it easier for couples when they attend for medical consultation. Not only have they had information about what to expect from the clinic but, hopefully, they feel that they know someone with whom they can talk over their fears and anxieties, or contact if they develop problems.

The first medical consultation involves a lengthy discussion with the medical team. The results of the tests are given and possible treatment options are discussed. If it is appropriate, the couple receives detailed information about the treatment regime that they will need in a future pregnancy. Patients are advised to contact me as soon as a pregnancy has been confirmed so that I can arrange for treatment to start if necessary. I also make an appointment for the miscarriage pregnancy clinic that is held every week. The consultant and his team of doctors who have a special interest in recurrent miscarriage attend this clinic.

Couples quite often feel overpowered by the amount of information that they receive. The fact that we have met earlier at the nurse clinic is helpful and I am able to go over anything that they have not understood. I reassure them that they can contact me at any time and this enables them to leave knowing that any questions that may crop up after they leave the clinic can be answered before their next appointment.

If the results come back negative, the couples are counselled about the likelihood of a future successful pregnancy. We appreciate that couples come to us looking for an explanation for previous pregnancy loss. It is not always possible to give this. What we do emphasise is the fact that a previous history of recurrent miscarriages does not mean that future pregnancies will fail. These patients are offered early ultrasound reassurance scans up to their twelfth week of pregnancy. This support on its own often proves beneficial and the majority of patients who attend fortnightly for surveillance scans achieve a successful outcome of their pregnancy.

Patients who have had a positive screen (eg. results that show that they will need treatment at some point in their pregnancy) are asked to contact me as soon as they become pregnant. I arrange an appointment for them to attend the next early pregnancy clinic where Mr Farquharson or one of his medical team sees them. An ultrasound scan will be done at six weeks gestation after serum HCG measurements and the appropriate treatment regime will begin. We make sure that the patient fully understands the reasons why the treatment is necessary and what it involves. One of the available treatments involves a daily injection. We encourage patients (or their partners) to administer these injections. We see self-injection as a means whereby the patient has an element of control over what is happening. It also gives greater freedom to the patient who does not have to plan her day around finding the time to visit the hospital or GP surgery. Patients often express reluctance at the suggestion that they do their own injections and it is very much their choice to do so. Once the initial reluctance has been overcome, patients become willing partners in their treatment. For some, the fact that they have mastered the skill of giving (as well as receiving) an injection is a source of great pride.

Ultrasound monitoring plays a large part in providing reassurance for patients. The scan is a tangible way of assessing the health of their baby. I undertook a scanning course last year and so I am now able to carry out scans on my patients. This has proven to be enormously beneficial as it provides even more continuity of care for the patient and gives me great job satisfaction. The down side, however, is that patients often feel tense in the day or so before their scan. Sadly, there are times when the scan shows that the fetus is no longer viable. It is at these times that the relationship that we have developed with our patients and their partners is at its strongest. Bad news is broken by someone who knows the couple and their history. We cannot take away the heartbreak but we can share in the loss.

I am directly involved with patients until the twelfth week of pregnancy when they are transferred to the Pregnancy Support Clinic in the antenatal department. I have close links with the midwifery staff in the hospital and patients know that they can contact me if they have any problems with treatment.

One cause of recurrent pregnancy loss is a weakness in the neck of the womb. This will be diagnosed from the medical history and further investigations. Patients receive a thorough explanation of this and are advised that treatment will need to be by a procedure called transabdominal cervical cerclage. Although only a fairly small number of our patients need this treatment, there is a support network available. This support group consists of patients who have had the procedure and those who are awaiting treatment. My role here is to put patients in contact with each other. As this procedure can only be carried out while the woman is pregnant there is, naturally, a great deal of anxiety on the part of patients waiting for treatment. Contact with others who have successfully undergone treatment and sharing anxiety with those who are also awaiting treatment can be a great source of support. It certainly works well for our patients who keep in touch with each other; attending christenings and children's birthday celebrations.

As I have already mentioned, there are times when our patients suffer a further miscarriage while under our care. We feel that it is important to acknowledge the loss of a much-wanted pregnancy and patients can if they wish, register the loss in the Book of Remembrance. If the patient is admitted I visit them on the ward.

Section II:
Clinical approach

5

Antiphospholipid syndrome and pregnancy loss: The Utah perspective

Ware Branch, Sean Esplin

This work is supported by a generous endowment from the HA and Edna Benning family.

Introduction

The first case reports documenting an association between antiphospholipid antibodies and pregnancy loss were published nearly a quarter of a century ago (Nilsson, 1975; Soulier and Boffa, 1980). This association was strengthened by the seminal publication of Lubbe in 1983. In the early 1980s, growing excitement about the relationship between antiphospholipid antibodies and thrombosis (Harris *et al*, 1983) led to the first in an ongoing series of international symposia on antiphospholipid antibodies and related medical problems. By the mid-1980s, rheumatologists had pregnancy loss as a clinical feature of the newly named antiphospholipid syndrome, with Harris listing a fetal loss as the pregnancy loss criterion for APS in his 1987 proposal entitled *The Syndrome of the Black Swan* (Harris, 1987).

We saw our first patient with antiphospholipid syndrome in 1983 — she had her only successful pregnancy treated with prednisone and low-dose aspirin and is alive and well today. Members of our group attended the second international symposium on antiphospholipid antibodies the following year in London. At that time, only a handful of obstetricians were actively involved in studying the relationship between antiphospholipid antibodies and pregnancy loss. Our group had primarily focused on fetal death as the obstetric feature of antiphospholipid syndrome (Branch, 1987). However, others assumed that antiphospholipid antibodies were associated with early pregnancy loss, and prospective treatment trials performed in the 1990s suggest that this relationship is real (Kutteh, 1996; Rai, 1997). During this same time period, we (Branch *et al*, 1989; Branch *et al*, 1992) and others (Lima, 1996) emphasised that antiphospholipid antibodies are associated with severe pre-eclampsia, placental insuffiency, fetal distress, and iatrogenic pre-term birth, sometimes resulting in neonatal death from complications of prematurity.

The 1999 clinical and laboratory criteria proposed at the International Antiphospholipid Symposium in Sapporo, Japan best reflect the current consensus. These criteria include any of the following three different types of pregnancy loss as a clinical criterion for APS:

1. One or more unexplained deaths of a morphologically-normal fetus at or beyond the tenth week of gestation with normal fetal morphology documented by ultrasound or direct examination of the fetus.
2. One or more premature births of a morphologically-normal neonate at or before the thirty-fourth week of gestation because of severe pre-eclampsia or placental insufficiency.
3. Three or more consecutive spontaneous abortions before the tenth week of gestation with maternal anatomic, hormonal abnormalities, and paternal and maternal chromosomal causes excluded (Wilson *et al*, 1999).

The purpose of this chapter is to analyse critically the relationship between antiphospholipid antibodies and these obstetric problems, point out areas of controversy, as well as to outline appropriate management plans when antiphospholipid antibodies are found in association with pregnancy loss.

Classification of pregnancy loss

Our group firmly believes that an important aspect of the future of recurrent pregnancy loss investigation requires thoughtful and consistent classification of pregnancy losses. The traditional grouping of all pregnancy losses prior to twenty weeks' gestation as 'abortions' may have been pragmatic in the past, but it is arbitrary and makes no sense in terms of what is now known about developmental biology and the nature of pregnancy loss. Rather, modern-day investigators should attempt whenever possible to group pregnancy losses into:

1. *Pre-embryonic:* from conception through the fourth week.
2. *Embryonic:* from the fifth week of gestation through the ninth week.
3. *Fetal:* from the tenth week of gestation until delivery.
4. *Neonatal:* live-born infant after twenty weeks' gestation. Such a classification system recognises the largely different nature of the biological events occurring during each of these periods and provides a sensible, although limited, approach to the modern study of pregnancy loss.

During the pre-embryonic period, the early trophoblast differentiates from the tissue destined to become the embryo (the inner cell mass) and accomplishes implantation into the maternal endometrium (day six–seven after fertilisation). The pre-embryo develops into a bilaminar disc of cells and microscopically observable alterations of the cell disc define the cranial end central neural axis of the pre-embryo. Oxygen and nutrient needs are met by diffusion across maternal tissues. During the embryonic period, with the exact beginning and end of the period debated by authorities according to developmental criteria used, the trilaminar disc folds to become cylindrical, the head and tail regions become recognisable as cranial and caudal folds, definite segmentation is seen, the heart forms, circulation is established through the umbilical cord and placenta, and all organs form. In contrast, the fetal period is characterised by relatively little organogenesis, but by substantial growth and differentiation of previously formed structures.

We admit this approach to classification of pregnancy loss is sometimes difficult because of the varieties of clinical presentation of pregnancy loss. The demise of the conceptus usually precedes the symptoms of miscarriage by at least several days, and often by a week or more. Transvaginal ultrasound has proven useful, but the distinction between late pre-embryonic and embryonic loss is often uncertain. Furthermore, fetal death may not always precede initial symptoms of pregnancy loss, as in cases of cervical incompetence where the fetus is usually alive at the time of presentation. Finally, the classification of a live, though pre-viable, infant at nineteen weeks' gestation, as may occur in cases of infection or cervical incompetence is problematic. Nonetheless, an approach using the above mentioned developmental stages to classify pregnancy losses has been used with modest success in the largest randomised, controlled treatment trial of women with recurrent pregnancy loss (Ober *et al*, 1999). Of 131 patients attaining pregnancy, fifty-nine had recurrent miscarriages, and more than half of these were pre-embryonic (or very early embryonic), 28% were embryonic, and 10% were fetal, though among the latter, fetal loss after fifteen weeks was rare.

Antiphospholipid antibodies, recurrent pregnancy loss, and pregnancy complications

There is widespread consensus that antiphospholipid antibodies cause, or at least are clearly associated with, pregnancy loss. However, a critical review of this association readily turns up some controversies regarding the type of pregnancy loss most closely associated with antiphospholipid antibodies. We reviewed published case reports and case series in 1987 and concluded that 30% to 40% of allegedly antiphospholipid-related pregnancy losses were second- or early third-trimester fetal deaths (Branch, 1987). Our series of well-characterised antiphospholipid syndrome patients confirms this; seventy-nine of 195 (41%) previous pregnancies were fetal deaths (Branch *et al*, 1992). Other of the abortions in these patients may have been fetal deaths as well (eg. losses at ten to thirteen weeks' gestation), but were recorded as 'spontaneous first-trimester abortions' because we could not be sure that live fetuses existed. The high rate of fetal death among patients with antiphospholipid syndrome contrasts sharply with the low rate of fetal death in most series of recurrent pregnancy loss patients. In our series, over 85% of women with well-characterised antiphospholipid syndrome have a history of at least one fetal death. Following up on this theme, Oshiro retrospectively analysed pregnancy losses in our highly-selected referral population of 366 women with two or more consecutive pregnancy losses, including seventy-six women with, and 290 women without lupus anticoagulant or ≥20 GPL units of anticardiolipin antibodies (Oshiro, 1996). Both groups of women had similar rates of prior pregnancy loss (84%), but 50% of the prior losses in women with antiphospholipid antibodies were fetal deaths, compared to less than

15% in women without antiphospholipid antibodies. More than 80% of women with antiphospholipid antibodies had at least one fetal death, compared with less than 25% of women without antiphospholipid antibodies. Finally, the specificity of fetal death for the presence of antiphospholipid antibodies was 76% compared to only 6% for two or more pre-embryonic or embryonic losses without fetal death. Thus, the women with moderate-to-high levels of antiphospholipid antibodies had significantly different pregnancy loss histories compared to women without high levels of antiphospholipid antibodies. We concluded that fetal death, not pre-embryonic loss or embryonic death, is the type of pregnancy loss most specific for antiphospholipid-related pregnancy loss.

No sooner had antiphospholipid syndrome been recognised as being associated with fetal death, than it was linked to recurrent early pre-embryonic and embryonic pregnancy loss. By the early 1990s, a number of studies that appear to have included women with recurrent pre-embryonic or embryonic losses, indicated that positive tests for lupus anticoagualant or IgG or IgM anticardiolipin antibodies were found in up to 20% of women with a recurrent pregnancy loss or a recurrent abortion (Petri *et al*, 1987; Out *et al*, 1991; Parazzini *et al*, 1991; Parke *et al*, 1991; Plouffe *et al*, 1992; MacLean *et al*, 1994). More recently, investigators have attempted to link antiphospholipid antibodies other than lupus anticoagulant and anticardiolipin to recurrent pregnancy loss, including antibodies to phosphatidylserine, phosphatidylethanolamine, phosphatidylinositol, phosphatidylglycerol, phosphatidylcholine, and phosphatidic acid (Kwak *et al*, 1992; Aoki *et al*, 1993; Yetman and Kutteh, 1996). We remain sceptical, finding that these antibodies are not associated with recurrent pregnancy loss once lupus anticoagulant and anticardiolipin antibodies have been excluded (Branch, 1997). Similarly, Khamashta and Hughes have recently found that multiple antiphospholipid tests do not increase the diagnostic yield in antiphospholipid syndrome (Bertolaccini, 1998).

The importance of low positive and only IgM antiphospholipid test results to the problem of recurrent pregnancy loss also generates controversy. Many studies of patients with recurrent pregnancy loss and antiphospholipid antibodies have included patients with low level IgG anticardiolipin or only IgM anticardiolipin isotype. The nature of the relationship between low positive IgG aCL antibodies or isolated IgM anticardiolipin antibodies is of uncertain (Yetman and Kutteh, 1996) or questionable (Silver *et al*, 1996) clinical significance. Our group found that women with low positive IgG anticardiolipin or isolated IgM anticardiolipin had no greater risk for antiphospholipid-related events than women who tested negative (Silver *et al*, 1996). In addition, their risk for antiphospholipid-associated complications was markedly lower than the risk in women with lupus anticoagulant or ≥20 GPL anticardiolipin antibodies. On the other hand, it is intriguing that two recent studies found a significant proportion of women with recurrent pregnancy loss (primarily pre-embryonic and embryonic losses) had normalised values indicating low levels of IgG anticardiolipin antibodies (defined as >95th or 99th percentiles) (Aoki *et al*, 1993; Branch *et al*, 1997). In one of these studies (Branch *et al*, 1997), those positive for low levels of IgG anticardiolipin antibodies did not have the clinical background typical of a population of women with well-characterised antiphospholipid syndrome (eg. systemic lupus erythematosus [SLE] thrombosis, autoimmune thrombocytopenia, etc).

Analyses of women with medium-to-high levels of antiphos-pholipid antibodies and past medical histories of systemic lupus erythematosus (SLE), fetal demise, or thrombosis have found that the obstetric complication rates in treated, prospectively-followed pregnancies are high. The rate of pre-eclampsia is 20% or greater (Lockshin *et al*, 1985; Branch *et al*, 1985; Branch *et al*, 1992; Caruso *et al*, 1993; Lima *et al*, 1996), and severe pre-eclampsia is a major contributor to the high rate of preterm delivery in this condition. Placental insufficiency as manifest by fetal growth impairment and fetal distress is also common, with some 30% of cases delivering a growth-restricted fetus (Branch *et al*, 1985; Branch *et al*, 1992; Caruso *et al*, 1993; Lima *et al*, 1996). In the two large series of women with antiphospholipid syndrome (Branch *et al*, 1992; Lima *et al*, 1996), half of all successfully treated pregnancies were complicated by fetal distress requiring delivery. A relationship between antiphospholipid antibodies and pre-eclampsia has been confirmed by two prospective studies of unselected obstetrical patients (Pattison *et al*, 1993; Yasuda *et al*, 1995), but not by another (Lynch, 1994). In one of these series (Yasuda *et al*, 1995), 12% of women testing positive for IgG aCL antibodies had small-for-gestational age infants compared to 2% of women testing negative. However, in two other series, investigators did not find a relationship between antiphospholipid antibodies and fetal growth impairment (Pattison *et al*, 1993; Lynch, 1994).

An important consequence of these complications in women with medium-to-high levels of antiphospholipid antibodies and past medical histories that included SLE, fetal demise, or thrombosis is the high rate of preterm birth. Even with treatment, preterm delivery occurs in approximately one-third of such patients (Branch *et al*, 1992; Lima *et al*, 1996). In one prospective, observational study of unselected obstetrical patients (Yasuda *et al*, 1995), 12% of sixty women testing positive for IgG anticardiolipin antibodies were delivered early compared to 4% of those testing negative.

Women with medium-to-high levels of antiphospholipid antibodies and SLE or previous fetal demise appear to be at increased risk for thrombosis in pregnancy, even if they do not have a history of prior thrombosis (Branch *et al*, 1992; Lima *et al*, 1996). We and others (Ginsberg and Hirsh, 1998) have advocated using thromboprophylaxis with heparin during pregnancy in these patients, even if they have no history of fetal loss in the past. Treatment should be continued during the postpartum period, probably for about six to eight weeks. Warfarin may be substituted for heparin during the postpartum period to limit further risk of heparin induced osteoporosis and fracture.

The last dozen women with antiphospholipid syndrome seen at our institution exemplify the type of patients discussed above. All have lupus anticoagulant and medium-to-high levels of anticardiolipin antibodies, and several have SLE, a history of thrombosis, or both. All have been treated with heparin and low dose aspirin during a next pregnancy. Among the outcomes are: miscarriage at eight weeks' gestation; fetal death at sixteen weeks' gestation; fetal demise at twenty-five weeks' gestation; severe pre-eclampsia requiring pregnancy termination at nineteen weeks' gestation; severe pre-eclampsia at twenty-three weeks' gestation; and worsening pre-eclampsia leading to delivery at thirty-four weeks' gestation.

In contrast, women with recurrent pre-embryonic or embryonic losses and antiphospholipid antibodies without a history of SLE or thrombosis seem to have very much reduced risks of the pregnancy complications mentioned above, A review of three recent studies is instructive. In Kutteh's study (1996), women with a history of thrombosis, SLE, or lupus anticoagulant were excluded, a move that would have excluded from the study at least 40% of the patients that we and others have seen (Branch *et al*, 1992; Lima *et al*, 1996). Women with anticardiolipin of either isotype and those with the less well-accepted antiphosphatidylserine antibodies were included. Most patients had recurrent pre-embryonic or embryonic loss, not fetal deaths; by comparison, we have found that well over 50% of our patients with antiphospholipid syndrome have a history of fetal death. Yet, as with antiphospholipid syndrome patients, the use of heparin treatment in the patients selected by Kutteh was associated with a dramatic improvement in successful pregnancy rates. Unlike the patients that we and others have reported (Branch *et al*, 1992; Lima *et al*, 1996), the patients studied by Kutteh did not have high rates of pre-eclampsia (10%) or premature birth (13%) due to obstetrical complications and no patient had a thrombosis. In a randomised study, Rai *et al* (1997) selected a population of women with antiphospholipid antibodies and predominantly recurrent pre-embryonic and embryonic loss for treatment with heparin versus no heparin. Once again, women with a history of thrombosis or SLE were not included, and no more than one-third of patients had a history of fetal death. Most of the patients had lupus anticoagulant by a sensitive assay, but only 10% had anticardiolipin antibodies. Thus, the patients studied comprised a different population with anti-phospholipid antibodies than would be typically identified in most US laboratories (Triplett, 1997). As in the study of Kutteh, the rate of obstetric complications was very low and no patient had a thrombosis, in spite of the fact that patients in the treatment group were treated with only 5,000 units of unfractionated heparin twice daily. Just as in the study of Kutteh, the patients treated with heparin had much better pregnancy outcomes than those who were not treated with heparin.

Recently, Pattison *et al* (2000) have shown that not all women with antiphospholipid antibodies and recurrent pregnancy loss require anticoagulation therapy for improved pregnancy outcomes. They included fifty women with predominantly pre-embryonic or embryonic losses, half of whom had only low levels of IgG or IgM aCL and would not qualify as having definite APS using the Sapporo criteria. As in the trials of Kutteh and Rai, women with prior thrombosis or SLE were excluded. The subjects were randomised to receive either low-dose aspirin or a placebo — no heparin was given. Live birth rates were over 80% in both the aspirin and placebo-treated women. The rate of serious obstetric or medical complication was very low. The authors appropriately emphasise that some women labelled as having antiphospholipid-related recurrent pregnancy loss do not require heparin treatment in order to have successful pregnancies.

This second population of women with antiphospholipid antibodies and pregnancy loss, described by Kutteh, Rai, and Pattison, are responsive to heparin in relatively modest doses or do not require heparin for favourable outcome. In either case, they do not appear at the same degree of risk for thrombosis, fetal demise, pre-eclampsia, or preterm birth as the patients seen by us. How does one resolve this apparent dichotomy? Some experts would argue that there is a single population of antiphospholipid syndrome patients existing on a continuum of clinical and laboratory characteristics and that different specialists are attracting different types of subsets of these women. But if this is true, why do the patients seen by our group, who tend to have both lupus anticoagulant and high levels of anticardiolipin antibodies, also tend to have a far greater proportion of past pregnancies that have progressed into the middle or early third trimesters? Are there differences in the specificities, and therefore the pathological effects of the antiphospholipid antibodies in different patients, with some low level antibodies being particularly damaging to the early trophoblast or embryo, but not triggering thrombosis or allowing pregnancy to progress into the fetal period? One can easily see how clinicians may be confused about the comparability of the respective patient populations in different studies. We believe that the full story is yet to be told and that clinical studies to better define the risks of different patients with antiphospholipid antibodies are desperately needed.

An alternative and equanimous interpretation of the current literature holds that the clinical and laboratory differences in antiphospholipid patients observable in the published studies points to two fundamentally different patient populations:

1. Definite (or classic) antiphospholipid syndrome: those with lupus anticoagulant or medium-to-high levels of IgG anticardiolipin antibodies and a fetal death, thrombosis, or neonatal death after delivery for severe pre-eclampsia or fetal distress.
2. Recurrrent pre-embryonic or embryonic pregnancy loss and antiphospholipid antibodies.

Management of patients with antiphospholipid antibodies in pregnancy

General principles of care

There are both similarities and differences in the overall management of women with definite antiphospholipid syndrome and women with antiphospholipid antibodies and recurrent early pregnancy loss. Patients in both groups should undergo preconceptional assessment and counselling. A detailed medical and obstetrical history should be obtained, and the presence of antiphospholipid antibodies should be confirmed. Although all women with antiphospholipid antibodies should be informed of the potential maternal and obstetrical problems, including fetal loss, thrombosis or stroke, pre-eclampsia, fetal growth impairment, and preterm delivery, it appears that those with definite antiphospholipid syndrome are at substantial risk for these complications. In those women who also have SLE, issues related to exacerbation of lupus should be discussed. All patients with anti-phospholipid syndrome should be assessed for evidence of anaemia and thrombocytopenia, since both may occur in association with antiphospholipid syndrome. Assessment for underlying renal disease (urinanalysis, a serum creatinine, twenty-four-hour urine for creatinine clearance and total protein) may be useful.

Once pregnant, the patient with antiphospholipid syndrome should be seen frequently by a physician and instructed to notify the physician immediately if she develops signs or symptoms of thrombosis or thromboembolism, severe pre-eclampsia, or decreased fetal movement. Once the antiphospholipid antibodies have been detected and confirmed, serial antiphospholipid antibody deter-minations are not useful.

A primary goal of the antenatal visits in antiphospholipid patients after twenty weeks' gestation is the detection of hypertension and/or proteinuria. Because of the risk of uteroplacental insufficiency, fetal ultrasounds should be performed every four to sixteen weeks starting at eighteen to twenty weeks' gestation. In otherwise uncomplicated antiphospholipid syndrome patients, standard antenatal surveillance for fetal compromise should be started at thirty to thirty-two weeks' gestation. Earlier and more frequent ultrasound and fetal testing is indicated in patients with poor obstetric histories, evidence of pre-eclampsia, or evidence of fetal growth impairment. In selected cases, fetal surveillance may be justified as early as twenty-four to twenty-five weeks' gestation.

Heparin and other therapies during pregnancy

Heparin is the treatment of choice during pregnancy for women with antiphospholipid antibodies. For women with recurrent pre-embryonic and embryonic losses and no history of thrombosis, relatively low, thromboprophylactic doses of heparin appear adequate. Excellent pregnancy outcomes in such a group were achieved by Rai *et al* (1997) using as little as 10,000 units of unfractionated heparin daily. We recommend that women with definite antiphospholipid syndrome but no history of thrombosis be treated with at least 15,000 units of unfractionated heparin per day, and we favour using higher doses (20,000 units per day) in the second and third trimesters, since 10,000 units per day of heparin may not provide adequate maternal thromboprophylaxis (Barbour, 1995). For women with antiphospholipid antibodies and a history of thrombosis, the American College of Chest Physicians (ACCP), recommends treatment during pregnancy with subcutaneously-administered heparin every twelve hours to prolong the activated partial thromboplastin time (aPTT) into the therapeutic range (Ginsberg and Hirsh, 1998). Low molecular weight heparin may be used in pregnancy, and it will likely replace unfractionated sodium heparin in APS. Doses of low molecular weight heparin that produce trough anti-Factor Xa activity levels of 0.1 to 0.15 U/mL would seem reasonable for patients requiring thromboprophylaxis (Dulitzki *et al*, 1996).

The use of high-dose intravenous immune globulin during pregnancy in women with antiphospholipid antibodies has generated interest because of anecdotal reports of successful pregnancy outcomes using this treatment, usually in combination with prednisone, heparin, or low-dose aspirin (Scott, 1988; Wapner *et al*, 1989; Clark *et al*, 1999). Most of these cases involve more severe cases of antiphospholipid-related pregnancy loss ('refractory' cases) who had failed other therapies. In the largest case series, patients treated with monthly intravenous immune globulin infusions, unfractionated heparin, and low dose aspirin had few pregnancy-related complications (Clark *et al*, 1999). None of sixteen pregnancies had fetal growth restriction, all were delivered after thirty-four weeks' gestation, and pre-eclampsia was diagnosed in only 25%. Similarly, investigators noted no cases of pre-eclampsia and few preterm deliveries in a small case series of women with definite antiphospholipid syndrome treated with a regimen that included intravenous immune globulin (Spinnato *et al*, 1995). However, a prospective, randomised, controlled pilot study of women with definite antiphospholipid syndrome, all of whom received heparin and low-dose aspirin, found no difference in obstetric or maternal outcomes between those who were treated with intravenous immune globulin *versus* placebo (5% albumin solution) (Pregnancy Loss Study Group, 1999). This study included sixteen well-characterised patients with lupus anticoagulant, medium-to-high levels of IgG anticardiolipin antibodies. All had successful pregnancies, and the rates of com- plications were fairly low, though one woman had a postpartum deep vein thrombosis. Thus, it appears that intravenous immune globulin is not of significant benefit beyond heparin treatment in women with antiphospholipid syndrome. It remains possible (and untested), that women who have failed previous heparin therapy during pregnancy might derive sufficient benefit from the addition of intravenous immune globulin for a successful pregnancy.

Summary

Over the last quarter of this century, the association between antiphospholipid antibodies and pregnancy loss has evolved from an interesting observation made by a few insightful clinicians to become part of a newly recognised autoimmune syndrome. It is our view that many past studies have suffered from inadequate characterisation of the specific types of pregnancy loss being reported, and we believe that the final relationship between antiphospholipid antibodies, pre-embryonic, embryonic, and fetal losses is a work still in progress. In women with recurrent pre-embryonic and embryonic loss and antiphospholipid antibodies, as little as 10,000 units per day of unfractionated heparin improves pregnancy outcome. Patients with definite antiphospholipid syndrome must be treated with adequate doses of heparin during pregnancy for the sake of the mother as well as the conceptus. The addition of intravenous immune globulin does not significantly improve maternal and fetal outcome in women with antiphospholipid syndrome, though its role in the patient with a prior treatment failure during pregnancy has not been studied.

References

Aoki K, Hayashi Y, Hirao Y, Yagami Y (1993) Specific antiphospholipid antibodies as a predictive variable in patients with recurrent pregnancy loss. *Am J Reprod Immunol* **29**: 82–7

Barbour LA, Smith JM, Marlar RA (1995) Heparin levels to guide thromboembolism prophylaxis during pregnancy. *Am J Obstet Gynecol* **173**: 1869–73

Bertolaccini ML, Roch B, Amengual O, Atsumi T, Khamashta MA, Hughes GR (1998) Multiple antiphospholipid tests do not increase the diagnostic yield in antiphospholipid syndrome. *Br J Rheumatol* **37**: 1229–32

Branch DW (1987) Immunologic disease and fetal death. *Clin Obstet Gynecol* **30**: 295

Branch DW, Silver RM, Pierangelli SS, van Leeuwen I, Harris EN (1997) Antiphospholipid antibodies other than lupus anticoagulant and anticardiolipin antibodies in women with recurrent pregnancy loss, fertile controls, and antiphospholipid syndrome. *Obstet Gynecol* **89**: 549–55

Branch DW, Scott JR, Kochenour NK, Hershgold E (1985) Obstetric complications associated with the lupus anticoagulant. *N Engl J Med* **313**: 1322–6

Branch DW, Andres R, Digre KB, Rote NS, Scott JR (1989) The association of antiphospholipid antibodies with severe preeclampsia. *Obstet Gynecol* **73**: 541–5

Branch DW, Silver RM, Blackwell JL, *et al* (1992) Outcome of treated pregnancies in women with antiphospholipid syndrome: An update of the Utah experience. *Obstet Gynecol* **4**: 614

Caruso A, De Carolis S, Ferrazzani S, Valesini G, Caforio L, Mancuso S (1993) Pregnancy outcome in relation to uterine artery flow velocity waveforms and clinical characteristics in women with antiphospholipid syndrome. *Obstet Gynecol* **82**: 970–7

Clark AL, Branch DW, Silver RM, Harris EN, Pierangeli S, Spinnato JA (1999) Pregnancy complicated by the antiphospholipid syndrome: outcomes with intravenous immunoglobulin therapy. *Obstet Gynecol* **93**: 437–41

Dulitzki M, Pauzner R, Langevitz P, Pras M, Many A, Schiff E (1996) Low-molecular-weight heparin during pregnancy and delivery: preliminary experience with 41 pregnancies. *Obstet Gynecol* **87**: 380–3

Ginsberg JS, Hirsh J (1998) Use of antithrombotic agents during pregnancy. *Chest* **114**(5 Suppl): 524S–530S

Harris EN (1986) Syndrome of the black swan. *Br J Rheumatol* **26**: 324

Harris EN, Gharavi AE, Boey ML, Patel BM, Mackworth-Young CG, Loizou S, Hughes GR (1983) Anticardiolipin antibodies: detection by radioimmunoassay and association with thrombosis in systemic lupus erythematosus. *Lancet* **2**: 1211–4

Kutteh WH (1996) Antiphospholipid antibody-associated recurrent pregnancy loss: treatment with heparin and low-dose aspirin is superior to low-dose aspirin alone. *Am J Obstet Gynecol* **174**: 1584–9

Kwak JYH, Gilman-Sachs A, Beaman KD, Beer AE (1992) Autoantibodies in women with primary recurrent spontaneous abortion of unknown etiology. *J Reprod Immunol* **22**: 15

Lima F, Khamashta MA, Buchanan NM, Kerslake S, Hunt BJ, Hughes GR. A study of sixty pregnancies in patients with the antiphospholipid syndrome. *Clin Exp Rheumatol* **14**: 131–6

Lockshin MD, Druzin ML, Goei S *et al* (1985) Antibody to cardiolipin as a predictor of fetal distress or death in pregnant patients with systemic lupus erythematosus. *N Engl J Med* **313**: 152–6

Lubbe WF, Palmer SJ, Butler WS, Liggins GC (1983) Fetal survival after prednisone suppression of maternal lupus anticoagulant. *Lancet* **i**: 1361

Lynch A, Marlar R, Murphy J, Davila G, Santos M, Rutledge J, Emlen W (1994) Antiphospholipid antibodies in predicting adverse pregnancy outcome. A prospective study. *Ann Intern Med* **120**: 470–5

MacLean MA, Cumming GP, McCall F, Walker ID, Walker JJ (1994) The prevalence of lupus anticoagulant and anticardiolipin antibodies in women with a history of first trimester miscarriages. *Br J Obstet Gynaecol* **101**: 103–6

Nilsson IM, Astedt B, Hedner U, Berezin D (1975) Intrauterine death and circulating anticoagulant ('antithromboplastin'). *Acta Med Scand* **197**: 153–9

Ober C, Karrison T, Odem RR *et al* (1999) Mononuclear-cell immunisation in the prevention of recurrent miscarriages: a randomised trial. *Lancet* **354**: 365–9

Oshiro BT, Silver RM, Scott JR, Yu H, Branch DW (1996) Antiphospholipid antibodies and fetal death. *Obstet Gynecol* **87**: 489–93

Out HJ, Bruinse HW, Christiaens GC *et al* (1991) Prevalence of antiphospholipid antibodies in patients with fetal loss. *Ann Rheum Dis* **50**: 553–7

Pattison NS, Chamley LW, Birdsall M, Zanderigo AM, Liddell HS, McDougall J (2000) Does aspirin have a role in improving pregnancy outcome for women with the antiphospholipid syndrome? A randomized controlled trial. *Am J Obstet Gynecol* **183**: 1008–12

Parazzini F, Acaia B, Faden D, Lovotti M, Marelli G, Cortelazzo S (1991) Antiphospholipid antibodies and recurrent abortion. *Obstet Gynecol* **77**: 854–8

Parke AL, Wilson D, Maier D (1991) The prevalence of antiphospholipid antibodies in women with recurrent spontaneous abortion, women with successful pregnancies, and women who have never been pregnant. *Arthritis Rheum* **34**: 1231–35.

Pattison NS, Chamley LW, McKay EJ, Liggins GC, Butler WS (1993) Antiphospholipid antibodies in pregnancy: prevalence and clinical associations. *Br J Obstet Gynaecol* **100**: 909–13

Petri M, Golbus M, Anderson R, Whiting-O'Keefe Q, Corash L, Hellmann D (1987) Antinuclear antibody, lupus anticoagulant, and anticardiolipin antibody in women with idiopathic habitual abortion. A controlled, prospective study of forty-four women. *Arthritis Rheum* **30**: 601–6

Plouffe L Jr, White EW, Tho SP, Sweet CS, Layman LC, Whitman GF, McDonough PG (1992) Etiologic factors of recurrent abortion and subsequent reproductive performance of couples: have we made any progress in the past 10 years? *Am J Obstet Gynecol* **167**: 313–20

Rai R, Cohen H, Dave M, Regan L (1997) Randomised controlled trial of aspirin and aspirin plus heparin in pregnant women with recurrent miscarriage associated with phospholipid antibodies. *Br Med J* **314**: 253–7

Scott JR, Branch DW, Kochenour NK, Ward K (1988) Intravenous immunoglobulin treatment of pregnant patients with recurrent pregnancy loss caused by antiphospholipid antibodies and Rh immunization. *Am J Obstet Gynecol* **159**: 1055–6

Silver RM, Porter TF, van Leeuwen I, Jeng G, Scott JR, Branch DW (1996) Anticardiolipin antibodies: clinical consequences of 'low titers'. *Obstet Gynecol* **87**: 494–500

Soulier JP, Boffa MC (1980) Avortements a repetition thromboses et anticoagulant circulant antithromboplastin. *Nouv Presse Med* **9**: 859

Spinnato JA, Clark AL, Pierangeli SS, Harris EN (1995) Intravenous immunoglobulin therapy for the antiphospholipid syndrome in pregnancy. *Am J Obstet Gynecol* **172**: 690

Triplett DA. Lupus anticoagulants: diagnostic dilemma and clinical challenge (1997) *Clin Lab Sci* **10**: 223–8

Wapner RJ, Cowchock FS, Shapiro SS (1989) Successful treatment in two women with antiphospholipid antibodies and refractory pregnancy losses with intravenous immunoglobulin infusions. *Am J Obstet Gynecol* **161**: 1271–2

Wilson WA, Gharavi AE, Koike T, Lockshin MD, Branch DW, Piette JC *et al* (1999) International consensus statement on preliminary classification criteria for definite antiphospholipid syndrome: report of an international workshop. *Arthritis Rheum* **42**: 1309–11

Yasuda M, Takakuwa K, Tokunaga A, Tanaka K (1995) Prospective studies of the association between anticardiolipin antibody and outcome of pregnancy. *Obstet Gynecol* **86**: 555–9

Yetman DL, Kutteh WH (1996) Antiphospholipid antibody panels and recurrent pregnancy loss: prevalence of anticardiolipin antibodies compared with other antiphospholipid antibodies. *Fertil Steril* **66**: 540–6

6

Laboratory diagnosis of the antiphospholipid syndrome

Michael Greaves

Antiphospholipid syndrome (APS) is present when recurrent miscarriage or arterial or venous thrombosis occur in a subject in whom laboratory tests for antiphospholipid antibody (aPL) are positive. The aPL tested for in most laboratories are anticardiolipin (aCL) and lupus anticoagulant (LA). Because transient aPL occur in subjects without APS, possibly associated with infections, it is essential to demonstrate antibody persistence over at least six weeks in a patient with relevant clinical manifestations. Additional clinical and laboratory features may be present in APS, including thrombocytopenia and an unusual, but not specific skin lesion — livedo reticularis. Where APS exists against a background of chronic inflammatory disease, especially systemic lupus erythematosus, the term secondary antiphospholipid syndrome distinguishes it from the primary syndrome, for which there is no evidence of another relevant underlying condition.

The nature of antiphospholipid antibodies

Although referred to as antiphospholipid it is now clear that LA and aCL consist of a family of antibodies reactive with proteins which are themselves complexed with negatively charged phospholipid (Roubey, 1996). For example, many aPL require beta2-glycoprotein I (beta2 GP I), a phospholipid-binding plasma protein with weak anticoagulant activity, for binding to acidic phospholipids (Galli *et al*, 1990; Matsuura *et al*, 1990; McNeil *et al*, 1990). The precise relationships between beta2 GP I, phospholipid and autoantibody are not fully determined. However the plastic of an ELISA plate can substitute for negatively charged phospholipid in this interreaction. This has allowed the development of possibly more specific assays for aPL which employ purified beta2 GP I. Other proteins share this property of binding to phospholipid in a manner that promotes interaction with aPL. These include the coagulation factor prothrombin, the anticoagulant protein C and its cofactor protein S, and annexin V.

This last, previously known as placental anticoagulant protein, could be especially relevant to the pathogenesis of pregnancy failure in APS.

LA is an *in vitro* phenomenon in which the antiphospholipid antibody slows clot formation resulting in lengthening of the clotting time. It can be due to antibodies reactive to beta2 GP I/phospholipid or to prothrombin/phospholipid. The beta2 GP I-dependent antibodies also bind in anticardiolipin assays, as the glycoprotein is present in test serum and often in assay reagents. LA due to prothrombin-reactive antibodies may be negative in anticardiolipin assays. As a result, the important clinical consequence is that some subjects with APS have LA and aCL and some LA only and others have aCL without LA, due to the presence of non-beta2 GP I and non-prothrombin-dependent antibody or possibly to relative insensitivity of the coagulation assays for LA. Because aPL are so heterogeneous a comprehensive laboratory approach is essential for their reliable detection. In most laboratories enzyme-linked immmuno-assays (ELISAs) employing cardiolipin and coagulation-based assays for LA remain the principal diagnostic tools. Beta2 GP I ELISA may offer improved specificity (Cabides *et al*, 1995; McNally *et al*, 1995; Tsutsumi *et al*, 1996; Guerin *et al*, 1997), but it is not essential for diagnosis.

Despite this improved understanding of the nature of aPL, the pathogenesis of pregnancy failure and thrombosis in APS is not fully explained (Greaves, 1999). Whether antibodies to beta2 GP I/phospholipid are causal is not conclusively proven. A range of pathogenetic prothrombotic mechanisms has been reported in subjects with APS, aPL induced resistance to the anticoagulant effect of protein C, vascular endothelial autoimmunity and activation, and impaired fibrinolytic capacity. Furthermore, although thrombosis in the uteroplacental vasculature has been implicated in the pathogenesis of miscarriage, placental infarction is not a universal finding and non-thrombotic mechanisms may be involved, such as failure of implantation or through autoantibody binding to tropho-blast. Although it is possible that, in at least some cases, aPL are surrogate markers for a prothrombotic syndrome with a multi-factorial pathogenesis. Their detection is frequently diagnostically and prognostically useful and remains the principal diagnostic tool. Some understanding of the limitations of these tests assists in the diagnostic process.

Diagnosis of antiphospholipid syndrome

Subjects with APS present to a wide range of clinical specialists, for example, obstetricians, clinical haematologists, neurologists, cardiologists, rheumatologists and dermatologists. A multidisciplinary approach to investigation and management is often appropriate.

It is essential to appreciate that aPL are not specific to APS. As well as the transient antibodies which may, for example, be triggered by intercurrent infection, APL may also arise apparently incidentally in healthy subjects as well as in relation to use of some drugs, particularly chlorpromazine. Persistent antiphospholipid antibody positivity may be a feature of chronic infection, for example, in syphilis, hepatitis C and HIV infection. This is important as these drug induced, transient and post-infective antibodies may not be associated with the clinical thrombotic manifestations of APS. In some cases they appear to be neither beta2 GP I nor prothrombin dependent.

Laboratory investigation

The diagnosis of APS relies on the demonstration of the presence of either LA by coagulation tests, or aPL by solid phase immunoassays. The latter typically employ cardiolipin as antigen (aCL assays). At present, these traditional tests remain the mainstay of laboratory investigation of APS, and it is clear that both LA and solid phase type assays must be employed for the detection of aPL. Reliance on just one type of assay may lead to false negative aPL assessments. There are detailed guidelines for the performance of assays for aPA, such as those prepared on behalf of the British Society for Standards in Haematology (Greaves *et al*, 2000). The methodological comments below are derived from that document.

Coagulation assays (lupus anticoagulant tests)

LA tests are indirect assays which rely upon the slowing of the clotting time of plasma through interaction of the autoantibody with phospholipid. Specificity and sensitivity are enhanced by choosing the most appropriate reagents and conditions. However, because these are indirect tests employing clot formation as an endpoint, factors other than aPL which lengthen or shorten clotting times potentially interfere in LA tests. Examples are anticoagulant drugs and clotting factor deficiencies and inhibitors, which lengthen clotting times and increased clotting factor levels, especially factor VIII, which shortens the time to clotting in some assays, potentially masking the presence of LA. High plasma concentrations of factor VIII occur in mid and late pregnancy and postoperatively, potentially masking the presence of LA.

In order to reduce the risks of false interpretation, in addition to prolongation of clotting time in a phospholipid dependent coagulation test, the criteria for LA positivity also include:

❖ Evidence of an inhibitor demonstrated by mixing studies with normal plasma. If the prolonged clotting time is due to factor deficiency, it corrects to normal in a mixture with equal parts of normal plasma. In contrast, normal plasma cannot generally correct a prolonged clotting time due to an inhibitor, such as LA.

❖ Confirmation of the phospholipid dependent nature of the inhibitor, for example by demonstration that excess phospholipid corrects the clotting time. This is to distinguish LA from other types of coagulation inhibitor, for example, factor VIII inhibitor.

The tests most frequently employed in LA testing are the activated partial thromboplastin time (APTT), the dilute Russell's viper venom time (DRVVT), and the kaolin clotting time (KCT).

No LA test consistently shows 100% specificity and sensitivity, and because of the heterogeneous nature of aPL, more than one test system should be used for detection of LA. Performance of the prothrombin time and thrombin time tests is also important as they are not usually affected by the presence of LA, and the results assist in the interpretation of LA tests. For example, abnormalities in these tests might indicate undisclosed anticoagulant therapy with warfarin or heparin which complicates the interpretation of LA tests.

Sample collection and handling and pre-analytical variables

Ex vivo coagulation activation affects clotting times and minimal venous stasis, rapid draw and immediate anticoagulation are therefore essential for the avoidance of artefact. Plasma should be prepared within one hour of blood collection, by centrifugation at room temperature at 2000g for fifteen minutes. Platelet activation causes exposure of negatively charged phospholipid at the cell surface and therefore contamination with platelets must be minimised, as these will limit the sensitivity of tests particularly after freezing plasma samples. Platelet depletion may be achieved in various ways, most commonly by careful double centrifugation. This is a particularly important step if the plasma is to be stored frozen for assay later.

Activated partial thromboplastin time

The APTT is frequently used as the initial screening test for LA. The principle of the test is activation of coagulation through exposure of recalcified plasma to a large surface area, such as kaolin, and provision of phospholipid to substitute for platelets in the coagulation reactions. This is provided as 'partial thromboplastin', so called to distinguish it from thromboplastin used in the prothrombin time test, which also contains tissue factor. The APTT is influenced by the levels of clotting factors in the intrinsic and common pathways, as well as by the presence of coagulation factor inhibitors and anticoagulants. When prolongation of the APTT is due to coagulation factor deficiency, the clotting time corrects when the test is repeated on an equal mixture of patient and normal plasma, whereas the prolongation above normal may persist with LA, consistent with its inhibitory activity. Correction in a mixing study does not exclude LA, however, as a weak antibody it is of course diluted out by addition of normal plasma and this may be sufficient to abolish its effect. Inhibitors to clotting factors, usually factor VIII, are associated with bleeding rather than thrombosis but also cause prolongation of the clotting times which may not be corrected by addition of normal plasma.

There is great variability in the composition of APTT reagents. The characteristics of the phospholipid component appear to be critical in determining LA sensitivity and reagents vary in both the types of phospholipid present and in their relative concentrations (Kelsey *et al*, 1984). This results in inconsistent sensitivity (Brandt *et al*, 1995). Also, the acute phase reaction and pregnancy are associated with increased levels of fibrinogen and factor VIII, which tend to shorten the APTT and could mask a weak lupus anticoagulant. It is essential that laboratories employ sensitive reagents. Even then, a normal APTT is insufficient to exclude LA and additional tests must be performed.

Dilute Russell's viper venom time (DRVVT)

In the DRVVT, Russell's viper venom (RVV) activates factor X, which in turn activates prothrombin in the presence of calcium ions, factor V and phospholipid, leading to the formation of a fibrin clot. The test does not involve the clotting factors of the intrinsic system, unlike the APTT, nor factor VII, like the prothrombin time. Any inhibition of the coagulant active phospholipid by LA results in a prolonged DRVVT. Like all LA tests, it is not specific. Deficiencies of the relevant clotting factors, for example, factors II and X due to warfarin therapy, will also prolong the DRVVT. The specificity is improved by repeating the test in the presence of a high concentration of phospholipid. This should result in partial or complete correction of the prolonged clotting time due to LA. This phospholipid is often provided as platelet membranes, the technique then being referred to as a platelet neutralisation procedure. In the presence of LA, the ratio of test to normal plasma clotting time is often >1.2, and corrects to <1.2, or at least partially, in the platelet neutralisation procedure. As with all coagulation tests, because of variations in reagents and techniques, it is essential that laboratories derive local normal ranges using a large number of plasma samples from healthy volunteers.

Kaolin clotting time (KCT)

In the KCT no additional phospholipid is employed. The test resembles the APTT in that it involves the intrinsic and common pathways of coagulation, but the sensitivity to LA is theoretically enhanced because the small amount of phospholipid present is only that derived from residual platelets in the test sample and plasma lipids. The test is also affected by clotting factor deficiencies and anticoagulants, but LA is identified when the KCT fails to correct even after relatively large proportions of normal plasma are added, whereas in factor deficiency the KCT is corrected with small amounts of normal plasma. Usually, control and patient plasmas are tested, as well as one mixture (80% control:20% test). A test/control ratio >1.2 generally indicates an abnormal result, and a mixture ratio of >1.2 should be considered as indicative of LA.

In some laboratories, alternative tests for LA are employed but these are not in general use. They include the tissue thromboplastin inhibition test and clotting tests, which use venoms other than Russell's viper venom. Examples are Taipan and Textarin venoms.

Despite attempts to standardise assays (Greaves *et al*, 2000) it should be appreciated that the performance of LA assays is far from ideal. Many 'weak' LA are overlooked and prolongation of clotting times due to coagulation factor deficiency is sometimes wrongly ascribed to the presence of LA (Jennings *et al*, 1997).

Solid phase assays (for aCL and beta2 GP I antibodies)

Solid phase assays for aPL, such as the aCL ELISA test have improved over time in terms of reproducibility (Loizou *et al*, 1985; Khamashta and Hughes, 1993). Unlike the coagulation assays for LA the results are not affected by factor deficiency or the use of anticoagulants. It is possible to test for IgG, IgM and IgA antibodies. Although there has been debate over the diagnostic relevance of IgM aCL, it seems possible that IgM aCL, like IgG antibody, is associated with clinical events and may be the only antibody detected in some patients. In contrast, IgA aCL may not be of clinical significance (Selva-O'Callaghan *et al*, 1998).

aCL tests are standardised by the use of international standards. This allows the calculation of aCL results in IgG or IgM anti-phospholipid units (GPLU and MPLU, respectively) related to a given concentration of affinity purified aCL immunoglobulin. Despite this, the user of these tests should be aware that they lack precision, and comparability between laboratories using different assays is not ensured.

The detection of aCL allows the diagnosis of APS in a subject with an appropriate clinical history, even when LA is absent. However, the aCL assay is not a substitute for the LA test, nor does it confirm that LA is present as different antibodies appear to be responsible for the two activities. Furthermore, the clinical significance of low titre aCL is doubtful. In cases where the aCL titre is less than 20 GPL units and tests for LA are negative, a diagnosis of APS may not be conclusive. Under these circumstances, it is particularly important to consider other causes of thrombosis or miscarriage.

A variety of specific assays for beta2 GP I antibodies have been developed (Roubey *et al*, 1996). Beta2 GP I antibody assays may show higher precision and better correlation with the thrombo-embolic complications in APS and SLE than assays for aCL, and are less likely to show transient positive results in association with infection. However, the problems of standardisation remain and at present these assays are not uniformly in routine use.

Antiprothrombin antibodies generally exhibit poor specificity for venous thrombosis and recurrent fetal loss, and may be found in patients with infection.

In summary, the important considerations in the interpretation of tests for aPL are:

❖ Firm diagnosis of APS requires a consistent clinical history and persistently positive tests for aPL.

❖ LA tests are indirect, not entirely specific and of variable sensitivity.

❖ More than one type of LA test is required, for example, APTT and DRVVT.

❖ Because of the inevitable prolongation of clotting times with their use, anticoagulant therapy generally precludes accurate detection of LA.

❖ Anticardiolipin assays are sensitive but transient positive tests are common.

❖ Both LA tests and aCL (IgG and IgM) assays are required to diagnose or exclude APS.

❖ Avoidance of misinterpretation of laboratory tests requires knowledge of their accuracy, reproducibility, sensitivity and specificity.

Antiphospholipid antibodies and pregnancy

Prevalence and indications for testing

A major feature of APS is recurrent pregnancy loss. The prevalence of aPL among women with recurrent miscarriage has been reported to be 7–42%. This variation is surprising but may be due to the lack of standardisation of laboratory protocols used to detect aPL and patient selection, including that of women with transiently positive test results. Using a comprehensive methodological approach with testing for both LA and aCL, the prevalence of persistently positive tests is around 15% (Rai *et al*, 1995). In women with recurrent miscarriage due to APS the prospective fetal loss rate has been reported to be as high as 90% (Rai *et al*, 1997). In contrast, the prevalence of positive tests for aPL in unselected women of child-bearing age is 3%. The tests are not therefore sensitive predictors of poor pregnancy outcome in women with no history of pregnancy complications (Creagh *et al*, 1991). Many women with recurrent pregnancy loss who exhibit aPL suffer only early miscarriages (<12 weeks' gestation); others have both early and late (>12 weeks) or late miscarriages only. Testing for aPL is applicable to all women with recurrent miscarriage, especially as effective treatment is available.

Because miscarriage is a common phenomenon, screening for aPL is not informative after a single event. In women with three or more consecutive pregnancy losses, testing for aPL should form part of the investigation of pathogenesis. It is possible that screening for aPL could be usefully extended to include women who do not fulfil the above strict criteria for APS but who have repeated miscarriage, defined as two miscarriages or three or more non-consecutive miscarriages. Unexplained loss of any morphologically normal fetus in the second or third trimester is also perhaps an indication for testing for aPL as are early, severe pre-eclampsia or severe placental insufficiency in any pregnancy. Because maternal aPL may fluctuate during pregnancy (Kwak *et al*, 1994; Topping *et al*, 1999), tests are best performed preconceptually or in the first trimester.

Conclusions

Antiphospholipid syndrome is an important diagnosis. Clinicians must be aware of the limitations of the available laboratory tests used to detect antiphospholipid antibodies and use this knowledge when interpreting test results alongside clinical evidence for the presence of the syndrome.

References

Brandt JT, Triplett DA, Alving B, Scharrer I (1995) Criteria for the diagnosis of lupus anticoagulants: an update. *Thromb Haemost* **74**: 1185–90

Cabides J, Cabral A, Alarcon-Segovia D (1995) Clinical manifestations of antiphospholipid syndrome in patients with systemic lupus erythematosus associate more strongly with anti beta2 glycoprotein I than with antiphospholipid antibodies. *J Rheumatol* **22**: 1899–1906

Creagh MD, Duncan SLB, Mc Donnell JM, Greaves M (1991) Failure of the detection of antiphospholipid antibodies alone to predict poor pregnancy outcome. *Br J Haematol* **77**: 4

Galli M, Comfurius P, Maassen C, Hemker HC, de Baets MH, van Breda-Vriesman PJ, Barbui T, Zwaal RF, Bevers EM (1990) Anticardiolipin antibodies directed not to cardiolipin but to a plasma protein cofactor. *Lancet* **335**: 1544–7

Greaves M (1999) Antiphospholipid antibodies and thrombosis. *Lancet* **105**: 664–6

Greaves M, Cohen H, Machin SJ, Mackie I (2000) Guidelines on the investigation and management of the antiphospholipid syndrome. *Br J Haematol* **109**: 704–15

Guerin J, Feighery C, Sim RB, Jackson J (1997) Antibodies to beta 2-glycoprotein I: a specific marker for the antiphospholipid syndrome. *Clin Exp Immunol* **109**(2): 304–9

Jennings I, Woods TAL, Kitchen S, Preston FE, Greaves M (1997) Potentially clinically important inaccuracies in testing for the lupus anticoagulant: an analysis of the results from the surveys of the UK national external quality assurance scheme (NEQAS) in blood coagulation. *Thromb Haemost* **77**: 810–11

Kelsey PR, Stevenson KJ, Poller L (1984) The diagnosis of lupus anticoagulant by the activated partial thromboplastin time. The central role of phosphatidyl serine. *Thromb Haemost* **52**: 172–5

Khamashta MA, Hughes GRV (1993) ACP Broadsheet No. 136. Detection and importance of anticardiolipin antibodies. *J Clin Pathol* **46**: 104–7

Kwak JYH, Barini R, Gilman-Sachs A, Beaman KD, Beer AE (1994) Down-regulation of maternal antiphospholipid antibodies during early pregnancy and pregnancy outcome. *Am J Obstet Gynecol* **171**: 239–46

Loizou S, McCrea JD, Rudge AC, Reynolds R, Boyle CC, Harris EN (1985) Measurement of anticardiolipin antibodies by enzyme-linked immunosorbent assay (ELISA): standardisation and quantitation of results. *Clin Exp Immunol* **62**: 738–45

Matsuura E, Igarashi Y, Fujimoto M, Ichikawa K, Koike T (1990) Anticardiolipin cofactor(s) and differential diagnosis of autoimmune disease. *Lancet* **336**: 177–8

McNally T, Mackie IJ, Machin SJ, Isenburg DA (1995) Increased levels of beta 2 glycoprotein-I antigen and beta 2 glycoprotein-I binding antibodies are associated with a history of thromboembolic complications in patients with SLE and primary antiphospholipid syndrome. *Br J Rheumatol* **34**: 1031–6

McNeil HP, Simpson RJ, Chesterman CN, Krilis SA (1990) Antiphospholipid antibodies are directed against a complex antigen that includes a lipid binding inhibitor of coagulation: beta 2-glycoprotein 1 (apolipoprotein H). *Proc Natl Acad Sci USA* **87**: 4120–4

Rai RS, Regan L, Clifford K, Pickering W, Dave M, Mackie I *et al* (1995) Antiphospholipid antibodies and beta2-glycoprotein-1 in 500 women with recurrent miscarriage: results of a comprehensive screening approach. *Hum Reprod* **10**: 2001–5

Rai R, Cohen H, Dave M, Regan L (1997) Randomised controlled trial of aspirin and aspirin plus heparin in pregnant women with recurrent miscarriage associated with phospholipid antibodies (or antiphospholipid antibodies). *Br Med J* **314**: 253–7

Roubey RAS (1996) Antigenic specificities of antiphospholipid autoantibodies: implications for clinical laboratory testing and diagnosis of the antiphospholipid syndrome. *Lupus* **5**: 425–30

Selva-O'Callaghan A, Ordi-Ros J, Monegal-Ferran F, Martinez N, Cortos-Hernandez F, Vilardell-Tarres M (1998) IgA anticardiolipin antibodies — relation with other antiphospholipid antibodies and clinical significance. *Thromb Haemost* **79**: 282–5

Tsutsumi A, Matsuura E, Ichikawa K, Fujisaku A, Mukai M, Kobayashi SL, Koike T (1996) Antibodies to beta2-glycoprotein I and clinical manifestations in patients with systemic lupus erythematosus. *Arthritis Rheum* **39**: 1466–74

7

Recurrent miscarriage: The Auckland approach to management

Neil S Pattison, Hilary Liddell

Introduction

Recurrent miscarriage (RM) is an emotionally charged disorder, plagued by poor classification, incomplete understanding of aetiology, and treatments which are not evidence-based. The strict definition of RM is three consecutive miscarriages prior to twenty weeks' gestation. Based on an incidence of spontaneous miscarriage of 15%, the risk of RM should be 0.4% — it is double this at 1%. This suggests that for some couples there is an underlying cause for their RM. For most couples finding an explanation for RM remains elusive and treatments are empirical. Many centres have established RM clinics (RMC) which coordinate management and improve outcomes (Liddell *et al*, 1991). The challenge for the future is a more comprehensive approach to evidence-based care.

Couples presenting with RM require empathy, recognition of their medical disorder, a clear explanation of their condition and careful investigation to exclude those infrequent causes of RM where specific therapies are available. All require guidance and support to enable them to embark on a subsequent pregnancy with confidence. The spontaneous cure rate for unexplained RM is above 50% — a critical factor in counselling.

This chapter will provide the approach to management for these couples that has been adopted and refined at the National Women's Hospital, Auckland, New Zealand.

Classification

For any disorder where the aetiology is frequently unexplained, a medical classification will remain elusive. This is particularly so for RM, where aetiological classifications have varied enormously. A recent approach by Bricker and Farquharson (2000), to provide a classification based solely on timing of the loss, is hopefully a step forward (*Table7.1*).

Table 7.1: Classification of recurrent miscarriage by gestation

Type of loss	Typical gestation (weeks)	Fetal heart activity	Principal diagnostic group	Beta HCG level
Pre-embryo	<6	Never	Idiopathic/chromo-somal/hormonal	Low then fall
Embryo	6–8	Never	Hormonal/ idiopathic	Initial rise then fall
Fetal	>8	Lost	Antiphospholipid syndrome/some trisomies	Rise then static or fall
Second trimester	>11	Lost	Antiphospholipid syndrome Anatomical and infective causes	Initial rise then fall

From Farquharson *et al*, 1998

RM is an area where a concise history alone will frequently lead to the diagnosis, but is often unavailable. Full details of every miscarriage should be recorded, including duration of pregnancy, ultrasound information, presence of fetal heart, histological confirmation, and chromosomal analysis of the products of conception if available. Family history of miscarriage, the birth weight of the mother herself, fetal abnormalities, procoagulant states, as well as personal medical history will aid diagnosis. Each pregnancy loss for every woman should — wherever possible — be formally classified as in *Table 7.2*.

The timing of the loss is the first step towards diagnosis (*Table 7.1*). **Pre-embryonic miscarriages**, often described as biochemical pregnancies, are those miscarriages where the pregnancy has been confirmed only by a positive human chorionic gonadotrophin (hCG) test. For women with RM who are attending the National Women's Hospital (NWH) early pregnancy clinic, pre-embryonic miscarriages occurs in 8.5% (42/491, 1994–96) with either a 'late menstrual bleed' or recognised miscarriage prior to six weeks.

Embryonic miscarriages are those where a fetal pole has been seen on ultrasound examination, or there has been a rise in hCG level. Miscarriage occurs usually before eight weeks. Here there has been failed development of the embryo with either early resorption (blighted ovum depending on when ultrasound performed) or small defective embryo with no fetal heart development. Typically hCG levels do not rise as expected.

Fetal miscarriages after eight weeks, are those where a fetal heart has been seen on ultrasound. These are less common. Miscarriages in the critical window between eight and ten weeks are often due to the less severe trisomies.

Second-trimester miscarriages are more commonly due to maternal factors relating to abnormal placentation, antiphospholipid antibodies (aPL) or cervical incompetence.

The presence of previous live births has lead to the description of primary RM, those women who have no successful pregnancies and secondary RM for women who after a successful first pregnancy/ies subsequently miscarry repetitively. This aspect is also of diagnostic importance. Only 40% of women referred to the NWH RM clinic have primary RM.

A practical approach to management is to assume that RM has been idiopathic but to formally exclude those infrequent conditions where specific therapy is required. This more positive approach leads easily into the supportive care management subsequently required.

Table 7.2: Classification by aetiology	
Anatomical	Cervical incompetence
	Uterine abnormalities
Endocrine	Polycystic ovarian disease
	Luteal phase defects
Infection	Bacterial vaginosis, Chlamydia,
	Ureaplasma
Chromosomal	Parental dislocations
	Oocyte aging
Immunological	Antiphospholipid syndrome
Vascular	Thrombophilia
Idiopathic	Environment, stress

Anatomical uterine defects

Anatomical uterine defects account for less than 5% of women attending a RM clinic and typically cause second-trimester mis-carriage. These women often have primary RM.

Cervical incompetence, the most common disorder in this group, can occur spontaneously or follow treatment for cervical intra epithelial neoplasia or recurrent termination of pregnancy. The aetiology of premature effacement and dilatation of the cervix is likely to be multi-factorial, with a number of contributing factors including infection, placental insufficiency, as well as any intrinsic cervical factor. There is evidence that regardless of the aetiology placing a cervical cerclage is likely to prolong pregnancy in women with a history of RM (RCOG trial; Althuisius, 2000). Cervical incompetence is best identified by a careful history of the timing and type of miscarriage. Cervical incompetence may be increasing due to many young women undergoing cervical procedures, such as Lletz and cone biopsy. Cervical incompetence is also documented following stilboestrol exposure. The diagnosis of cervical incompetence remains difficult, with no single diagnostic test having a high degree of accuracy.

Uterine abnormalities, in contrast, are easy to diagnose with high resolution ultrasound and diagnostic hysteroscopy. The incidence in the general population is still unknown. Uterine anomalies, including the mullerian development anomalies — such as septate uterus, unicornuate and bicornuate uterus, when they cause RM cause second-trimester miscarriage. Recent studies of patients with uterine anomalies report birth rates of 68% in untreated women with RM. This is indeed our experience, although we have found a high preterm delivery rate. These women tend to have their losses at progressively later gestations and often carry a subsequent pregnancy to term without treatment.

Acquired lesions, such as synechiae and fibroids do not cause RM. All women attending our RMC between 1993 and 1996 with RM said to be secondary to fibroids had successful pregnancies. Eighty five percent (n=13) of women with uterine fusion defect had successful outcomes, however 36% were delivered preterm.

Hormonal disorders

The maternal endocrine disorders, diabetes and thyroid disease, rarely cause RM. Women with diabetes mellitus and hypothyroidism are reported to have an increased incidence of RM but it is uncommon for women with undiagnosed disease to have their primary presentation to a RMC. Even women with severe disease are unlikely to have RM. Thyroid antibodies are not an infrequent finding in the work up for RM. Rushworth *et al*, 2000, found 19% (162/870) women with RM to have thyroglobulin antibodies, only 28 of these women had a history of thyroid disorders or abnormal function tests.

The presence of antibodies did not effect subsequent pregnancy outcome. Live births occurred in 58% (14/24) of women with antibodies and 58% (47/81) in those women without antibodies.

Controversial areas of RM are polycystic ovarian disease (PCO) and luteal phase defects. The recognition that inadequate or delayed production of progesterone by the corpus luteum may contribute to failed implantation and early miscarriage is historically important in the causation of RM. However, the diagnosis of this condition is unreliable. Traditionally, endometrial biopsies in the luteal phase of the cycle showing a lack of synchrony between the secretory endometrial maturation and the supposed time of ovulation, has been taken to indicate defective luteal phase. Absolute levels of progesterone measured in peripheral blood are unlikely to show any discrimination between normal cycles and cycles of defective luteal phases. These subtle hormone aberrations are associated with infertility and recurrent pre-embryonic or embryonic loss.

In PCO it appears that the elevated luteinising hormone (LH) level is associated with poor reproductive outcome, but there is debate over the best method of testing for this and attempts to lower the LH level prior to pregnancy have not resulted in an improved outcome (Clifford *et al*, 1996).

Screening women with RM for PCO shows an incidence of 36–40% (Liddell *et al*, 1997; Rai *et al*, 2000) however the presence of PCO on ultrasound is not predictive of outcome in the subsequent monitored pregnancy (Liddell *et al*, 1997).

The question remains: are the low progesterone or hCG levels in early pregnancy due to a hormone deficiency or a failing pregnancy for another reason?

Progesterone and hCG therapy have been subjected to many randomised-controlled trials which showed no benefit. However, our knowledge of early pregnancy development has improved to the extent that design flaws in these studies are now apparent. Inadequate early pregnancy monitoring, poor selection of patients and inappropriate timing of treatment blighted these trials. They were performed prior to accurate ultrasound dating and chromosomal evaluation. Often therapy was commenced when a fetal heart was detectable; by which stage all the critical hormonal events were complete. Also, both drugs were used indiscriminately rather than in women specifically selected for supposed luteal phase deficiency. If hormonal supplementation is effective it should be given from the time of ovulation and continued throughout the critical stage of implantation up until the nine weeks stage when the corpus luteum becomes less important. The most recent review in the Cochrane Library, 2001 based on three small studies failed to find sufficient evidence to advocate the use of hCG (Scott and Pattison, 2001). This may be a question of insufficient power. Only one of these randomised-controlled studies addressed RM in the subgroup of women with oligoamenorrhoea (Quenby and Farquharson, 1994). These authors reported a benefit from hCG therapy (75% success in hCG treated group versus 59% in the placebo arm).

Genital tract infection

Maternal genital tract infection is an unlikely cause of RM but has been suspected of causing second-trimester miscarriages (Kurki *et al*, 1992) and preterm labour. Bacterial vaginosis (BV), Chlamydia and Ureaplasma have been described in association with RM. In an attempt to address this issue authors have sampled women with RM and made comparisons between those with first- and second-trimester losses (Llahi-Camp *et al*, 1996). The incidence of BV was higher in the group with at least one second-trimester loss (21%, 27/130) compared with 8% (31/370, p<0.001). Social and racial factors influence the incidence of BV and local figures should be ascertained. For an infection to cause RM it would need to be relatively asymptomatic and long term. RM is an unlikely sequel from infections such as herpes, rubella etc.

Chromosomal disorders

Chromosomal factors account for the majority of spontaneous miscarriages. Typically, chromosomal abnormalities cause pre-embryonic miscarriages. An excellent study by Johnson *et al*, 1990, employing chorionic villous sampling pre-completion of a spontaneous miscarriage, found that 75% of miscarriages were aneuploidy. The more serious the chromosomal abnormality, the earlier the miscarriage occurs. Sensitive hCG assays reveal a pregnancy loss rate of 30% in healthy women. The majority of these losses are unavailable for study as two thirds occurred before the first missed period (Wilcox *et al*, 1988). Bryne *et al* (1985) from a study of 3472 miscarriages found that 56% of embryonic miscarriages (crown rump length [CRL] less than 30mm) had chromosomal abnormalities. This contrasts with second-trimester miscarriages (CRL>30mm) where the incidence of chromosomal abnormality was only 2%.

For couples to have RM from chromosomal abnormalities, either one partner must have a chromosomal abnormality, or there must be a tendency to produce recurrent abnormalities in their offspring — such as age or environmental factors. The risk of miscarriage when one partner has a balanced translocation depends on which partner and which chromosome/s. Expert genetic counselling is required. The maternal age related increase in chromosomal abnormalities is often of concern for women with RM who because of RM are attempting pregnancy later in life than planned. This adds to their existing risk. The average age at presentation at the RMC at NWH is thirty-four years.

Fetal chromosomal analysis after miscarriage in women with RM shows an increased incidence of abnormality. Carp *et al* (2001) found that 29% (36/125) of miscarriages had a chromosomal abnormality. Vidal *et al* (2000) in a similar study found the incidence of abnormalities in women with RM to be 53%. These factors suggest an increased tendency to chromosomal anomalies apart from age in some women with RM. This is a critical factor in counselling women with RM.

Thrombophilias

The procoagulant disorders of acquired and hereditary thrombophilia are both associated with RM. The hereditary thrombophilia are a group of genetic disorders of blood coagulation resulting in an increased incidence of thrombosis. This diverse group includes deficiencies of antithrombin111, protein C and S, and the most common — resistance to activated protein C (APC). At present, there is insufficient data on timing of fetal loss in women with this disorder. It does appear that these women typically have second-trimester miscarriages. Recent data from the EPCOT study group (European Prospective Cohort on Thrombophilia) investigated 1384 women with thrombophilia (Preston *et al*, 1996). They used as controls the female partner of the males who had thrombophilia. In the time period, 571 of the female cohort with thrombophilia conceived. The odds ratio for pregnancy loss (prior to twenty-eight weeks) was 1.35 (1.01–1.82). This was 29% (168/571) compared with 23.5% (93/395) in the controls. This control group may have been inappropriate as some of the fetuses would have inherited thrombophilia from their father and these fetuses may be more likely to miscarry than non-affected fetuses. Ridker *et al* (1998) in a study of 113 women with RM found factor V Leiden mutation in 8% of women. The incidence of fetal loss is highest in women with antithrombin III deficiency, and lowest in women with APC resistance

Antiphospholipid syndrome

The antiphospholipid syndrome (APS) is an acquired thrombophilia causing RM. This is a more common cause of fetal loss than hereditary disorders. APS is thought to exist in 10–15% of RM populations. Of the two antibodies, anticardiolipin and lupus anti-coagulant, we find anticardiolipin antibodies more frequently. These disorders are associated with pregnancy loss throughout the pregnancy, and also pregnancy complications — including growth retardation, and pre-eclampsia.

In the period 1993–1996, 122 women miscarried with the pregnancy being monitored through the early pregnancy clinic at NWH. Five percent (6/122) had an ectopic pregnancy, 8.9% (15/122) had a pre-embryonic miscarriage, 24% (29/122) an embryonic miscarriage and 60% (72/122) a fetal miscarriage. Chromosomal anomalies were common whenever testing was possible (31% [6/22] of the tested embryonic miscarriages and 80% [42/58] of the tested fetal miscarriages). This data confirms our clinical impression that fetal miscarriages are typically due to the less severe trisomies.

Investigation

All pregnancy losses should be investigated. After a single embryonic or pre-embryonic loss, most women only require a detailed history. Management should include a careful explanation, empathy and emotional support. The favourable prognosis with a live birth rate of 80% or more for subsequent pregnancies should be explained. For some women, depending on previous obstetric history and the details of this miscarriage, a more comprehensive individual approach is required. Clearly, it is inappropriate to request invasive investigations after one pre-embryonic loss, but it is also inappropriate not to investigate a single fetal loss after sixteen weeks' gestation.

The investigation of RM has become more streamlined in recent years. Previously, patients were subjected to a large battery of tests that seemed more designed to reassure the patient that something was being done, rather than yielding true information about proven aetiology of RM. There is controversy over the best investigations to diagnose specifically conditions that are now recognised as being relevant to the causation of RM, especially PCO and APS. It is likely that, as we understand more about the aetiology of RM, the types of investigations will become more specific.

The protocol for investigation of RM at NWH is illustrated in *Table 7.3*. Where possible these investigations are performed prior to pregnancy. Test for aPL antibodies should be repeated six weeks after an initial positive result, at the beginning of each new pregnancy and at twelve weeks' gestation as 5% of patients with positive antibodies only show these antibodies during pregnancy.

Table 7.3: Protocol for investigation

Investigation	Any fetal loss after 13 weeks*	Two first-trimester miscarriages	Three first-trimester miscarriages
Detailed history	y	y	y
Family history	y	y	y
Menstrual history	y	y	y
Antiphospholipid antibodies	y	y	y
Thrombophilia screen	y	y	y
Endocervical swab	y		y
Luteinising hormone and luteal phase progesterone			
Pelvic ultrasound scan	y		y
Hysterosalpingogram	?		y
Parental karyotypes			y
Cervical sounding	?		y

* true mid-trimester loss
? history dependent

Management

Couples with RM should be seen and investigated prior to pregnancy. A management plan should be made for the subsequent pregnancy. The security that this approach gives to couples is of great importance. Many couples will not have the courage to attempt another pregnancy unless they feel that all avenues have been investigated, and that there is a reasonable prospect of a successful pregnancy. Most couples can be confidently reassured that regardless of the cause, there is a 70–80% chance of a successful pregnancy with each pregnancy. This statistic is often considerably higher than couples expect.

The chance of a successful pregnancy is largely dependent on the number of previous miscarriages and the age of the female partner (Brigham *et al*, 1999; Quenby and Farquharson, 1993). However, at or above the age of forty, there is still a 50% chance of a successful pregnancy with each attempt (NWH 1993–1996 data).

Supportive care

There is general agreement that supportive care should be the mainstay of treatment, both for couples with an identifiable and non-identifiable cause. The model of supportive care used at NWH (*Table 7.4*), is based upon the following principles.

1. Pre-pregnancy assessment

All couples are encouraged to attend a pre-pregnancy RMC for full history, examination and investigation as described above. Subsequently, a management plan for the future pregnancy is discussed.

2. Early pregnancy clinic

Continuity of care with the same personnel responsible for both the pre-pregnancy RMC and the early pregnancy clinic is an important issue. The point of contact for the couple should be an experienced nurse/counsellor, with twenty-four-hour availability. Early diagnosis is essential. The woman is asked to contact immediately when pregnancy is suspected in order to start early pregnancy care as soon as possible, in most cases twenty-eight to thirty-five days from the last period.

3. Pregnancy care plan

After diagnosis of pregnancy, the couple meets with the nurse/ counsellor who discusses activity levels and plans for the pregnancy, as previously discussed with the couple.

4. Pregnancy monitoring

The patient is offered specific monitoring of her pregnancy including weekly clinic visits, twice-weekly HCG levels, ultrasound to detect the fetal heart is offered at around six weeks' gestation, and thereafter offered weekly for maternal reassurance. Scans are brief, measure only the presence of a fetal heart and a crown-rump length, and document any retroplacental or subchorionic bleeding.

5. Relaxation and stress reduction

Each week a physiotherapy relaxation class is held, which teaches general relaxation techniques and creative visualisation of the baby growing. Patients are also encouraged to use a relaxation tape, and have a specific period of stress reduction relaxation therapy each day.

6. Rapid response team

If there are any concerns about the pregnancy, eg. bleeding (40% of women with an on-going pregnancy will experience first-trimester bleeding, NWH 1993–1996 data), they are encouraged to contact their nurse/counsellor from the clinic immediately, and appropriate reassurance is arranged via ultrasound.

During the pre-pregnancy discussion and the initial pregnancy discussion, avoidance of common and known associations of bleeding in RM patients are discussed. These include travelling, work stresses — including shift work, long hours, and interpersonal relationship conflicts — stressful family dynamics, inappropriate advice from non-medical friends and relatives, sexual intercourse, aerobic activity and exercise.

7. Miscarriage in monitored pregnancy

If a failed pregnancy is recognised on ultrasound, at the earliest opportunity an evacuation of the uterus is performed to obtain samples for chromosomes. A post-operative visit is then organised to discuss these results, and whether anything further can be offered in the next pregnancy. Chromosomal anomalies are common in these women.

For ongoing pregnancies at thirteen weeks the women graduate to a high risk clinic or appropriate specialist.

Table 7.4: Supportive care in pregnancy
⌘ Pre-pregnancy assessment
⌘ Early pregnancy clinic
⌘ Pregnancy care plan
⌘ Pregnancy monitoring
⌘ Relaxation and stress reduction
⌘ Rapid response team
⌘ Chromosome analysis of miscarriage monitored

Management of specific disorders

Chromosome abnormalities: Parents who have identifiable chromosome abnormalities are referred for genetic counselling. On the whole, those with a balanced translocation have a good chance of successful outcome in the next pregnancy (75% deliver a live baby next time; NWH data). Despite appropriate genetic counselling, it is difficult to take into account the different biological behaviour of a specific translocation in different couples. It is apparent that with the same inherited translocation poor reproductive outcome may be confined to only one of several female descendants. There is evidence that balanced translocations carried by the father have a lesser reproductive effect than maternal carriage of translocations. There is also evidence that peripheral blood carrier typing may not be reflecting what is truly happening at the level of the ovum.

Fetal genetic factors are overwhelmingly important as a cause of RM, and will become increasingly so with the ageing obstetric population. Ageing of the ova is variable among women of the same chronological age, and it is apparent that some RM women start forming recurrent trisomies in their mid-thirties.

There are also non-chromosomal genetic problems with the embryo that are more common for women with RM. A family history of RM, stillbirth, neonatal death or chromosomal abnormality is more common in the families of women who suffer from RM. The incidence of fetal abnormality in the live births of women who have a history of RM is double that of the background obstetric population (NWH data). This would tend to support the theory that some RM are due to carriage of lethal genes. There is evidence from animal and fertility work that male sperm abnormalities may be causative in RM. Sperm separation to eliminate obvious abnormalities such as diploid or dyspermy, which could contribute to molar pregnancy and partial-molar pregnancy or more subtle abnormalities, is an important research area.

Antiphospholipid syndrome: Treatment of aPS remains controversial. Aspirin therapy has been shown by some trials to improve fetal outcome however our recent studies suggest that for women with low or medium-level aCL antibodies, the reproductive outcome is not improved by the addition of aspirin. There is evidence from the study by Rai *et al* (1997), in a population who were largely lupus anticoagulant positive, that the addition of heparin improved reproductive outcome. However, given that this therapy has potential for serious complications, the population with whom it is appropriate needs to be very carefully defined. Our practice is to reserve heparin for those women with both high level aPL antibodies (aCL +/- lupus anticoagulant) and a past or current obstetric history suggesting placental vascular problems. These include previous thrombotic events, antepartum haemorrhage, intrauterine growth retardation and fetal or second-trimester miscarriages only. Most women referred to our clinic have low to medium level aCL antibodies and we obtain excellent results in this population with either aspirin 150mg a day, or supportive therapy alone (Pattison *et al*, 2000).

Hormonal disorders: The evidence for hCG or progesterone treatment for all women with RM is clear — it is not associated with improved outcomes. However, replacement therapies for women with PCO or proven luteal phase defects remains controversial. Our practice is to use 5000µ hCG from first visit to ten weeks' gestation in this subgroup of women.

Uterine structural anomalies: Surgical treatment is usually not required for women with RM and the finding of a uterine shape anomaly. Recent studies of patients with uterine anomalies and RM report birth rates of 62% (Heinonen, 1997). The procedure of open uterine metroplasty is no longer advised in view of the likelihood of adhesions with open uterine surgery, and the reported infertility, which may be in excess of 30%. Specific patients, taking into account the timing of their pregnancy losses — especially the occurrence of mid-trimester miscarriage with a normal fetus or preterm labour — may be successfully treated with hysteroscopic septal division. Further information is needed to establish long-term outcomes after hysteroscopic metroplasty, but this appears to be the procedure of choice in carefully selected patients with known uterine anomalies.

Cervical incompetence: The MRCOG trial had as its inclusion criteria that the obstetrician concerned with the management of the patient, considered placing a cervical cerclage to be in the patient's interest. The study reinforces the view that clinical judgement in each case is of importance, and that evidence from the patient's past history, as well as events that are occurring in the current pregnancy, should be taken into account before the decision is made. Cervical cerclage is accompanied by increasing maternal morbidity, largely related to infection. In cases where there is doubt, ultrasound monitoring to detect such events as early funnelling of the cervix, may be of value. Our data shows that women having had cervical sutures placed at the National Women's Hospital's RM clinic, 44% had had previous Lletz or laser therapy to cervix, 50% had previous chorioamnionitis and 31% had had previous multiple terminations of pregnancy.

In cases where placement of a vaginal cerclage is difficult due to loss of the vaginal cervix, trans-abdominal cervical cerclage has been shown to have excellent reproductive outcomes (see *Chapter 16*). This operation involves laparotomy during pregnancy, and placement of the stitch at the level of the internal os can be difficult and potentially haemorrhagic. Recently laparoscopic cervical cerclage in the pre-pregnancy stage has been developed (Lesser, 1998). This new technique may offer the advantages of less traumatic interval surgery, and easier anatomical placement with decreased adhesion formation.

Conclusion

We have a lot to learn about both the diagnosis and treatment of RM. We hope that a more evidence-based approach will improve outcomes and avoid unnecessary therapies. This is an area where more trials are required. Reassurance and supportive care should not be overlooked as successful therapies

References

Althuisius SM, Dekker GA, van Geijn HP, Bekedam DJ, Hummel P (2000) Cervical incompetence prevention randomized cerclage trial (CIPRACT): study design and preliminary results. *Am J Obstet Gynecol* **183**(4): 823–9

Bricker L and Farquharson RG (2000) Recurring Miscarriage, The Obstetrician and Gynaecologist. *RCOG press* **2**: 17–23

Brigham SA, Conlon C, Farquharson RG (1999) A longitudinal study of pregnancy outcome following idiopathic recurrent miscarriage. *Hum Reprod* **14**(11): 2868–71

Bryne J, Warburton D, Kline J, Blanc W *et al* (1985) Morphology of early fetal deaths and their chromosomal characteristics. *Teratology* **32**: 297–315

Carp H, Toder V, Aviram A, Daniely M, Mashiach S, Barkai G (2001) Karyotype of the abortus in recurrent miscarriage. *Fertil Steril* **75**(4): 678–82

Clifford K, Rai R, Watson H, *et al* (1996) Does suppressing luteinising hormone secretion reduce the miscarriage rate? Results of a randomised controlled trial. *Br Med J* **312**(7045): 1508–11

Heinonen PK (1997) Reproductive performance of women with uterus anomalies after abdominal or hysteroscopic metroplasty or no treatment. *J Am Assoc Gynecol Laparosc* **4**: 311–7

Johnson MP, Drugan A, Koppitch FC, *et al* (1990) Postmortem chorionic villus sampling is a better method for cytogenetic evaluation of early fetal loss than culture of abortus material. *Am J Obstet Gynecol* **163**(5 Pt 1): 1505–10

Kurki T, Sivonen A, Renkonen O, *et al* (1992) Bacterial vaginosis in early pregnancy and pregnancy outcome. *Obstet Gynaecol* **80**: 173–7

Lesser KB, Childers JM, Surwit EA (1998) Transabdominal cerclage: a laparoscopic approach. *Obstet Gynecol* **91**(5 Pt 2): 855–6

Liddell HS, Pattison NS, Zanderigo A (1991) Recurrent miscarriage-outcome after supportive care in early pregnancy. *Aust N Z J Obstet Gynaecol* **31**(4): 320–2

Liddell HS, Sowden K Farquhar C (1997) Recurrent miscarriage: screening for polycystic ovaries and subsequent pregnancy outcome. *Aust N Z J Obstet Gynaecol* **37**(4): 402–6

Llahi-Camp JM, Rai R, Ison C, Regan L, Taylor-Robinson D (1996) Association of bacterial vaginosis with a history of second trimester miscarriage. *Hum Reprod* **11**(7): 1575–8

Pattison NS, Chamley LW, Birdsall M, *et al* (2000) Does aspirin have a role in improving pregnancy outcome for women with the antiphospholipid syndrome? A randomized controlled trial. *Am J Obstet Gynecol* **183**(4): 1008–12

Preston FE, Rosendaal FR, Walker ID, Brief E, Berntorp E *et al* (1996) Increased fetal loss in women with heritable thrombophilia. *Lancet* **348**(9032): 913–6

Quenby S, Farquharson RG (1994) Human chorionic gonadotropin supplementation in recurring pregnancy loss: a controlled trial. *Fertil Steril* **62**(4): 708–10

Quenby S, Farquharson RG (1993) Predicting recurrent miscarriage: What is important? *Obstet and Gynaecol* **82**: 132–8

Rai R, Backos M, Rushworth F, Regan L (2000) Polycystic ovaries and recurrent miscarriage — a reappraisal. *Hum Reprod* **15**(3): 612–5

Rai R, Cohen H, Dave M, Regan L (1997) Randomised controlled trial of aspirin and aspirin plus heparin in pregnant women with recurrent miscarriage associated with phospholipid antibodies (or antiphospholipid antibodies). *Br Med J* **25**, 314(7076): 253–7

Ridker PM, Miletich JP, Buring JE *et al* (1998) Factor V Leiden mutation as a risk factor for recurrent pregnancy loss. *Ann Intern* **128**(12 Pt 1): 1000–3

Rushworth FH, Backos M, Rai R, Chilcott IT, Baxter N, Regan L (2000) Prospective pregnancy outcome in untreated recurrent miscarriers with thyroid autoantibodies. *Hum Reprod* **15**(7): 1637–9

Scott JR, Pattison N (2001) *Human chorionic gonadotrophin for recurrent miscarriage* (Cochrane Review). In: The Cochrane Library, Issue 2, Update Software, Oxford

Vidal F, Rubio C, Simon C, Gimenez C, Minguez Y, Pellicer A, Santalo J, Remohi J, Egozcue J (2000) Is there a place for preimplantation genetic diagnosis screening in recurrent miscarriage patients? *J Reprod Fertil Suppl* **55**: 143–6

Wilcox AJ, Weinberg CR, O'Connor JF *et al* (1988) Incidence of early loss of pregnancy. *N Engl J Med* **319**(4): 189–94

8

The pathogenic mechanism(s) of antiphospholipid antibodies in causing recurrent miscarriage

Larry W Chamley, Neil S Pattison

In most cases of recurrent miscarriage the molecular mechanisms that cause fetal demise are not known. Antiphospholipid antibodies (aPL) are believed to be involved in up to 40% of recurrent miscarriages (Birdsall *et al*, 1992). The mechanism(s) by which aPL cause miscarriage, or late fetal death, is also unknown but we are beginning to discover some of the molecular activities of these antibodies that lead to fetal demise.

Definition of antiphospholipid antibodies

There are various definitions of aPL but in this chapter we define the term to include lupus anticoagulant and antibodies that react with the phospholipids cardiolipin or phosphatidyl serine and are detected by ELISA. Antiphospholipid antibodies do not react directly with phospholipid but rather with phospholipid/protein complexes. The most studied protein involved in these complexes is β_2 glycoprotein I (β_2GPI). The significance of β_2GPI in the pathogenesis of aPL will also be discussed.

Antiphospholipid antibodies: cause or association?

Antiphospholipid antibodies are associated with a variety of obstetric complications including recurrent miscarriage, stillbirth, pre-eclampsia and intrauterine growth retardation (IUGR) (Branch *et al*, 1989; Pattison *et al*, 1993). There is also growing evidence that these antibodies are associated with recurrent IVF implantation failure (Birdsall *et al*, 1996; Birkenfeld *et al*, 1994; Stern *et al*, 1998). Antiphospholipid antibodies are also associated with thrombotic disorders such as stroke and pulmonary embolism in the systemic circulation (Asherson and Harris, 1986; Levine *et al*, 1995; Horbach *et al*, 1996).

The first demonstration that aPL are directly pathogenic and not just markers of a disease came with the demonstration by Branch *et al* (1990) that passive transfer of aPL to pregnant mice caused fetal death. Others have confirmed the effects of aPL on pregnancy in a variety of murine models (Bakimer *et al*, 1992; Blank *et al*, 1994; Sthoeger *et al*, 1996). There is also evidence from murine models that aPL have procoagulant effects in the systemic circulation (Pierangeli *et al*, 1995; 1996) and that they can inhibit periimplantation events (Sthoeger *et al*, 1993; Tartakovsky *et al*, 1996). From these various murine models we can conclude with reasonable certainty that aPL are directly pathogenic and are not just markers of the conditions with which they are associated.

The significance of phospholipid-binding proteins (cofactors)

A major step towards a clearer understanding of how aPL cause disease came with the discovery that these antibodies do not react directly with phospholipids, such as cardiolipin or phosphatidyl serine. Rather, aPL bind to phospholipid-binding proteins (Galli *et al*, 1990; McNeil *et al*, 1990; Matsuura *et al*, 1990). The first of these proteins shown conclusively to be involved with aPL binding was β_2 glycoprotein I (β_2GPI). β_2 glycoprotein I was originally thought to be a cofactor that was required to allow aPL to bind to phospholipids (McNeil *et al*, 1990; Matsuura *et al*, 1990). It has now been shown that β_2GPI is itself the antigen for aPL (Matsuura *et al*, 1994; Roubey *et al*, 1995; Tincani *et al*, 1996; Chamley *et al*, 1999).

β_2 glycoprotein I is a plasma protein that is present in normal blood at 150–300µg/ml (Cleve and Rittner, 1969). If β_2GPI is the antigen for aPL, how is it then that patients can have both the antibody and antigen in their circulation and the two do not form immune complexes? The answer to this question lies in the finding that β_2GPI only becomes antigenic for aPL after if is immobilised on a negatively-charged surface, such as, cardiolipin or phosphatidyl serine (Matsuura *et al*, 1994; Roubey *et al*, 1995; Chamley *et al*, 1999). Immobilisation of β_2GPI on negatively charged surfaces is thought to cause a conformational change in the protein (shape change) which exposes cryptic sites in the β_2GPI to which aPL bind (Chamley *et al*, 1999). Thus, circulating β_2GPI is not antigenic for apL (Chamley *et al*, 1999). Normally, negatively charged phospholipids are found only on the inner leaflet of cell membranes (the outer leaflet being made up of primarily phosphatidyl choline and phosphatidyl ethanolamine). When a cell becomes activated, damaged or apoptotic negatively-charged phospholipids are exposed on the outer leaflet. If the cell in question is in contact with the blood then β_2GPI can bind to the exposed phospholipid and undergo the conformational alteration that allows aPL binding (*Figure 8.1a, b*). A disease process is then initiated. Exactly what the disease process is that causes pregnancy complications remains unknown but some clues have been found from *in vitro* experiments. Some of these possible mechanisms are discussed in the following sections.

The finding that β_2GPI is only antigenic for aPL when bound to negatively charged phospholipid answers another riddle posed by these antibodies. Namely, why do patients with aPL have significant clinical episodes, such as fetal death or thrombosis, interspersed with periods of good health yet their antibody levels do not change? The answer is that the antibodies only become pathogenic when a triggering event(s) has led to the exposure of negatively-charged cellular phospholipids. These triggering events are probably unrelated to the antibodies.

Pregnancy is a time of considerable tissue remodelling, a process that is associated with the exposure of negatively-charged phospholipids, and may be in itself a triggering event. This might explain why there appears to be a significant group of women who have pregnancy complications as their only clinical manifestation of the antiphospholipid antibody syndrome (APS).

How do antiphospholipid antibodies cause miscarriages?

Is the current concept correct?

The mechanism of action of aPL is unknown but it is a widely held view that aPL causes fetal death and other obstetric complications by inducing thrombosis in the uterine spiral arteries (De Wolf *et al*, 1982). It is proposed that thrombosis leads to infarction of the placental lobes supplied by the artery in question and subsequent fetal demise (*Figure 8.2*).

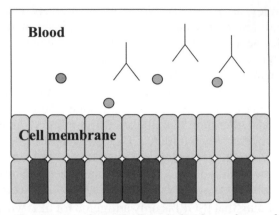

Figure 8.1a: Negatively charged phospholipids such as phosphatidyl serine are found only in the inner leaflet of the membrane bi-layer of resting cells. Thus, negatively charged surfaces are not available to immobilise β₂GPI which circulates in the blood in a form that is not antigenic for antiphospholipid antibodies

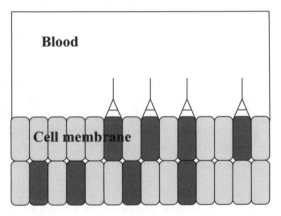

Figure 8.1b: Following cellular activation, tissue damage, tissue remodelling or apoptosis phosphatidyl serine is transported to the outer leaflet providing a surface for immobilisation of β₂GPI. The immobilised β₂GPI then undergoes a conformational change exposing cryptic epitopes

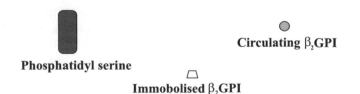

Phosphatidyl serine

Circulating β₂GPI

Immobolised β₂GPI

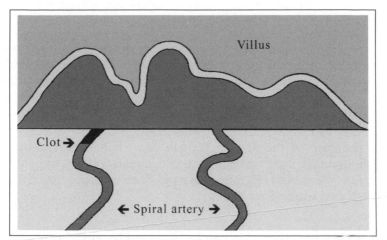

Figure 8.2: It is commonly, but probably incorrectly, suggested that aPL induce fetal demise by inducing thrombosis of the uterine spiral arteries. This thrombosis would then lead to infarction of the lobe of the placenta supplied by the spiral artery and consequent fetal death

Although thrombosis of the spiral arteries might explain how aPL c hypothesis in explaining early miscarriage (or IVF implantation failure). Firstly, significant blood flow to the intervillous space does not occur until the end of the first trimester of pregnancy (Hustin and Schaaps, 1987; Rodesch *et al*, 1992). During the first weeks of pregnancy trophoblast plugs occlude the spiral arteries and only allow percolation of blood/plasma to the implantation site. Thus, it is unlikely that aPL could cause early miscarriages or IVF implantation failure by a thrombotic mechanism. Secondly, the available histological evidence is not supportive of a thrombotic mechanism. Out *et al* (1991), in a survey of 17 placentae from women with aPL found no evidence of thrombosis in 18% of cases. Another study found no evidence of thrombosis in any placentae studied where the pregnancies ended prior to sixteen weeks of gestation (Salafia and Cowchock, 1997). While it is possible that thrombosis could contribute to the pathogenesis of aPL-mediated fetal death (particularly late fetal losses) it is unlikely that thrombosis is the primary cause of recurrent early miscarriage. Any proposed mechanism by which aPL disrupt pregnancy must account for first-trimester losses or propose a dual mechanism of action.

In vitro clues about possible alternative mechanisms.

β_2 glycoprotein I is expressed primarily by the liver but it has been shown that other cell types including trophoblasts also synthesise this protein (Chamley *et al*, 1997). Several immunohistochemical studies have shown that β_2GPI is localised to syncytiotrophoblast, extravillous cytotrophoblasts and macrophages in normal placentae (Chamley *et al*, 1993; Chamley *et al*, 1997; Donohoe *et al*, 2000). The presence of the antigen for aPL on trophoblasts raises the possibility that these antibodies could directly affect trophoblast functions. A number of groups have provided evidence that aPL do, indeed, alter trophoblast biology.

Trophoblast proliferation can be inhibited by antiphospholipid antibodies

The first function of trophoblasts is proliferation, ie. cellular replication. Following implantation, at which point the blastocyst contains in the order of 100 cells, trophoblasts rapidly proliferate so that there are many millions of these cells at the end of the first trimester. Syncytiotrophoblasts, cover the placenta and do not proliferate. These cells represent a barrier to transfer of antibodies into the placenta during the first trimester of pregnancy. In contrast, villous cytotrophoblasts and those extravillous cytotrophoblasts that are proximal to the villi proliferate (Bulmer *et al*, 1988). Chamley *et al* (1998) have shown that human aPL and monoclonal murine aPL inhibit the proliferation of choriocarcinoma cell lines (malignant trophoblasts) in a concentration-dependent fashion. If aPL have the same effect *in vivo*, the development of extra villous trophoblast populations would be disrupted leading to inadequate implantation, while the syncytiotrophoblast layer of the placenta would prevent the aPL attacking villous cytotrophoblasts allowing relatively normal development of the villous placenta (Chamley *et al*, 1998).

Effects of antiphospholipid antibodies on syncytiotrophoblasts

The presence of the hormone human chorionic gonadotrophin (hCG) is one of the first biochemical markers of pregnancy. Human CG is essential during the first weeks of pregnancy to maintain the corpus luteum. The β chain of hCG is produced by the syncytiotrophoblast layer of the placenta. Antiphospholipid antibodies have been shown to reduce the level of hCG secreted by isolated trophoblasts and placental explants in culture (Shurtz-Swirski *et al*, 1993; Di Simone *et al*, 1995). The evidence that aPL directly effect syncytiotrophoblast function is complemented by reports showing that monoclonal aPL can inhibit the ability of choriocarinoma cells to form into syncytiotrophoblast-like multinucleated clumps (Adler *et al*, 1995). These two lines of evidence suggest that aPL can adversely affect the function and/or formation of syncytiotrophoblasts.

Effects of antiphospholipid antibodies on trophoblast invasion

In order to establish the utero-placental circulation cytotrophoblasts break through the syncytiotrophoblast layer and invade the decidua attaching the placenta to the uterus. These extravillous trophoblasts also spread out from the implantation site and when they encounter decidual spiral arteries invade both the lumen and extramural portions of these vessels. These trophoblasts then convert the spiral arteries to non-vasoactive, flaccid, large-bore tubes. This process is called the 'physiological changes of pregnancy' (Brosons *et al*, 1967). It has been demonstrated that murine monoclonal aPL can inhibit the invasion of trophoblasts into the basement membrane substance Matrigel, which is used to model the invasive actions of trophoblast (Katsuragawa *et al*, 1997). Human polyclonal aPL have also been shown to have an adverse effect on the *in vitro* invasion of trophoblasts (Di Simone *et al*, 2000b).

Antiphospholipid antibodies and interleukin 3

Several lines of evidence have suggested that the cytokine interleukin 3 (IL-3) may play an important role in antiphospholipid antibody-mediated pregnancy complications. Fishman *et al* (1992; 1993; 1996) have shown that both women and mice with aPL have reduced circulating levels of IL-3 and that administration of IL-3 to mice with aPL can correct the adverse effects of the antibodies on pregnancy. It has also been shown that one of the effects of aspirin, which is used to treat women with aPL, is to increase IL-3 levels (Fishman *et al*, 1995). Furthermore, IL-3 has been reported to overcome the inhibitory effect of aPL on trophoblast invasion and hCG secretion in cell culture models (Di Simone *et al*, 2000a). However, IL-3 does not reverse the effects of aPL on trophoblast proliferation *in vitro* (Chamley *et al*, 2001). Current *in vitro* evidence therefore suggests that IL-3 may have some role to play in the pathogenesis of fetal demise caused by aPL.

Conclusion

It is not yet apparent how aPL, at the molecular level, cause recurrent pregnancy failure but we are beginning to see possible explanations emerge. It is becoming clear that at the cellular level aPL can, at least *in vitro*, affect trophoblast biology in ways that could disrupt pregnancy, but it is not yet clear whether these processes occur *in vivo*. There are other possible mechanisms that we have not described that could also be equally important. For example, we have not discussed the role of other 'cofactor' proteins, such as annexin V, in the pathogenesis of aPL-mediated recurrent miscarriage.

Does it matter how aPL cause miscarriage? Current therapies, particularly heparin prophylaxis, appear to be reasonably successful but may have significant side-effects. If thrombosis of the utero-placental circulation is not the mechanism by which aPL cause early fetal loss how does heparin benefit these women? It has been suggested that heparin may promote trophoblast growth or invasion. If heparin promotes implantation is it still needed during the third trimester for women without a history of thrombotic disease? Further research is required to answer these questions.

References

Asherson RA, Harris EN (1986) Anticardiolipin antibodies — clinical associations. *Postgrad Med J* **62**: 1081–7

Adler RR, Ng AK, Rote NS (1995) Monoclonal antiphosphatidylserine antibody inhibits intercellular fusion of the choriocarcinoma line. *JAR Biol Reprod* **53**: 905–10

Bakimer R, Fishman P, Blank M, Sredni B, Djaldetti M, Shoenfeld Y (1992) Induction of primary antiphospholipid syndrome in mice by immunization with a human monoclonal anticardiolipin antibody (H-3). *J Clin Invest* **89**: 1558–63

Birdsall MA, Pattison NS, Chamley LW (1992) Antiphospholipid antibodies and adverse pregnancy outcome. *Aust N Z J Obstet Gynaecol* **32**: 328–30

Birdsall MA, Lockwood GM, Ledger WL *et al* (1996) Antiphospholipid antibodies in women having in vitro fertilisation. *Hum Reprod* **11**: 1185–9

Birkenfeld, A, Mukaida T, Minichiello M, Jackson M, Kase NG, Yemini M (1994) Incidence of autoimmune antibodies in failed embryo transfer cycles. *Am J Reprod Immunol* **31**: 65–8

Blank M, Faden D, Tincani A, Kopolovic J, Goldberg I, Gilburd B, Allegri F, Balestrieri G, Valesini G, Shoenfeld Y (1994) Immunization with anticardiolipin cofactor (beta-2-glycoprotein I) induces experimental antiphospholipid syndrome in naive mice. *J Autoimmun* **7**: 441–55

Branch DW, Andres R, Digre KB, Rote NS, Scott JR (1989) The association of antiphospholipid antibodies with severe pre-eclampsia. *Obstet Gynecol* **73**: 541–5

Branch DW, Dudley DJ, Mitchell M, Creighton K, Abbott TM, Hammond EH, Dynes RA (1990) Immunoglobulin G fraction from patients with antiphospholipid antibodies cause fetal death in Balb/C mice; a model for autoimmune fetal loss. *Am J Obstet Gynecol* **163**: 210–16

Brosens I, Robertson WB, Dixon HG (1967) The physiological response of the vessels of the placental bed to normal pregnancy. *J Pathol Bacteriol* **93**: 569–79

Bulmer JN, Morrison L, Johnson PM (1988) Expression of the proliferation markers Ki67 and transferrin receptor by human trophoblast populations. *J Reprod Immunol* **14**: 291–302

Chamley LW, Pattison NS, McKay EJ (1993) Elution of anticardiolipin antibodies and their cofactor β_2 glycoprotein 1 from the placentae of patients with a poor obstetric history. *J Reprod Immunol* **25**: 209–20

Chamley LW, Allen JL, Johnson PM (1997) Synthesis of β_2 glycoprotein 1 by the human placenta. *Placenta* **18**: 403–10

Chamley LW, Duncalf A, Mitchell M, Johnson PM (1998) Action of anticardiolipin and antibodies to β_2 glycoprotein I on trophoblast proliferation as a mechanism for fetal death. *Lancet* **352**: 1037–8

Chamley LW, Duncalf A, Konarkowska B, Mitchell M, Johnson PM (1999) Conformationally altered β_2 glycoprotein I is the antigen for anticardiolipin autoantibodies. *Clin Exp Immunol* **115**: 571–6

Chamley LW, Konarkowska B, Duncalf A, Mitchell M, Johnson PM (2001) Is Interleukin-3 important in antiphospholipid antibody-mediated pregnancy failure? In press

Cleve H, Rittner C (1969) Further family studies on the genetic control of beta 2-glycoprotein I concentration in human serum. *Humangenetik* **7**: 93–7

De Wolf F, Carreras LO, Moerman P, Vermylen J, Van Assche A, Renaer M (1982) Decidual vasculopathy and extensive placental infarction in a patient with repeated thromboembolic accidents, recurrent fetal loss, and a lupus anticoagulant. *Am J Obstet Gynecol* **142**: 829–42

Di Simone N, De Carolis S, Lanzone A, Ronsisvalle E, Giannice R, Caruso A (1995) In vitro effect of antiphospholipid antibody-containing sera on basal and gonadotrophin releasing hormone-dependent human chorionic gonadotrophin release by cultured trophoblast cells. *Placenta* **16**: 75–83

Di Simone N, Caliandro D, Castellani R *et al* (2000a) Interleukin-3 and human trophoblast: in vitro explanations for the effect of interleukin in patients with antiphospholipid antibody syndrome. *Fertil Steril* **73**: 1194–1200

Di Simone N, Meroni PL, de Papa N, Raschi E, Caliandro D, De Carolis CS, Khamashta MA, Atsumi T, Hughes GR, Balestrieri G et al (2000b) Antiphospholipid antibodies affect trophoblast gonadotropin secretion and invasiveness by binding directly and through adhered beta2-glycoprotein I. *Arthritis Rheum* **43**: 140–50

Donohoe S Kingdom, JC, Mackie IJ, Burrell S, Quenby S, Jauniaux E, Machin SJ (2000) Ontogeny of beta 2 glycoprotein I and annexin V in villous placenta of normal and antiphospholipid syndrome pregnancies. *Thromb Haemost* **84**: 32–8

Fishman P, Bakimer R, Blank M, Sredni D, Djaldetti M, Shoenfeld Y (1992) The putative role of cytokines in the induction of primary anti-phospholipid syndrome in mice. *Clin Exp Immunol* **90**: 266–70

Fishman P, Falach-Vaknin E, Sredni B, Meroni PL, RudnikiC, Shoenfeld Y (1995) Aspirin modulates interleukin-3 production: additional explanation for the preventive effects of aspirin in antiphospholipid antibody syndrome. *J Rheumatol* **22**: 1086–90

Fishman P, Falach-Vaknin E, Sredni B, Meroni PL, Tincani A, Dicker D, Shoenfeld Y (1996) Aspirin-interleukin-3 interrelationships in patients with anti-phospholipid syndrome. *Am J Reprod Immunol* **35**: 80–4

Fishman P, Falach-Vaknine E, Zigelman R, Bakimer R, Sredni B, Djaldetti M, Shoenfeld Y (1993) Prevention of fetal loss in experimental antiphospholipid syndrome by in vivo administration of recombinant interleukin-3. *J Clin Invest* **91**: 1834–7

Galli M, Comfurius P, Maassen C, Hemker HC, De Baets MH, Van Breda-Veriesman PJ, Barbui T, Zwaal RF, Bevers EM (1990) Anticardiolipin antibodies (ACA) directed not to cardiolipin but to a plasma protein cofactor. *Lancet* **335**: 1544–7

Horbach DA, van Oort E, Donders RC, Derksen RH, de Groot PG (1996) Lupus anticoagulant is the strongest risk factor for both venous and arterial thrombosis in patients with systemic lupus erythematosus. Comparison between different assays for the detection of antiphospholipid antibodies. *Thromb Haemost* **76**: 916–24

Hustin J, Schaaps JP (1987) Echographic [corrected] and anatomic studies of the maternotrophoblastic border during the first trimester of pregnancy. *Am J Obstet Gynecol* **157**: 162–8

Katsuragawa H, Kanzaki H, Inoue T, Hirano T, Mori T, Rote NS (1997) Monoclonal antibody against phosphatidylserine inhibits in vitro human trophoblastic hormone production and invasion. *Biol Reprod* **56**: 50–8

Levine SR, Brey RL, Sawaya KL, Salowich-Palm L, Kokkinos J, Kostrzema B, Perry M, Havstad S, Carey J (1995) Recurrent stroke and thrombo-occlusive events in the antiphospholipid syndrome. *Ann Neurol* **38**: 119–24

Matsuura E, Igarashi Y, Fujimoto M, Ichikawa K, Koike T (1990) Anticardiolipin cofactor(s) and differential diagnosis of autoimmune disease. *Lancet* **336**: 177–8

Matsuura E, Igarashi Y, Yasuda T, Triplett DA, Koike T (1994) Anticardiolipin antibodies recognise β_2 glycoprotein 1 structure altered by interacting with an oxygen modified solid phase surface. *J Exp Med* **179**: 457–62

McNeil HP, Simpson RJ, Chesterman CN, Krilis SA (1990) Antiphospholipid antibodies are directed against a complex antigen that includes a lipid-binding inhibitor of coagulation: β_2 Glycoprotein 1(apolipoprotein H). *Proc Natl Acad Sci* (USA) **87**: 4120–4

Out HJ, Kooijman CD, Bruinse HW, Derksen RH (1991) Histopathological findings in placentae from patients with intra-uterine fetal death and anti-phospholipid antibodies. *Eur J Obstet Gynaecol Reprod Biol* **41**: 179–86

Pattison NS, Chamley LW, Liggins GC, Butler WS, McKay EJ (1993) Antiphospholipid antibodies in pregnancy: prevalence and clinical associations. *Br J Obstet Gynaecol* **100**: 909–13

Pierangeli SS, Liu SW, Anderson G, Barker JH, Harris EN (1996) Thrombogenic properties of murine anti-cardiolipin antibodies induced by beta 2 glycoprotein 1 and human immunoglobulin G antiphospholipid antibodies. *Circulation* **94**: 1746–51

Pierangeli SS, Liu XW, Barker JH, Anderson G, Harris E (1995) Induction of thrombosis in a mouse model by IgG, IgM and IgA immunoglobulins from patients with the antiphospholipid syndrome. *Thromb Haemost* **74**: 1361–7

Rodesch F, Simon P, Donner C, Jauniaux E (1992) Oxygen measurements in endometrial and trophoblastic tissues during early pregnancy. *Obstet Gynecol* **80**(2): 283–5

Roubey RAS, Eisenberg RA, Harper MF, Winfield JB (1995) 'Anticardiolipin' autoantibodies recognise β_2 glycoprotein 1 in the absence of phospholipid. *J Immunol* **154**: 954–60

Salafia CM, Cowchock FS (1997) Placental pathology and antiphospholipid antibodies: a descriptive study. *Am J Perinatol* **14**: 435–41

Shurtz-Swirski R, Inbar O, Blank M, Cohen J, Bakimer R, Shoenfeld Y (1993) In vitro effect of anticardiolipin autoantibodies upon total and pulsatile placental hCG secretion during early pregnancy. *Am J Reprod Immunol* **29**: 206–10

Stern C, Chamley LW, Hale L, Norris H, Dunlop L, Kloss M, Grover S, Speirs A, Baker HWG (1998) Antibodies to β_2 glycoprotein I are significantly associated with in-vitro-fertilisation implantation failure as well as recurrent miscarriage: results of a prospective prevalence study. *Fertil Steril* **70**: 938–44

Sthoeger ZM, Mozes E, Tartakovsky B (1993) Anti-cardiolipin antibodies induce pregnancy failure by impairing embryonic implantation. *Proc Natl Acad Sci* (USA) **90**: 6464–7

Sthoeger ZM, Tartakovsky B, Fogel M, Lasri Y, Mozes E (1996) Anticardiolipin, but not the 16/6 Id anti-DNA antibody induces pregnancy failure. *Immunol Lett* **49**: 117–22

Tartakovsky B, Bermas BL, Sthoeger Z et al (1996) Defective maternal-fetal interaction in a murine autoimmune model. *Hum Reprod* **11**: 2408–11

Tincani A, Spatola L, Prati E et al (1996) The anti-beta2-glycoprotein I activity in human anti-phospholipid syndrome sera is due to monoreactive low-affinity autoantibodies directed to epitopes located on native beta2-glycoprotein I and preserved during species' evolution. *J Immunol* **157**: 5732–8

9

Abnormal genital tract flora and pregnancy loss

Paul E Adinkra, Ronnie F Lamont

Introduction

In the developed world, preterm birth (PTB) remains the major cause of perinatal morbidity and mortality. Preterm birth is defined as delivery before thirty-seven completed weeks' gestation and occurs in approximately 10% of all births, but accounts for up to 75% of perinatal mortality in normally formed fetuses (Guyer *et al*, 1997). The rate of PTB has not changed over the last twenty years, but the survival of preterm infants has increased, and those born prior to thirty-two weeks' gestation and of a birthweight less than 1500g account for most of the deaths or disabilities (Goldenberg *et al*, 2000). In one large cohort of infants who were born before twenty-six weeks' gestation, the most common outcome was stillbirth or death before admission to a neonatal intensive care unit (Wood *et al*, 2000). In the surviving infants who were assessed neurologically and developmentally at thirty months of age, a degree of disability was present in almost 50% of the infants, and in 50% of these, the disability was severe.

Preterm birth has a multifactorial aetiology and the process encapsulates several heterogeneous variables that play a part in initiating spontaneous preterm labour (SPTL), including bio-chemical, immunological and pathological factors that result in an insult to the feto-maternal unit. This has been described as the preterm labour syndrome (Romero *et al*, 1994). The theory proposes that the interaction of these mechanisms stimulates preterm labour through a variety of pro-inflammatory mediators such as cytokines, growth factors and bacterial products. Maternal factors such as black race, cigarette smoking, age and a previous spontaneous PTB are known to be associated with an increased risk of SPTL and PTB, but there is now undeniable evidence to implicate infection as a cause of SPTL (Lamont *et al*, 1986; Andrews *et al*, 1995) possibly accounting for up to 40% of cases (Lettieri *et al*, 1993). Little can be done to reverse any changes in the cervix uteri once a woman presents in

SPTL, and any intervention using tocolytics or antimicrobial therapy at this stage may be too late to arrest the process. A more proactive approach could be adopted by identifying women in early pregnancy with abnormal genital tract flora who are at an increased risk of SPTL, and in whom, by administering appropriate antimicrobial treatment, the process might be prevented.

Infection as a cause of preterm labour

It is generally accepted that term labour is a normal physiological process resulting from stimulation of a prostaglandin cascade resulting in uterine contractility, cervical dilatation and rupture of fetal membranes. Preterm labour may also share this physiological pathway but with a signal occurring too early in pregnancy. Conversely, SPTL may be due to a pathological process triggered by an abnormal signal such as infection. The nearer to thirty-seven weeks' gestation that SPTL occurs, the more likely the process is to be physiological, whereas SPTL nearer to twenty-four weeks' gestation is more likely to be due to a pathological signal (*Figure 9.1*).

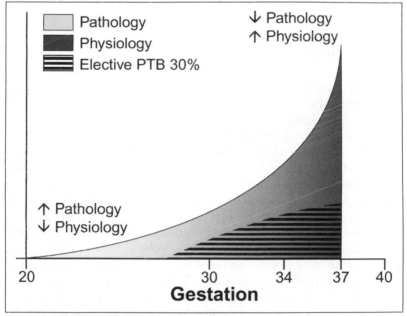

Figure 9.1: Heterogeneity of preterm birth

Although maternal systemic infection and intrauterine infection have both been linked to SPTL and PTB, ascending genital tract infection is thought to be the route through which the bacteria spread. The proposed mechanism is that pathogenic bacteria ascend from the vagina and cervix, colonise the fetal membranes and decidua then invade the amniotic sac and liquor amnii, eventually reaching the fetus by aspiration or seeding through other sites into the fetal circulation (Romero and Mazor, 1988). One source of evidence comes from the introduction of bacterial endotoxins into pregnant animals, which result in SPTL and preterm birth (Dombroski *et al*, 1990). A wide range of bacteria have also been isolated from the amniotic fluid of women in SPTL who have histological chorio-amnionitis (Romero *et al*, 1989). In neonates with congenital sepsis and who are born preterm, bacteria similar to those of the lower genital tract of their mothers have been isolated, further strengthening the role of infection. Maternal systemic infections such as pyelonephritis (Fan *et al*, 1987) and subclinical intrauterine infections (Miller *et al*,1980) are commonly associated with increased rates of SPTL and preterm birth. The antibiotic treatment of ascending genital tract infections under experimental conditions has been shown in some cases to prevent preterm birth (Romero *et al*, 1994).

Normal vaginal flora

The vaginal micro-ecosystem is dynamic and complex and various micro-organisms may be present transiently, making it difficult to distinguish between normal and abnormal flora. There are distinct patterns of bacteria found in pregnant and non-pregnant women, but the normal vaginal flora is dominated by the *Lactobacillus* spp., which maintain an acidic environment in the vagina by producing substances such as lactic acid and hydrogen peroxide (H_2O_2), both of which possess antibacterial properties. In women with normal flora, anaerobic bacteria such as *Mobiluncus* spp., *Bacteroides* spp. and *Prevotella* spp. are usually present in small numbers and anaerobic cocci such as *Peptostreptococcus* spp. can be found in up to 75% of these women. The genital mycoplasmas, *Mycoplasma hominis* and *Ureaplasma urealyticum*, can also be found in small numbers in some women. Facultative aerobes such as *Staphylococcus epidermidis* and *Gardnerella vaginalis* can also be detected in some women. In pregnancy there is a ten-fold increase in the numbers of *lactobacilli*.

The anaerobic bacteria become less common and the numbers of anaerobes remain virtually constant. These alterations make the flora more benign, consisting of organisms of low virulence, which present no risk to the fetus.

Microbiology of prematurity

A variety of micro-organisms that can be found in the lower genital tract have been associated with adverse obstetric sequelae, including preterm birth (Gibbs *et al*, 1992). Sexually transmitted infections caused by micro-organisms such as *Chlamydia trachomatis* and *Neisseria gonorrhoeae* have been linked to increased rates of SPTL and preterm birth (Hardy *et al*, 1984), and the current guidelines from the Centers for Disease Control and Prevention based in Atlanta recommend screening for *C trachomatis* and *N gonorrhoeae* if certain risk factors are present (MMWR, 1997). These include a prior history of a sexually transmitted infection, late prenatal care, age <20 years, low socio-economic status, unmarried women, a history of douching, a partner with a known infection or inconsistent use of barrier contraception.

Maternal infection with group B streptococcus (GBS) is an important cause of perinatal morbidity and mortality by causing early onset GBS disease, but its role in causing preterm prelabour rupture of membranes (PPROM) and PTB is still debatable (McDonald *et al*, 1989; Regan *et al*, 1981). The largest study to date as part of the vaginal infections in pregnancy study group, found that only heavy colonisation of GBS at twenty-three to twenty-six weeks' gestation was associated with an increased likelihood of delivering a preterm low birthweight infant and were more likely to deliver preterm (Regan *et al*, 1996).

Most of the evidence with respect to GBS relates to intrapartum chemoprophylaxis for the prevention of early onset GBS infection of the neonate, and this has been the subject of recently revised guidelines. Published in part by the Centers for Disease Control and Prevention, they recommend adopting a risk-based or a screening-based approach to GBS prevention (CDC, 1996). The first approach involves the use of intrapartum chemoprophylaxis for women with any of the following risk factors: a history of a previous infant with invasive GBS disease, PTB, PPROM for eighteen hours or longer, fever during labour (≥38C) or GBS bacteriuria in the current pregnancy. The screening-based approach recommends low vaginal and rectal cultures between thirty-five to thirty-seven weeks for all women, and intrapartum treatment for all those identified as GBS carriers, even in the absence of any risk factors. Intrapartum chemo-prophylaxis with intravenous penicillin until delivery is recommended due to its narrow spectrum of activity, and the risk of developing resistant strains with the use of ampicillin.

Role of cytokines and neonatal implications

It is generally accepted that bacterial products or endotoxins are capable of triggering the prostaglandin cascade, resulting in labour (Romero *et al*, 1987). Enzymes such as phospholipase A_2 and phospholipase C can cause the release of arachidonic acid, the precursor of prostaglandin synthesis, and both enzymes have been shown to be elevated in the lower genital tract of women with abnormal flora (McGregor *et al*, 1991;1992).

As only a proportion of women with positive amniotic fluid cultures or with PPROM will have an overt clinical infection or even progress to SPTL, there must be other factors that control the mechanism of SPTL other than the presence of the bacteria alone. This has been established as the role of endogenous cytokines, regulatory proteins which mediate inflammation and the host response to infection. This host response results in the production of microbial products, which activate macrophages to produce cytokines. These cytokines are involved in activating the inflammatory cascade that results in prostaglandin production, and subsequent SPTL and term labour.

Proinflammatory cytokines such as interleukin-1β (IL-1β), IL-6 and tumour necrosis factor-α (TNF-α) have been detected in amniotic fluid in term labour, and elevated levels can be found in SPTL in the absence of infection and with intact membranes (Opsjon *et al*, 1993; Romero *et al*, 1992). The levels of amniotic fluid cytokines detected in SPTL in association with intra-amniotic infection are even more markedly elevated (Hillier *et al*, 1993). In one study, women with chorioamnionitis who delivered preterm had significantly higher levels of serum IL-6 compared to those women in SPTL in the absence of infection (Greig *et al*, 1997).

Increased levels of cytokines and prostaglandins in cervico-vaginal secretions may also play a role in subsequent preterm birth (Platz-Christensen *et al*, 1993; Inglis *et al*, 1994). Significantly, higher levels of IL-1b and IL-6 in vaginal secretions were found in women during labour compared to those women not in labour (Imseis *et al*, 1997). In women with BV, vaginal IL-1b was significantly raised, particularly in those who were not in labour. The detection of an allelic variant of gene for TNF-α has been found to be associated with an increased predisposition to PPROM in a subgroup of women, resulting in preterm birth (Roberts *et al*, 1999).

Micro-organisms associated with PTB have been detected by polymerase chain reaction within the amniotic fluid in over 50% of women in SPTL, including even those with intact membranes (Markenson *et al*, 1997), and these bacteria are capable of infecting the fetus during pregnancy. This microbial invasion may stimulate the production of proinflammatory cytokines such as IL-6 in the fetus, resulting in what is described as a fetal inflammatory response syndrome. This acute response is characterised by multi-organ failure and sepsis, and is a major risk factor for neonatal morbidity and mortality (Gomez *et al*, 1998).

Infection-related SPTL and PTB have also been linked to the development of periventricular leucomalacia (PVL), a form of neonatal white matter damage seen near the lateral ventricles, and an important contributing factor to the development of cerebral palsy. The underlying cause of this lesion is unknown, but an increased expression of IL-6 and TNF-α has been observed in infants with PVL compared to those without the condition (Yoon *et al*, 1997). Exposure to intra-amniotic inflammation manifest by funisitis, increased white blood cell count, and increased cytokine concentration in amniotic fluid during labour were strong risk factors for the subsequent development of cerebral palsy at the age of three years (Yoon *et al*, 2000).

Bronchopulmonary dysplasia (BPD) is another neonatal complication of PTB resulting in morbidity and mortality. A link between infection and BPD was proposed, based on the discovery that higher numbers of infants who had acquired nosocomial infections also had BPD, compared to those infants without infection (Rojas *et al*, 1995). There is now increasing evidence to show that exposure to intrauterine inflammation in association with increased levels of proinflammatory cytokines, and histological chorio-amnionitis are associated with the development of BPD in neonates

(Yoon *et al*, 1997). The similarity of cytokine expression in both PVL, BPD and the initiation of SPTL suggests that there may be a common pathway involved (Vigneswaran *et al*, 2000).

Bacterial vaginosis

Bacterial vaginosis (BV) is a polymicrobial condition resulting in an alteration in the vaginal flora, characterised by a decrease in the normally dominant *Lactobacillus* spp. and a one-thousand-fold overgrowth of anaerobes, accompanied by a smaller rise in the number of aerobes. This results in a rise in vaginal pH, and in some women this is accompanied by a vaginal discharge. Micro-organisms associated with BV include Gram-negative anaerobes and facultative anaerobes such as *Gardnerella vaginalis*, *Bacteroides* spp., *Peptostreptococcus* spp., *Mobiluncus* spp. and *Prevotella* spp. The genital mycoplasmas associated with BV include *Mycoplasma hominis* and *Ureaplasma urealyticum*.

Using gram stain of vaginal secretions, three recognised grades of vaginal flora can be recognised: grade I: normal (made up of flora dominated by *lactobacilli*), grade II: intermediate (reduced *lactobacilli* numbers mixed with other bacterial morphotypes) and grade III: bacterial vaginosis (few or absent *lactobacilli* and predominantly other morphotypes) (Rosenstein *et al*, 1996). Certain bacteria can be detected with the same frequency in all three grades of gram stain, whereas some organisms such as *M hominis* and some anaerobes were detected less frequently in grades I and II, and were only manifest in high numbers in grade III or florid bacterial vaginosis. The study recognised a subgroup of women described as 'revertants', where the flora was observed to change from grade III or grade II to grade I within a few weeks.

The prevalence of BV varies widely depending on the population studied but in an unselected population, this averages between 10% and 20% (Mead *et al*, 1993). The figures represented in the table show a very random population selection and prevalence only at a point in time, and it may be that asymptomatic BV may occur in the majority of the population at any time (*Table 9.1*).

Bacterial vaginosis has been implicated in adverse obstetric sequelae including early and late miscarriage, chorioamnionitis, PPROM, SPTL and preterm birth. It has also been associated with adverse gynaecological outcomes such as post-hysterectomy vaginal cuff infection, pelvic inflammatory disease and post-abortal sepsis (Lamont *et al*, 1995). It has also been implicated as a cofactor in the transmission of the human immunodeficiency virus (Sewankambo *et al*, 1997). The normal vaginal environment is acidic with a pH of about 4.5, maintained by glycogen metabolism to acidic products such as lactic acid. In BV, there is a dramatic reduction in H_2O_2-producing *lactobacilli*, which renders the vaginal milieu more alkali and encourages the growth of pathogenic bacteria. At a high pH, this is often accompanied by a fishy odour due to production of volatile amines such as trimethylamine, which are more stable at low pH.

Table 9.1: Incidence rates of bacterial vaginosis

Year of study	Population studied	Incidence of BV
Embree *et al*, 1984	Women attending an STD clinic, USA	64%
Eschenbach *et al*, 1988	Symptomatic college students attending gynaecology clinic, USA	15%
Eschenbach *et al*, 1988	Asymptomatic college students, USA	4%
Bump *et al*, 1988	Group of virginal post-menarchal girls, USA	12%
Hay *et al*, 1992	Low risk gynaecology clinic, Harrow, UK	11%
Blackwell *et al*, 1993	Group of women undergoing termination of pregnancy, USA	28%
Hay *et al*, 1994	A routine antenatal clinic, Harrow, UK	15%
Lamont *et al*, 2000	Group of asymptomatic women attending general practitioner for cervical cytology, UK	9%

Natural history and pathogenesis

The natural history of BV is still not fully understood and varying patterns of behaviour have been observed in women, both in pregnancy and the non-pregnant state. In non-pregnant women, BV has been found to develop usually at the time of menstruation, with the condition resolving at mid-cycle (Keane *et al*, 1997), but is also known to recur (Cook *et al*, 1992). In pregnancy, BV has been shown to develop and resolve spontaneously, but may recur.

There are several factors that increase the risk of acquisition of BV such as increased numbers of lifetime sexual partners and vaginal douching, smoking and the use of an intrauterine contraceptive device, but the underlying aetiology of BV remains unclear. Phage viruses have been shown *in vitro* to lyse vaginal *Lactobacillus* spp. strains, resulting in a fall in the numbers of *lactobacilli* (Pavlova *et al*, 1997). The levels of phages were found to be higher in BV-infected women compared to healthy women and phage infection may account for the reduction of vaginal *lactobacilli*. Another theory centres on a toxin specific to *Gardnerella vaginalis* (Gvh), the most prevalent BV-associated microorganism. This toxin has been implicated in the pathogenesis of BV in association with sialidase activity (Cauci *et al*, 1998). Some women with BV demonstrated an impaired immune defence in which there was high sialidase activity and no anti-Gvh IgA response, and these women were at the greatest risk of preterm birth.

The diagnosis of BV has been based on composite clinical criteria devised by Amsel *et al* in 1983, and has been accepted as the gold standard for the diagnosis of bacterial vaginosis. This is based on finding three out of four of the following:

- a white homogenous vaginal discharge
- a vaginal pH >4.5
- an amine odour following the addition of an alkaline solution of 10% potassium hydroxide to a sample of vaginal secretions
- the presence of clue cells (bacteria so adherent to vaginal epithelial cells as to make the cell wall indistinct) on a wet prep of a vaginal smear.

This method of diagnosis tends to be cumbersome, unpleasant and irreproducible and diagnosis by gram stain is increasingly becoming the preferred choice. Spiegel *et al* (1983) formulated a method of quantification of different bacterial morphotypes as seen on gram–stained vaginal smears. The Gram-stain has been shown to have a higher degree of sensitivity and specificity when compared to other methods of diagnosis, being simple and cheap to perform, and easily reproducible (Lamont *et al*, 1999).

Bacterial vaginosis and pregnancy loss

First-trimester miscarriage

There have been very few studies carried out to assess the association between BV diagnosed in the first trimester and adverse pregnancy outcome. In one study, women attending an assisted conception unit for IVF were recruited in order to evaluate the influence of BV on conception and first-trimester miscarriage (Ralph *et al*,1999). The subjects were screened for BV by Gram-stain prior to egg collection, and 24.6% (190/771) of the women were found to be BV-positive. Although the results showed no difference in the conception rates between those with BV and those with normal flora, there was a significantly increased risk of a first-trimester miscarriage in BV-positive women (31.6%), compared to those with normal flora (18.5%). After adjusting for confounding factors, there was an adjusted relative risk of miscarriage of 2.03 (95% confidence interval 1.09–3.78) in those women with bacterial vaginosis.

Another study found a strong association between the presence of BV diagnosed at less than fourteen completed gestational weeks, and subsequent early pregnancy loss (relative risk 5.4, 95% confidence interval 2.5–11.0) (Donders *et al*, 2000). Of the women who suffered a pregnancy loss, 38% had clinical BV at their first visit compared to 5.3% of the women without bacterial vaginosis. Organisms associated with BV such as *G vaginalis*, *U urealyticum* and *M hominis* were cultured from almost 50% of those women who had an early pregnancy loss compared to 8.25% of the control group. The study also showed that in those women who suffered a pregnancy loss, a higher number had a history of a previous early pregnancy loss compared to those with a normal pregnancy outcome, raising the possibility of an association between recurrent BV and recurrent spontaneous miscarriages.

Second-trimester loss

In a UK study, a significant association was found between abnormal genital tract colonisation and late miscarriage (Hay *et al*,1994). Over 700 women were screened between nine and twenty-four weeks' gestation for the presence of BV or intermediate abnormal flora using Gram stain of vaginal secretions. In the women in whom BV was detected around sixteen weeks' gestation, there was a five-fold increased risk of a second-trimester miscarriage and a three-fold increased risk of preterm birth. In the USA, the presence of BV was associated with a three-fold increased risk of pregnancy loss at less than twenty-two weeks' gestation (McGregor *et al*,1995). In another group of women with a history of at least three consecutive pregnancy losses, the incidence of BV-positive women was found to be significantly higher in those with at least one second-trimester miscarriage compared to those who had suffered only recurrent first-trimester pregnancy losses (Llahi-Camp *et al*, 1996).

Prediction of preterm birth

The identification of a marker of PTB in early pregnancy or even prior to pregnancy may provide a means of early intervention and hence the prevention of any adverse outcome. The traditional maternal and fetal risk factors such as multiple pregnancy, intrauterine growth restriction and pre-eclampsia account for only a proportion of all preterm births. A history of a previous spontaneous PTB remains the best predictor of a subsequent SPTL and PTB, but primiparous women with no past obstetric history as a guide, account for up to 45% of births.

Various biochemical markers such as fetal fibronectin, sialidase and cervical lactoferrin have been proposed as useful predictors of preterm birth (Goldenberg *et al*, 2000). A shortened cervical length measured by transvaginal ultrasound in pregnancy has also been shown to be associated with a shortened gestation (Anderson *et al*, 1990). Interleukin-6 (Lockwood *et al*, 1994) and IL-8 (Rizzo *et al*, 1997) in cervicovaginal secretions have also been shown to be of value in the detection of abnormal flora in the amniotic cavity, and may be helpful predictors of preterm birth. Amniotic fluid IL-6 has also been proposed as a reliable marker for the diagnosis of the onset of preterm labour (Romero *et al*, 1993).

A large number of trials have used the presence of bacterial vaginosis (BV) as a predictor of SPTL and PTB of infectious aetiology, and most have concluded that there is a statistically significant association between abnormal genital tract colonisation and adverse pregnancy outcome. One Indonesian study demonstrated a two-fold increased risk of PTB in women with BV detected between sixteen and twenty weeks compared to women with BV diagnosed later in pregnancy (Riduan *et al*, 1993). In another study, BV found in early pregnancy was associated with a 2.6-fold increased risk of SPTL, and a 6.9-fold increased risk of preterm birth (Kurki *et al*, 1992). In a UK study, BV was associated with a five-fold increased risk of PTB and late miscarriage when detected prior to sixteen weeks' gestation, independent of other risk factors such as a previous PTB, black race or smoking (Hay *et al*, 1994). The overall trend suggests that the earlier in pregnancy at which BV is detected, the greater the risk of an adverse outcome (*Figure 9.2*). Another possible marker of inflammation is provided by the presence of insulin-like growth factor binding protein-1 (IGFBP-I) in the cervical secretions of BV-positive pregnant women. This protein was found to be associated with a significant increase in the risk of infectious morbidity when compared to women who had BV but were negative for IGFBP-1 (Kekki *et al*, 1999).

Author	Max GA. of sampling		RR + CI
Gravett *et al*, 1986	32	$0^{2.0}$	(1.1–3.5)
McDonald *et al*, 1992	28	$0^{1.8}$	(1.0–3.2)
Hillier *et al*, 1995	26	$0^{1.4}$	(1.2–1.8)
Krohn *et al*, 1995	26	$0^{1.5}$	(1.1–2.2)
Germaine *et al*, 1994	26	$0^{1.2}$	(1.0–1.3)
Hillier *et al*, 1995	26	$0^{1.5}$	(0.8–3.0)
McGregor *et al*, 1990	24	$0^{2.0}$	(1.1–6.5)
Riduan *et al*, 1993	20	$0^{2.0}$	(1.0–3.9)
Hay *et al*, 1994	20		$0^{5.5}$ (2.3–13.30)
Kurki *et al*, 1992	17		$^{6.9}0$(2.5–19)

1 2 3 4 5 6 7

Figure 9.2: Relationship of abnormal colonisation to preterm delivery or preterm labour according to gestational age at screening

Treatment of BV in pregnancy

A number of studies have been performed to try to reduce the incidence of pregnancy loss using antibiotics (*Table 9.2*). The choice of different antibiotics in varying doses and regimens given by different routes to women with differing degrees of risk has achieved variable success so far. This has been compounded by the use of different methodologies of antibiotic intervention, timing of treatment and the variable methods of diagnosis of BV that are used in practice. In the recently published ORACLE study, the choice of erythromycin and co-amoxiclav to treat PPROM and SPTL raises certain questions (Kenyon *et al*, 2001). Erythromycin is bactericidal and co-amoxiclav is bacteriostatic and this property may result in their respective activities cancelling out each other. The use of tocolytic therapy in less than 50% of those purported to be in SPTL combined with a median gestational age at delivery of greater than thirty-eight weeks, implies that a lot of these women were not actually in SPTL, and of those who were, less than half were in SPTL due to infection. By giving antibiotics at such a late stage, irreversible cervical changes would have occurred already, making it difficult to prevent both PPROM and SPTL from occurring.

The current guidelines issued by the CDC in Atlanta propose that it is reasonable to screen and treat women with BV who are thought to be at high risk of preterm birth (CDC).

Treatment trials using metronidazole

The efficacy of oral metronidazole was investigated in eighty pregnant women who were BV-positive and considered to be high risk of PTB due to a history of a previous spontaneous preterm birth (Morales *et al*, 1994). The subjects were randomised between thirteen and twenty weeks' gestation to receive 250mg of metronidazole three times daily for seven days or a placebo. There were significantly fewer admissions in the treatment group for PTB (18% vrs 39%), SPTL (27% vrs 38%), PPROM (14% vrs 33%) and low birthweight infants (5% vrs 33%). Hauth *et al* (1995) recruited over 600 women with a history of a previous spontaneous PTB or low maternal weight of less than 50kg to a randomised controlled study using oral metronidazole and erythromycin or placebo. Women in this trial were randomised regardless of whether they had BV or not. Of the women with BV, the rate of PTB was 31% in those receiving the combined treatment regimen, compared to 49% in those receiving placebo (p=0.006). Of the women who did not have BV, there was no significant difference in the rate of preterm birth.

In the largest randomised trial of antibiotics for the prevention of PTB in women with asymptomatic BV, it was found that the metronidazole therapy of low and high-risk women in pregnancy did not reduce the rate of PTB or adverse neonatal outcome (Carey *et al*, 2000). The administration of two 2-gram doses of oral metronidazole between sixteen and twenty-four weeks' gestation and repeated at twenty-four to thirty weeks, though effective in eliminating BV, did not reduce the rate of spontaneous preterm labour. However, up to 85% of the women recruited were Black or Hispanic, which is not representative of a general obstetric population and the subjects were not treated before sixteen weeks' gestation, the time when risk of adverse outcome is most likely the greatest. These findings were supported by an earlier trial by McDonald *et al* in Australia in which women were recruited on the basis of a heavy growth of the BV-associated organism, *G vaginalis* (McDonald *et al*, 1997). In this study, women were given twice daily 400mg doses of metronidazole for two days at twenty-four weeks' gestation, and only repeated if *G vaginalis* was still present four weeks after the first course. Although it was concluded that in women with a previous spontaneous PTB, metronidazole did reduce the likelihood of a subsequent PTB, the overall PTB rate in the treatment arm was not reduced when compared to those receiving placebo.

Treatment trials using clindamycin

Clindamycin given orally or vaginally has been the choice of antibiotic for the treatment of BV in several studies, since it is effective against most of the bacteria associated with BV and achieves good tissue penetration. The use of clindamycin has been associated with variable success at reducing the rate of SPTL and PTB, but the optimum timing, dose and route of treatment has not as yet been identified.

In a non-randomised controlled trial in more than 1000 women in whom BV was treated with oral clindamycin (300mg twice daily for seven days) from twenty weeks' gestation, screening for abnormal vaginal flora including syphilis, gonorrhoea and chlamydia took place in the first phase of the trial and appropriate treatment was given (McGregor *et al*, 1995). Similarly, women who were symptomatic for BV were treated with clindamycin. In the second or treatment phase, women were screened and periodically sampled for BV and other abnormal flora and the same clindamycin treatment was given to BV-positive women. Treatment with oral clindamycin was associated with a 50% fall in the rate of preterm birth (9.8% vrs 18.8%). Women between fourteen and twenty-six weeks' gestation

Table 9.2: Summary of treatment trials in pregnancy

Author	Study design	Subject nos.	Inclusion criteria	Gestation at treatment	Treatment regime	Outcome measures of pregnancy expressed as a percentage (%)
McGregor *et al*, 1994	Multicentre RDBPCT	271 enrolled	Composite criteria: >20% CC and two out of three of HD, pH>4.5, AO and Gram stain	16–27/40	5gm CLIN 2% nocte for 7 days vs placebo	PTB at<37/40 PROM CLIN: 15.0 Clin 15.0 Placebo: 7.2 Placebo: 16.2 Birthwgt<2.5kg CLIN: 13.6 Placebo: 44.0
Morales *et al*, 1994	RDBPCT in women with PTB in pre-ceding pregnancy from idiopathic PTL or PROM	94 eligible 80 enrolled	Composite criteria: HD, vag pH>4.5, CC, AO and no Trich	13–20/40	250mg MET tdds for 7 days vs placebo (vit C)	PTB at <34/40 Birthwgt<2.5 MET:5 kg Placebo: 1.1 MET: 14 PTB at <37/40 Placebo: 33 MET: 18 PROM Placebo: 39 MET: 5 Placebo: 33
Hauth *et al*, 1995	RDBPCT in women with previous spontaneous PTB or maternal weight <50kg before pregnancy	624 enrolled	Three out of four of composite criteria: HD, pH<4.5, CC, AO no GC, Trich or yeast	22–24/40 for 1st rx. If BV+, 2nd tx at 2–4 weeks after end of first course	250mg MET tds for 7 days + 333mg ERY tds for 14 days vs placebo (lactose filler) in ratio of 2:1	PTB<37/40+ BV MET + ERY: 31 Placebo: 49 PTB<37/40+BV+previous PTB MET+ERY: 39 Placebo: 57 PTB<37/40+BV+mat.wgt. <50kg MET+ERY: 14 Placebo: 33

Table 9.2: cont.

Joesoef et al., 1995	Multicentre RDBPCT	745 enrolled	PH>4.5 and GS (Nugent's criteria)	14–26/40	5gm CLIN 2% noce for 7 days vs p'acebo	PTB<37/40 CLIN: 15.0 Placebo: 13.5	PTB<32/40 CLIN: 4.7 Placebo: 2.6
McDonald et al. 1997	Multicentre RDBPCT in women with previous PTB	1734 eligible 879 enrolled	GS or heavy growth of G. vaginalis on LVS	24/40 and 28/40 if further tx required	400mg MET bd for 2 days and 2nd course after one month vs placebo	PTB<37/40 MET: 9.1 Placebo: 41.7	PPROM MET: 4.5 Placebo: 12.5
Carey et al., 2000	RDBPCT in pregnancy	1953 enrolled	GS and pH	16–24/40 for 1st tx 2nd tx at 24–30/40	2gm MET (two doses) vs placebo. 2nd course if BV+	PTB<37/40 MET: 12.2 Placebo: 12.5 PROM MET: 4.2 Placebo: 3.7 PTB<32/40 MET: 2.3 Placebo: 2.7	

Abbreviations: RDBPCT: randomised double-blind placebo-controlled trial; CC: clue cells; HD: homogeneous discharge; AO: amine odour; CLIN: clindamycin; MET: metronidazole; ERY: erythromycin; PTB: preterm birth; PTL: preterm labour; PRCM: preterm rupture of membranes; Trich: trichomonas; GC: gonococcus; GS: gram stain who had BV were recruited to a study using clindamycin 2% vaginal cream for seven days (Joesoef *et al*, 1995). Although effective at eradicating BV (85% cure rate), the rate of PTB was not decreased in the treatment group (15%) compared to the placebo group (13.5%). There was also no significant difference in the rate of low birthweight between the two groups, but 60% of the women were treated after twenty weeks' gestation. In another randomised trial, 271 pregnant women were recruited between sixteen to twenty-seven weeks' gestation and were randomised to receive clindamycin 2% vaginal cream or placebo (McGregor *et al*, 1994). The treatment was effective at eliminating BV, but did not reduce the rate of PTB or perinatal morbidity, yet all of the women were beyond twenty weeks' gestation when treatment was administered.

In a multicentre randomised placebo-controlled trial, clindamycin 2% vaginal cream was given prophylactically to women with a previous spontaneous PTB at between twenty-six and thirty-two weeks' gestation for one week (Vermeulen *et al*, 1999). In the women who completed the trial, clindamycin failed to prevent PTB and there was a higher rate of neonatal morbidity in the treatment group. None of the women who delivered preterm had BV, making it a self-fulfilling prophecy that non-infected women are not helped by antibiotics. It is likely that the antibiotics used in this study caused more harm than good, because rather than eradicating abnormal colonisation, they actually decimated normal colonisation. Treatment beyond twenty-six weeks' gestation will not prevent late miscarriage or very early PTB and will therefore be less likely to contribute to a reduction in neonatal morbidity or mortality. This strengthens the concept that treatment given early in pregnancy to women with abnormal genital tract colonisation is the most appropriate approach to management and should not be on the basis of multifactorial risk of preterm birth.

Two studies so far published only in abstract form have shown statistically significant benefit from treating BV with clindamycin, either intravaginally (Lamont, personal communication) or orally (Hay, personal communication) early in pregnancy.

The results from antibiotic trials so far are very contrasting, but there seems to be enough evidence to screen and treat women in early pregnancy that have abnormal genital tract flora, and are at high risk of adverse obstetric sequelae.

Conclusion

There is now sufficient evidence to implicate abnormal genital tract flora, and in particular BV, in adverse obstetric sequelae such as SPTL and preterm birth. However, PTB may be a poor outcome measure since many preterm infants are born healthy, and the object should be to prevent neonatal infection, whether term or preterm, since it is in these babies that cytokines may cause tissue damage and long-term handicap. Antibiotic treatment should be targetted at those women with abnormal genital tract colonisation in early pregnancy.

References

Amsel R, Totten PA, Spiegel CA, Chen KCS, Eschenbach DA, Holmes KK (1983) Nonspecific vaginitis. Diagnostic criteria and microbial and epidemiologic associations. *Am J Med* **74**: 14–22

Anderson HF, Nugent CE, Wanty SD, Hayashi RH (1990) Prediction of risk for preterm delivery by ultrasonographic measurement of cervical length. *Am J Obstet Gynecol* **163**: 859–67

Andrews WW, Goldenberg RL, Hauth JC (1995) Preterm labor: Emerging role of genital tract infections. *Infect Agents Dis* **4**: 196–211

Blackwell AL, Thomas PD, Wareham K *et al* (1993) Health gains from screening for infection of the lower genital tract in women attending for termination of pregnancy *Lancet* **342**: 206–10

Bump RC, Buesching WJ (1988) Bacterial vaginosis in virginal and sexually active adolescent females: evidence against exclusive sexual transmission. *Am J Obstet Gynecol* **158**: 935–9

Carey JC, Klebanoff MA, Hauth JC *et al (2000)* Metronidazole to prevent preterm delivery in pregnant women with asymptomatic bacterial vaginosis. *N Engl J Med* **342**: 534–40

Cauci S, Monte R, Driussi S, Lanzafame P, Quadrifoglio F (1998) Impairment of the mucosal immune system: IgA and IgM cleavage detected in vaginal washings of a subgroup of patients with bacterial vaginosis. *J Infect Dis* **178**: 1698–1706

Centers for Disease Control and Prevention (1993) 1993 Sexually transmitted diseases treatment guidelines. *MMWR Morb Mortal Wkly Rep* **42**: 27–46

Centers for Disease Control and Prevention (1996) Prevention of perinatal group B streptococcal disease: a public health perspective. *Morb Mortal Wkly Rep* **45** (RR-7): 1–24

Cook RL, Redondo-Lopez V, Schmitt C *et al* (1992) Clinical, microbiological, and biochemical factors in recurrent bacterial vaginosis. *J Clin Microbiol* **30**: 870–7

Dombroski RA, Woodward DS, Harper JK *et al* (1990) A rabbit model for bacterial-induced abortion by treatment of mice with antisera. *Am J Obstet Gynecol* **163**: 1938–47

Donders GG, Van Bulck B, Caudron J, Londers L, Vereecken A, Spitz B (2000) Relationship of bacterial vaginosis and mycoplasmas to the risk of spontaneous abortion. *Am J Obstet Gynecol* **183**: 431–7

Embree J, Caliando JJ, McCormack WM (1984) Nonspecific vaginitis among women attending a sexually transmitted diseases clinic. *Sex Trans Dis* **11**: 81–4

Eschenbach DA, Hillier SL, Critchlow C *et al* (1988) Diagnosis and clinical manifestations of bacterial vaginosis. *Am J Obstet Gynecol* **158**: 819

Fan YD, Pastorek JG, Miller JM, Mulvey J (1987) Acute pyelonephritis in pregnancy. *Am J Perinatol* **4**: 324–6

Gibbs RS, Romero R, Hillier SL, Eschenbach DA, Sweet RL (1992) A review of premature birth and subclincal infection. *Am J Obstet Gynecol* **166**: 1515–28

Goldenberg RL, Hauth JC, Andrews WM (2000) Intrauterine infection and preterm delivery. *N Engl J Med* **342**: 1500–7

Goldenberg RL, Andrews WW, Guerrant RL *et al* (2000) The Preterm Prediction Study: cervical lactoferrin concentration, other markers of lower genital tract infection, and preterm birth. *Am J Obstet Gynecol* **182**: 631–5

Gomez R, Romero R, Ghezzi F, Yoon BH, Mazor M, Stanley M (1998) The fetal inflammatory response syndrome. *Am J Obstet Gynecol* **179**: 194–202

Gravett MG, Hummel D, Eschenbach DA, Holmes KK (1986) Preterm labor associated with subclinical amniotic fluid infection with bacterial vaginosis. *Obstet Gynecol* **67**: 229–37

Greig PC, Murtha AP, Jimmerson CJ, Herbert WNP, Roitman-Johnson B, Allen J (1997) Maternal serum interleukin-6 during pregnancy and during term and preterm labour. *Obstet Gynecol* **90**: 465–9

Guyer B, Martin JA, Macdorman MF, Anderson RN, Strobino DM (1997) Annual summary of vital statistics — 1996. *Pediatrics* **100**: 905–18

Hardy PH, Hardy JB, Nell EE, Graham DA, Spencer MR, Rosenbaum RC (1984) Prevalence of six sexually transmitted disease agents among pregnant inner-city adolescents and pregnancy outcome. *Lancet* **2**: 333–7

Hauth JC, Goldenberg RL, Andrews WW, DuBard MB, Copper RL (1995) Reduced incidence of preterm delivery with metronidazole and erythromycin in women with bacterial vaginosis. *N Engl J Med* **333**: 1732–6

Hay PE, Taylor-Robinson D, Lamont therefore (1992) Diagnosis of bacterial vaginosis in a gynaecology clinic. *Br J Obstet Gynaecol* **99**: 63–6

Hay PE, Lamont RF, Taylor-Robinson D, Morgan DJ, Ison C, Pearson J (1994) Abnormal bacterial colonisation of the genital tract and subsequent preterm delivery and late miscarriage. *Br Med J* **308**: 295–8

Hay PE, Lamont RF, Taylor-Robinson D, Morgan DJ, Ison C, Pearson J (1994) Abnormal bacterial colonisation of the genital tract and subsequent preterm delivery and late miscarriage. *Br Med J* **308**: 295–8

Hillier SL, Witkin SS, Krohn MA, Watts DA, Kiviat NB, Eschenbach DA (1993) The relationship of amniotic fluid cytokines and preterm delivery, amniotic fluid infection, histologic chorioamnionitis, and chorioamnion infection. *Obstet Gynecol* **81**: 941–8

Hillier SL, Nugent RP, Eschenbach D A *et al* (1995) Association between bacterial vaginosis and preterm birth of a low birthweight infant. *N Engl J Med* **333**: 1737–42

Imseis HM, Greig PC, Livengood CH III *et al* (1997) Characterization of the inflammatory cytokines in the vagina during pregnancy and labour and with bacterial vaginosis. *J Soc Gynecol Invest* **4**: 90–4

Inglis SR, Jeremias J, Kuno K *et al* (1994) Detection of tumor necrosis-alpha, interleukin-6 and fetal fibronectin in the lower genital tract during pregnancy: relation to outcome. *Am J Obstet Gynecol* **171**: 5–10

Joesoef MR, Hillier SL, Wiknjosastro G *et al* (1995) Intravaginal clindamycin treatment for bacterial vaginosis: effects on preterm delivery and low birth weight. *Am J Obstet Gynecol* **173**: 1527–31

Keane FE, Ison CA, Taylor-Robinson D (1997) A longitudinal study of the vaginal flora over a menstrual cycle. *Int J STD AIDS* **8**: 489–94

Kekki M, Kurki T, Paavonen J, Rutanen EM (1999) Insulin-like growth factor binding protein-1 in cervix as a marker of infectious complications in pregnant women with bacterial vaginosis. (letter) *Lancet* **353**: 1494

Kenyon SL, Taylor DJ, Tarnow-Mordi, for ORACLE Collaborative Group (2001) Broad-spectrum antibiotics for spontaneous preterm labour: the ORACLE II randomised trial. *Lancet* **357**: 989–94

Krohn MA, Hillier SL, Nugent RP *et al* (1995) The genital flora of women with intraamniotic infection. Vaginal infection and Prematurity Group. *J Infect Dis* **171**: 1475–80

Kurki T, Sivonen A, Renkonen O *et al* (1992) Bacterial vaginosis in early pregnancy and pregnancy outcome. *Obstet Gynecol* **80**: 173–7

Lamont RF, Taylor-Robinson D, Newman M, Wigglesworth J, Elder MG (1986) Spontaneous early preterm labour associated with abnormal genital bacterial colonization. *Br J Obstet Gynaecol* **93**: 804–10

Lamont RF (1995) Bacterial vaginosis. In: Studd JWW (ed) (1994) *The Yearbook of the Royal College of Obstetricians and Gynaecologists*. Parthenon Publishing Group, London: 149–60

Lamont RF, Hudson EA, Hay PE *et al* (1999) A comparison of the use of Papanicolaou-stained cervical cytological smears with Gram-stained vaginal smears for the diagnosis of bacterial vaginosis in early pregnancy. *Int J STD AIDS* **10**: 93–7

Lamont RF, Morgan DJ, Wilden SD, Taylor-Robinson D (2000) Prevalence of bacterial vaginosis in women attending one of three general practices for routine cervical cytology. *Int J STD AIDS* **11**: 495–8

Lettieri L, Vintzileos AM, Rodis JF, Albini SM, Salafia CM (1993) Does 'idiopathic' preterm labor resulting in preterm birth exist? *Am J Obstet Gynecol* **168**: 1480–5

Llahi-Camp JM, Rai R, Ison C, Regan L, Taylor-Robinson D (1996) Association of bacterial vaginosis with a history of second trimester miscarriage. *Hum Reprod* 11: 1575–8

Lockwood C, Ghidini A, Wein R, Lapinski R, Casal D, Berkowitz R (1994) Increased interleukin-6 concentrations in cervical secretions are associated with preterm delivery. *Am J Obstet Gynecol* 171: 1097–102

McDonald H, Vigneswaran R, O'Loughlin JA (1989) Group B streptococcal colonization and preterm labour. *Aust N Z J Obstet Gynaecol* 29: 291–3

McDonald HM, O'Loughlin JA, Jolley P *et al* (1992) Prenatal microbiological risk factors associated with preterm birth. *Br J Obstet Gynaecol* 99: 190–6

McDonald HM, O'Loughlin JA, Vigneswaran R *et al* (1997) Impact of metronidazole therapy on preterm birth in women with bacterial vaginosis flora (Gardnerella vaginalis): a randomised, placebo controlled trial. *Br J Obstet Gynaecol* 104: 1391–7

McGregor JA, French JI, Richter R *et al* (1990) Antenatal microbiologic maternal risk factors associated with prematurity. *Am J Obstet Gynecol* 163: 1465–73

McGregor J, Lawellin D, Franco-Buff A, Todd J (1991) Phospholipase C activity in microorganisms associated with reproductive tract infection. *Am J Obstet Gynecol* 164: 682–6

McGregor J, French J, Jones W, Parker R, Patterson E, Draper D (1992) Association of cervicovaginal infections with increased vaginal fluid phospholipase A2 activity. *Am J Obstet Gynecol* 167: 1588–94

McGregor JA, French JI, Jones W *et al* (1994) Bacterial vaginosis is associated with prematurity and vaginal fluid mucinase and sialidase: results of a controlled trial of topical clindamycin cream. *Am J Obstet Gynecol* 170: 1048–60

McGregor JA, French JI, Parker R *et al* (1995) Prevention of premature birth by screening and treatment of common genital tract infections: Results of a prospective controlled evaluation. *Am J Obstet Gynecol* 173: 157–67

Markenson GR, Martin RK, Tillotson-Criss M, Foley KS, Stewart RS Jr., Yancey M (1997) The use of polymerase chain reaction to detect bacteria in amniotic fluid in pregnancies complicated by preterm labour. *Am J Obstet Gynecol* 177: 1471–7

Mead PB (1993) Epidemiology of bacterial vaginosis. *Am J Obstet Gynecol* 169: 446–9

Miller JM, Pupkin MJ, Hill GB (1980) Bacterial colonization of amniotic fluid from intact fetal membranes. *Am J Obstet Gynecol* 136: 796–804

Morales WJ, Schorr S, Albritton J (1994) Effect of metronidazole in patients with preterm birth in preceding pregnancy and bacterial vaginosis: a placebo-controlled, double-blind study. *Am J Obstet Gynecol* 171: 345–9

Morbidity and Mortality Weekly Report (1997) 1998 Guidelines for treatment of sexually transmitted diseases. *Morb Mortal Wkly Rep* 47 (RR-1)

Opsjon SL, Wathen NC, Tingulstad S *et al* (1993) Tumor necrosis factor, interleukin-1, and interleukin-6 in normal human parturition. *Am J Obstet Gynecol* 169: 397–404

Platz-Christensen J, Mattsby-Baltzer I, Thomsen P, Wiqvist N (1993) Endotoxin and interleukin-1a in the cervical mucus and vaginal fluid of pregnant women with bacterial vaginosis. *Am J Obstet Gynecol* **169**: 1161–6

Pavlova SI, Kilic SO, Mou SM, Tao L (1997) Phage infection in vaginal lactobacilli: an in vitro study. *Infect Dis Obstet Gynecol* **5**: 36–44

Ralph SG, Rutherford AJ, Wilson JD (1999) Influence of bacterial vaginosis on conception and miscarriage in the first trimester: cohort study. *Br Med J* **319**: 2203

Regan JA, Cho S, James LS (1981) Premature rupture of membranes, preterm delivery, and group B streptococcal colonization of mothers. *Am J Obstet Gynecol* **141**: 184–6

Regan JA, Klebanoff MA, Nugent RP *et al* (1996) Colonization with group B streptococci in pregnancy and adverse outcome. *Am J Obstet Gynecol* **174**: 1354–60

Riduan JM, Hillier SL, Utomo B, Wiknjosastro G, Linnan M, Kandun N (1993) Bacterial vaginosis and prematurity in Indonesia: association in early and late pregnancy. *Am J Obstet Gynecol* **169**: 175–8

Rizzo G, Capponi A, Vlachopoulou A, Angelini E, Grassi C, Romanini C (1997) The diagnostic value of interleukin-8 and fetal fibronectin concentrations in cervical secretions in patients with preterm labor and intact membranes. *J Perinat Med* **25**: 461–8

Roberts AK, Monzon-Bordonaba F, Van Deerlin PG *et al* (1999) Association of polymorphism within the promoter of the tumor necrosis factor alpha gene with increased risk of preterm premature rupture of the fetal membranes. *Am J Obstet Gynecol* **180**: 1297–302

Rojas MA, Gonzalez A, Bancalari E, Claure N, Poole C, Silva-Neto G (1995) Changing trends in the epidemiology and pathogenesis of neonatal chronic lung disease. *J Pediatr* **126**: 605–10

Romero R, Kadar N, Hobbins JC, Duff GW (1987) Infection and labour: the detection of endotoxin in amniotic fluid. *Am J Obstet Gynecol* **157**: 815–9

Romero R, Mazor M (1988) Infection and preterm labor. *Clin Obstet Gynecol* **31**: 553–82

Romero R, Sitori M, Oyarzun E et al (1989) Infection and labor: V. Prevalence, microbiology and clinical significance of intraamniotic infection in women with preterm labor and intact membranes. *Am J Obstet Gynecol* **161**: 817–24

Romero R, Mazor M, Brandt F *et al* (1992) Interleukin-1a and interleukin-1b in preterm and term human parturition. *Am J Reprod Immunol* **27**: 117–23

Romero R, Yoon BH, Mazor M *et al* (1993) The diagnostic and prognostic value of amniotic fluid white blood cell count, glucose, interleukin-6, and gram stain in patients with preterm labor and intact membranes. *Am J Obstet Gynecol* **169**: 805–16

Romero R, Munoz H, Ramirez M *et al* (1994) Antibiotic therapy reduces the rate of infection-induced preterm delivery and perinatal mortality. *Am J Obstet Gynecol* **70**: 390

Romero R, Mazor M, Munoz H, Gomez R, Galasso M, Sherer DM (1994) The preterm labor syndrome. *Ann N Y Aca Sci* **734**: 414–29

Rosenstein IJ, Morgan DJ, Sheehan M, Lamont RF, Taylor-Robinson D (1996) Bacterial vaginosis in pregnancy: distribution of bacterial species in different gram-stain categories of the vaginal flora. *J Med Microbiol* **45**: 120–6

Sewankambo N, Gray RH, Wawer MJ *et al* (1997) HIV-infection associated with abnormal vaginal flora morphology and bacterial vaginosis. *Lancet* **350**: 546–50

Spiegel CA, Amsel R, Holmes KK (1983) Diagnosis of bacterial vaginosis by direct gram stain of vaginal fluid. *J Clin Microbiol* **18**: 170–7

Vermeulen GM, Bruinse-HW (1999) Prophylactic administration of clindamycin 2% vaginal cream to reduce the incidence of spontaneous preterm birth in women with an increased recurrence risk: a randomised placebo-controlled double-blind trial. *Br J Obstet Gynaecol* **106**: 652–7

Vigneswaran R (2000) Infection and preterm birth: evidence of a common causal relationship with bronchopulmonary dysplasia and cerebral palsy. *J Paediatr Child Health* **36**: 293–6

Wood NS, Marlow N, Costeloe K, Gibson AT, Wilkinson AR (2000) Neurologic and developmental disability after extremely preterm birth. EPICure study group. *N Engl J Med* **343**: 378–84

Yoon BH, Romero R, Kim CJ *et al* (1997) High expression of tumor necrosis factor-a and interleukin-6 in periventricular leukomalacia. *Am J Obstet Gynecol* **177**: 406–11

Yoon BH, Romero R, Jun JK *et al* (1997) Amniotic fluid cytokines (interleukin-6, tumor necrosis factor-a, interleukin-1b and interleukin-8) and the risk for the development of bronchopulmonary dysplasia. *Am J Obstet Gynecol* **177**: 825–30

Yoon BH, Romero R, Park JS *et al* (2000) Fetal exposure to an intra-amniotic inflammation and the development of cerebral palsy at the age of three years. *Am J Obstet Gynecol* **182**: 675–81

10

Early pregnancy assessment units

Jayne Shillito, James J Walker

Introduction

Miscarriage is the commonest complication of pregnancy affecting 12–15% of all recognised pregnancies and a substantially greater proportion (perhaps 40%) of biochemical pregnancies (Regan *et al*, 1989). Despite this, no specialised services were available for women presenting with problems of early pregnancy until relatively recently. The last five years have seen a significant rise in the number of hospitals developing early pregnancy assessment units (EPAU) which appears to benefit patients, healthcare professionals and the NHS. A recent survey by the National Association of Early Pregnancy Units identified 174 such units within Britain. Of these, 103 returned the survey and we now have a much clearer idea of the facilities offered in different centres around the country (Moshy, 2001).

Modern treatment of miscarriage should provide rapid, sympathetic diagnosis, a choice of management options and adequate counselling and follow-up. First-trimester pregnancy loss is associated with significant psychological morbidity (Turner, 1989) similar to that following stillbirth and neonatal death (Cuisinier *et al*, 1993). It is therefore important that women seen in an early pregnancy unit receive sympathetic and considerate care in order to minimise long term sequelae. However, it is found that more than half of all women attending the EPAU will have a continuing pregnancy and they will have different needs and anxieties to those suffering a miscarriage. This short chapter aims to describe the assessment, diagnosis, management and follow-up of women attending an EPAU in order to best meet their needs.

The need for an early pregnancy assessment unit

Previously, women with early pregnancy bleeding were admitted to hospital via A&E, waited several hours for a viability scan and were fasted for prolonged periods prior to surgery. In 1995 in Leeds, prior to the introduction of our EPAU, the majority of women (90%) stayed at least one night in hospital with a maximum length of stay of five days. All evacuations were surgical and 40% were performed after 10.00 pm (Walker and Shillito, 1997). Most women saw only the most junior doctor and were often given conflicting and confusing advice.

An EPAU is an outpatient service for women with early pregnancy problems, providing sensitive and efficient management and minimising unnecessary admissions. It can result in a reduction in out of hours work and operating for junior doctors and leads to cost savings for managers by reducing the number of in-patient beds required for gynaecological emergencies.

How common are problems of early pregnancy?

In 1994 the OPCS survey indicated that 18.2% of conceptions in Britain miscarried, 16.1% ended through termination and 0.7% resulted in stillbirth, leaving only 65% of recognised conceptions with a live birth (HMSO, 1994). During the year 2000, the EPAU at St James's Hospital in Leeds saw 3,016 women with pain or bleeding in early pregnancy. Of these, 1179 (39%) had a viable pregnancy confirmed on their first visit and another 215 after follow-up scans (*Figure 10.1*). In the same year there were 3,637 deliveries in the hospital suggesting that as many as one third of women with a continuing pregnancy experience first-trimester bleeding. During the same year there were forty-five ectopic pregnancies identified through the unit, and a further thirty admitted directly to the wards. Since ectopic pregnancy remains a significant cause of maternal mortality, this important condition should never be overlooked.

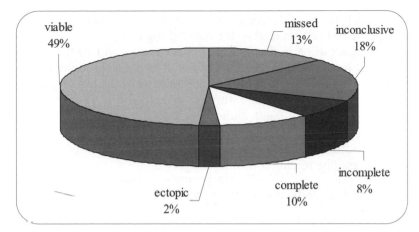

Figure 10.1: Type of scan preferred by women attending the EPAU

Assessment

An EPAU is predominantly an outpatient unit and the majority of women are fit and well with minimal bleeding and can be seen on the next working day. However, there must be mechanisms in place for rapid admission of women who are unwell, have heavy bleeding, severe pain, signs of shock or a suspected ectopic pregnancy. There will also be a proportion of women who are frightened by the blood loss or who are socially or geographically isolated and prefer direct admission.

Most referrals come directly from GPs or A&E although the EPAU survey found that 52% of units accept referrals direct from patients. The most common presenting symptoms are bleeding or pain in early pregnancy but others attend for scans for uncertain dates, reassurance scans for poor obstetric history and previous ectopic pregnancy (*Table 10.1*). Most units limit referrals to bleeding or pain only, others incorporate all gynaecological acutes and see non-pregnant women with pelvic pain and suspected pelvic inflammatory disease

Like most units, the EPAU in St James's University hospital in Leeds is open five days per week, although a small number of units offer a seven-day service which should be the ultimate aim. The main work of the unit occurs between 8.00 am and 12.30 pm but ward staff are available to deal with any telephone inquiries until 5.00 pm. The workload varies considerably but we see an average of fifty patients per week and find that to allow adequate time for counselling and reassurance we need two nurse specialists during the morning clinic.

An EPAU should have a waiting area, an examination room, a scan room and private rooms for counselling (*Table 10.2*). Women should expect to be in the unit for between one and two hours and those that have a viable pregnancy should be seen throughout by a single practitioner. The admitting practitioner can take a short history and arrange the appropriate further investigations (*Table 10.3*). Women prefer to be dealt with by a specialist team (Davies and Geoghegan, 1994) who should be sympathetic nursing or midwifery staff providing personal care. This has been shown to improve both outcome and the retention of information.

Table 10.1: Details of patients attending EPAU

Mean gestational age	8.77 weeks	(Range 5–18)
Source of referral	GP	46%
	A&E	34%
	Wards	10%
	Midwives/ANC	5%
Reason for referral	Bleeding	84%
	Pain alone	11%
	Past history	5%

Table 10.2: Requirements and location of an early pregnancy assessment unit

Required facilities

- ⌘ Easy and rapid access — ideally on the same or next working day
- ⌘ Direct telephone access
- ⌘ Dedicated staff
- ⌘ Access to dedicated operating time
- ⌘ All facilities within a single unit or area
- ⌘ Venupuncture
- ⌘ Urine and serum pregnancy testing
- ⌘ Appropriate referral to other health professionals

Points to consider in the location of an EPAU

- ⌘ Acceptability to patients
- ⌘ Adequate privacy
- ⌘ Need for examination
- ⌘ Availability of toilets
- ⌘ Resuscitation facilities
- ⌘ Possible need for recovery of post-op patients

Possible locations for an EPAU

- ⌘ Out-patient department
- ⌘ Purpose built unit
- ⌘ Gynaecology day care unit
- ⌘ Antenatal day care unit
- ⌘ Obstetric ward
- ⌘ Gynaecology ward

Table 10.3: patient details and investigations required on admission	
Admission details collected	**Initial investigations**
Name, address and date of birth	Temperature, pulse and BP
GP: name and address	Pregnancy test (if none previously)
Parity	Haemoglobin
Relevant past obstetric/gynae history	Rhesus grouping
LMP/date of positive pregnancy test	Ultrasound
Usual cycle	
Present symptoms	

If the unit is to be nurse led, there needs to be in-put from middle grade or senior medical staff. However, early pregnancy complications form a significant portion of gynaecology and all junior doctors should spend time on the unit in order to gain experience in counselling skills and in the diagnosis and management of miscarriage and ectopic pregnancy. The medical staff associated with the unit are not necessarily part of the consultant team that the patient will be booked under. This is similar to the design of antenatal day units (Walker, 1994). Consistency of information and care is imperative if patient satisfaction is to be kept to a maximum.

It is surprising how much administrative work is generated by an EPAU particularly with regard to obtaining hospital notes and communicating with GPs. A multidisciplinary admission proforma is extremely useful, as is a computer with access to the patient administration system (PAS). A computer can be used to develop a database of information about patients attending the unit and to generate a discharge letter. A system for referring women with viable pregnancies through to the antenatal clinic for on-going care would be ideal and save time for the patient, her GP and her midwife.

Diagnosis

Ultrasound assessment is the mainstay of diagnosis in early pregnancy bleeding. However, there is continuing debate about the method of scanning to use in early pregnancy. Much will depend on the equipment available and the experience of the operator. Transvaginal scanning can be performed immediately and with the patient fasting, as a full bladder is not necessary (*Table 10.4*). It will produce clear images particularly at very early gestations and is no more uncomfortable than abdominal scanning, particularly when pressure is applied over a full bladder. It is often unacceptable to pregnant women who are bleeding especially as they already fear the pregnancy is at risk. For a transabdominal scan time must be allowed for the bladder to fill, the patient is not fasted and the images obtained may be inconclusive. It is though familiar to many women and therefore more acceptable.

Table 10.4: Advantages/disadvantages of vaginal and abdominal scans

Transvaginal	Transabdominal
⌘ Accurate at all gestations	⌘ Only accurate beyond eight weeks
⌘ Clear images	⌘ Images may be unclear, esp to patient
⌘ Can be performed instantly	⌘ Requires a full bladder
⌘ May not have been met before	⌘ Familiar to most women
⌘ Requires patient to undress	⌘ Underwear can be left on
⌘ Well tolerated	⌘ Uncomfortable with full bladder
⌘ Safe	⌘ Safe
⌘ Requires separate probe and therefore expense	⌘ Equipment universally available

Both methods are available at St James's and we found that if given a choice many women had no preference as to the type of scan performed although a small minority would refuse a transvaginal scan (*Figure 10.2*). It is worth noting that with transabdominal scanning up to 42% of women will require a vaginal scan either because the bladder is not sufficiently full or the scan is inconclusive (*Figure 10.3*).

It is important that all personnel performing early pregnancy ultrasound should have adequate training, access to suitable equipment and recourse to expert help if necessary. At St James's Hospital, scans are performed by radiologists who operate according to set guidelines agreed in the wake of the South Glamorgan Inquiry (RCOG/RCR Guidelines, 1995). This report came about following problems with misdiagnosis as women may be sure of the date of the last menstrual period but can never be sure of when they conceived.

The guidelines state that:

❖ A missed miscarriage can only be diagnosed when absent fetal heart movements are confirmed by **two** qualified, independent observers.

❖ A missed miscarriage cannot be diagnosed if the fetal pole is less than 6mm.

❖ An empty sac (anembryonic pregnancy/early fetal demise/blighted ovum) cannot be diagnosed if the mean sac diameter is less than 2cm.

In some units gynaecologists, nurses or midwives perform scans.

Other investigations should be kept to a minimum. Following a brief history, blood is taken for haemoglobin estimation and rhesus grouping. In our series, only 40% of women knew their blood group even amongst those who had been pregnant before. Urine pregnancy testing should be available on the ward. If the scan is inconclusive and the pregnancy test positive, serial B-hCG estimation may be necessary to exclude ectopic pregnancy or confirm a complete miscarriage. There is no need to carry out a vaginal or clinical assessment unless there is medical concern or the woman requires a general anaesthetic. In this way, women do not need to undress while in the unit apart from what is necessary during ultrasound assessment.

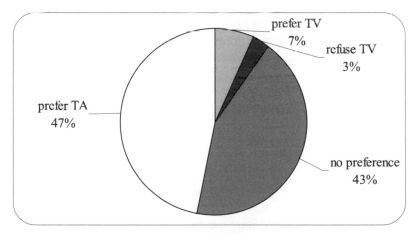

Figure 10.2: Type of scan preferred by women attending the EPAU

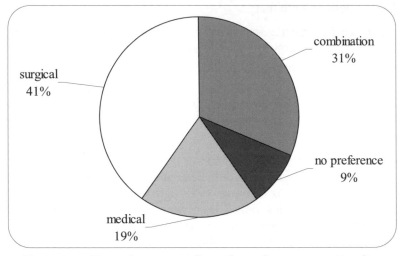

Figure 10.3: Type of scan actually performed on women attending the EPAU

Management

Women should be informed of the diagnosis sensitively and as soon as possible. They should be allowed to see the scan images, have simple explanations of the findings and be given the opportunity to obtain photographs. In addition, they should be given sufficient written and verbal information so that they can make choices about their subsequent management. The development of unit specific leaflets has greatly helped this but ones available from the Miscarriage Association and the Ectopic Pregnancy Trust are clear and informative.

Viable pregnancies

If the ultrasound scan positively identifies the fetal heart the outcome is usually good. Previous studies have suggested that early pregnancy bleeding is associated with adverse pregnancy outcome (Silpia *et al*, 1992). We retrospectively reviewed 200 women who had bled in early pregnancy and found no increase in adverse perinatal outcomes and a subsequent miscarriage rate of around 2%.

However, many women continue bleeding or have pain after leaving the unit and telephone for further advice or to request a further scan. Many women express concern that the bleeding has in some way damaged the baby and require continued support. We provide a short information leaflet answering commonly asked questions such as when they can return to work, whether they can bath/shower and is it safe to continue intercourse. The opportunity to give health advice should not be overlooked and women should be encouraged to take folic acid supplements, to stop smoking and to eat a healthy diet.

Non-viable pregnancies

Once a pregnancy has been diagnosed as being non-viable women should be offered a choice of further management. There is no hurry to empty the uterus and women should be allowed to return home to come to terms with the miscarriage prior to return for evacuation. There is no increased risk of infection or clotting disturbance even if products are retained for several weeks. Some women find the diagnosis hard to accept and repeat scanning or serial β-hCG should be offered until there is no doubt in a woman's mind that the pregnancy is non-viable.

Once the diagnosis has been made, the options currently available are surgical or medical evacuation of the uterus or expectant management (*Table 10.5*) (Hughes *et al*, 1996; Chipchase and James, 1997). The majority still choose surgical evacuation (*Figure 10.4*).

Table 10.5: Advantages of different methods of uterine evacuation			
	Medical	**Conservative**	**Surgical**
effectiveness	94%	50%	96%
acceptability	85%	90%	95%
amount of bleeding	moderate	moderate	minimal
degree of pain	moderate	minimal	minimal
complications	retained products heavy bleeding	retained products	infection retained products
time taken	24–48 hours	up to four weeks	within four hours

Medical methods of uterine evacuation are now available for women with both missed and incomplete miscarriages. Regimes employing combinations of mifepristone and prostaglandin similar to those used for first-trimester termination of pregnancy can be effective although employing smaller doses (El Refaey and Templeton, 1994; Hughes *et al*, 1996). We have found this method to be well tolerated and have only required evacuation in around 6% of cases. At present, there is no consensus as to which preparation, dose or route of prostaglandin administration is needed in order to achieve miscarriage in an acceptable time interval with minimal gastro-intestinal side-effects.

Conservative management is increasingly chosen. It is highly successful for those with an incomplete miscarriage and may be recommended above medical management as there is no need for admission or medication. Clinical follow-up is all that is required and repeat scans or β-hCGs used only where there is persistent bleeding. However, for delayed miscarriage the success rate is relatively low and spontaneous evacuation may take several weeks. Women require regular review, either by telephone or on the unit, until the uterus is empty. In our experience, almost half of those who choose this method will eventually request more active management.

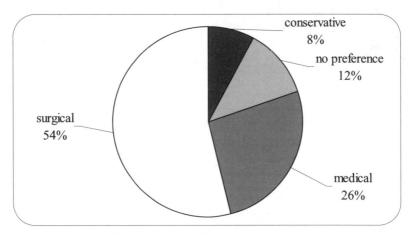

Figure 10.4: Preferred method of uterine evacuation

Inconclusive results

Patients are often frustrated when a diagnosis of pregnancy viability cannot be reached. If a gestation sac is seen, but viability cannot be confirmed, a rescan should be arranged for one week irrespective of menstrual data. Growth of the sac should be seen in seven days and a longer delay is not indicated.

Where the pregnancy test is positive but the scan shows an empty uterus, careful clinical assessment is necessary to distinguish between early pregnancy, complete miscarriage and ectopic pregnancy. Follow-up with serial β-hCG measurements is appropriate provided that the patient is asymptomatic and has been adequately counselled. Review by a senior member of the team should occur after forty-eight hours as although a significant number of ectopic pregnancies will resolve spontaneously, tubal rupture can still occur with falling β-hCG levels.

Both Mol and Ankum (Mol *et al*, 1999; Ankum *et al*, 1993) have suggested the use of diagnostic algorithms in this situation and report a sensitivity of 93% with a specificity of 97% for a diagnosis of ectopic pregnancy. The signs, symptoms and investigation results are so varied in this patient population that an inflexible algorithm may not be clinically useful. The algorithm currently used in our unit is shown in *Figures 10.5* and *10.6*.

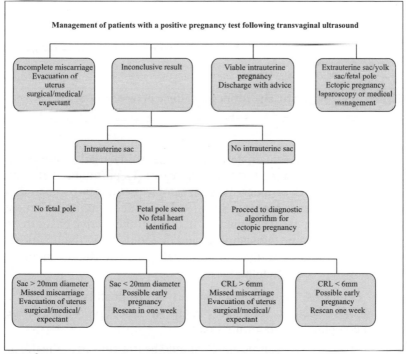

Figure 10.5: Management of patients on the EPAU

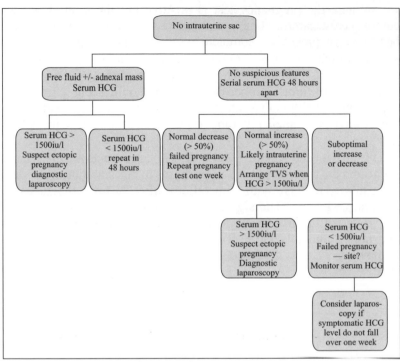

Figure 10.6: Diagnostic algorithm for ectopic pregnancy

Ectopic pregnancy

Ectopic pregnancy remains a major cause of maternal mortality in the first trimester. In the last triennial report (Department of Health, 1998) there were twelve deaths from ectopic pregnancy compared to eight in the previous report (1991–1993), and accounting for almost half the deaths in early pregnancy. In eight of the twelve cases there was considered to be substandard care due to delay in the diagnosis and inappropriate investigation and treatment. The Report includes the following recommendations:

❖ All clinicians, including GPs and A&E doctors, consider a diagnosis of ectopic pregnancy in any woman of reproductive age who complains of abdominal pain.

❖ Women in hypovolaemic shock should be transferred to theatre as soon as possible. Delay while attempting to restore the circulatory volume may lead to deterioration in the woman's condition.

❖ The decision to perform laparoscopic surgery should be based on the surgeon's experience and expertise and a judgement about the suitability of the procedure for the individual woman.

The diagnosis is often difficult to make, particularly among women attending the EPAU who may have had no pain or discomfort prior to admission.

Where an ectopic pregnancy is diagnosed but the woman is haemodynamically stable it is still possible to offer a choice of management options including medical or surgical treatment. Conservative management, while successful in up to 67% of cases, is associated with a tubal rupture or major haemorrhage rate of 24% and persistent trophoblast in a further 2–20%. Hence, it cannot be recommended as a safe treatment (Hajenius, 2000).

For surgical treatment, the laparoscopic approach is recommended where possible as there is a shorter hospital stay, a rapid return to normal activities and subsequent intrauterine pregnancy rates greater than or equal to that following open surgery. There is still considerable debate as to whether salpingostomy or salpingectomy offers the best long-term prognosis, whether open or laparoscopic treatment is performed. Salpingostomy has a slightly higher rate of subsequent intrauterine pregnancy; 57% versus 52% following salpingectomy (Yao and Tulandi, 1997). However, there is a significant incidence of persistent trophoblast and marginally higher rates of subsequent ectopic pregnancy (13% versus 9%).

Medical treatment is offered in some centres around the UK but has been more widely used in the USA. While methotrexate is the most commonly used agent, mifepristone, misoprostol and hyperosmolar glucose instillation have all been used. Methotrexate is the treatment of choice for a stable cervical ectopic pregnancy and can be considered for a cornual pregnancy. The American College of Obstetricians and Gynaecologists has recently produced specific guidelines (ACOG, 1999) on the selection criteria for offering medical treatment (*Table 10.6*). Most centres use a cut-off level of initial HCG of 2000IU/l as above this treatment is more likely to fail. There are two commonly used regimens:

1. Single dose methotrexate — a single intramuscular dose calculated according to the body surface area.
2. Variable dose methotrexate — given on alternate days with folinic acid rescue on the intervening days.

Women should be warned that abdominal pain may increase around the third or fourth day after treatment but there is no necessity to repeat the hCG before day seven, as there is usually an initial rise after treatment.

Adverse side-effects following methotrexate include nausea and vomiting, stomatitis, photosensitive skin reactions and rarely impaired liver function, neutropenia and alopecia. Patients should be monitored by regular full blood counts, liver and renal function tests. At present, the use of methotrexate should be reserved for a selected group of patients.

Follow-up care

Table 10.6: Criteria for selection of patients for methotrexate treatment
Absolute indications
✴ Haemodynamically stable
✴ No active bleeding
✴ No haemoperitoneum
✴ Non-laparoscopic diagnosis
✴ Patient desires future fertility
✴ General anaesthesia poses significant risk
✴ Patient is able to return for follow-up care
✴ Patient has no contraindications to methotrexate
Relative indications
✴ Unruptured mass < 3.5cm in size on scan
✴ No fetal cardiac activity
✴ HCG does not exceed a predetermined value

Of the women who attended our EPAU, 89% were discharged home the same day, 80% immediately and a further 9% after same day evacuation (*Figure 10.7*). As found by others (Bigrigg and Read, 1991), admission times for those requiring evacuation can be reduced from a three-night in-patient to one day as an out-patient. Those with a viable pregnancy can go home the same morning. However, an EPAU should not simply be seen as a way of streamlining the care of women needing evacuation (Maclean and Cumming, 1993).

Psychological care becomes an important part of the care of women seen in an EPAU. Research has shown that psychological distress following sporadic miscarriage is reduced by appropriate counselling and support (Turner *et al*, 1991). Denied grief or a failure to recognise the loss leads on to long-term depressive illness and psychological disturbance (Welch, 1991). Even less is known about the psychological effects of bleeding where the pregnancy continues.

In order to establish the amount of distress generated by bleeding in the first trimester we conducted a survey using hospital anxiety and depression ratings on women attending the EPAU for the first time. As expected we found elevated anxiety levels when compared to women attending antenatal clinic for a first-trimester dating scan

(*Figure 10.8*). We assumed that an ultrasound scan would provide reassurance but when followed up one to two weeks after a scan confirming a viable pregnancy, we found anxiety levels had not decreased at all. These findings suggest that an EPAU may need to offer follow-up after both threatened and complete miscarriage, although this may be by telephone contact rather than repeat visits.

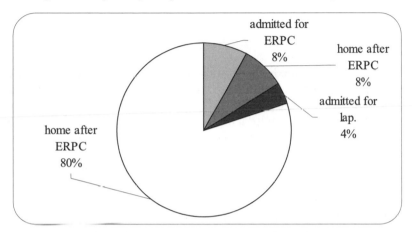

Figure 10.7: Outcome of women seen on the EPAU

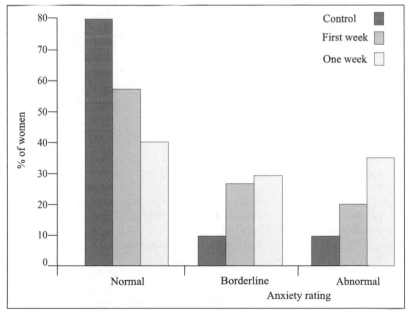

Figure 10.8: Anxiety scores after a threatened miscarriage

A number of women attending an EPAU will have experienced two or more miscarriages. They are often anxious to know more about their future prognosis. We have introduced a Recurrent Miscarriage Clinic run by staff from the EPAU to provide counselling and information, investigation where appropriate and support in future pregnancies.

Conclusions

Early pregnancy bleeding and miscarriage affect a large percentage of pregnant women and early pregnancy units were developed to overcome many of the problems of women who miscarry. Pregnancy bleeding is associated with a high level of anxiety whether there is a continuing pregnancy or not. To overcome this, an EPAU needs to provide easy access for women and sympathetic dedicated staff in all areas. Ultrasound scanning is the mainstay of diagnosis and must be provided on site. Since the majority of women that attend have viable pregnancies, there needs to be a smooth transition to antenatal care facilities. It has to be remembered that many women will have continuing anxiety and they should be provided with clear information about what to expect in the days to come. If a miscarriage occurs, the woman should be offered time to come to terms with the news and different choices of management. After a miscarriage, early pregnancy support should be offered in the subsequent pregnancy.

References

Ankum WM, Van der Veen F, Hamerlynck JVTH, Lammes FB (1993) Laparoscopy: a dispensable tool in the diagnosis of ectopic pregnancy? *Hum Reprod* **8**: 1301–6

Anonymous (1999) Medical management of tubal pregnancy. American College of Obstetricians and Gynaecologists. ACOG Practice Bulletin, number 3. *Int J Gynaecol Obstet* **65**: 97–103

Bigrigg MA, Read MD (1991) Management of women referred to early-pregnancy assessment unit — care and cost-effectiveness. *Br Med J* **302**: 577–9

Chipchase J, James D (1997) Randomised trial of expectant versus surgical management of spontaneous miscarriage. *Br J Obstet Gynaecol* **104**: 840–1

Cuisinier MCJ, Kuijpers JC, Hoogduin CAL, Degraauw CPHM, Janssen HJEM (1993) Miscarriage and stillbirth — time since the loss, grief intensity and satisfaction with care. *Eur J Obstet Gynecol Reprod Biol* **52**: 163–8

Davies M, Geoghegan J (1994) Developing an early pregnancy unit. *Nurs Times* **90**: 36–8

Department of Health (1998) *Why Mothers Die — Report on Confidential Enquiries into Maternal Deaths in the United Kingdom 1994–1996*. HMSO, London

El Refaey H, Templeton A (1994) Early abortion induction by a combination of mifepristone and oral misoprostol — a comparison between 2 dose regimens of misoprostol and their effect on blood-pressure. *Br J Obstet Gynaecol* **101**: 792–6

Hajenius PJ, Mol BW, Bossunt PM *et al* (2000) *Interventions for tubal ectopic pregnancy*. Cochrane Database of Systematic Reviews, CD 000324

Hughes J, Ryan M, Hinshaw K, Henshaw R, Rispin R, Templeton A (1996) The costs of treating miscarriage — a comparison of medical and surgical-management. *Br J Obstet Gynaecol* **103**: 1217–21

Maclean MA, Cumming GP (1993) Providing for women following miscarriage. *Scott Med J* **38**: 5–7

Mol BWJ, Van der Veen F, Bossuyt premium (1999) Implementation of probabilistic decision rules improves the predictive values of algorithms in the diagnostic management of ectopic pregnancy. *Hum Reprod* **14**(11): 2855–62

Moshy R (2001) Survey of Early Pregnancy Units on behalf of the National Association of Early Pregnancy Units. Personal communication

Office of Population Consenses and Surveys, Birth Statistics, Series FM1 and DH3 annual reference volumes. HMSO, London, 1994

Regan L, Braude PR, Trembath PL (1989) Influence of past reproductive performance on risk of spontaneous abortion. *Br Med J* **299**: 541–4

Royal College of Radiologists/Royal College of Obstetricians & Gynaecologists (1995) *Guidance on Ultrasound procedures in early pregnancy*. RCOG, London

Sipila P, Hartikainen-Sorri AL, Oja H *et al* (1992) Perinatal outcome of pregnancies complicated by vaginal bleeding. *Br J Obstet Gynaecol* **99**: 959–63

Turner M (1989) Spontaneous miscarriage — this hidden grief. *Ir Med J* **82**:145

Turner MJ, Flannelly GM, Wingfield M *et al* (1991) The miscarriage clinic — an audit of the 1st-year. *Br J Obstet Gynaecol* **98**: 306–8

Walker JJ, Shillito J (1997) Early Pregnancy Units: service and organisational aspects. In: Grudzinskas JG, O'Brien PMS, eds. *Problems in Early Pregnancy: Advances in Diagnosis and Management*. RCOG Press, London: 160–73

Walker JJ (1994) Daycare assessment and hypertensive disorders of pregnancy. *Fetal Maternal Med Rev* **6**: 57–70

Welch ID (1991) Miscarriage, stillbirth or newborn death: starting a healthy grieving process. *Neonatal Netw* **9**(8): 53–7

Yao M, Tulandi T (1997) Current status of surgical and non-surgical management of ectopic pregnancy. *Fertil Steril* **67**: 421–33

11

Pregnancy outcome following idiopathic recurring miscarriage

Sara Brigham, Roy G Farquharson

Introduction

Spontaneous miscarriage occurs in approximately 15% of all pregnancies, as recorded by hospital episode statistics. The actual figure, from community-based assessment, may well be higher than this as some women miscarry at home and remain unreported to hospital (Everett, 1997). Between 1% and 2% of fertile women will experience recurring pregnancy loss and, despite a wide range of investigations no cause can be found in approximately 50% of cases (Stirrat, 1990; Quenby and Farquharson, 1993). Recurrent loss of pregnancy is distressing for the patient and frustrating for the clinician, especially where treatment options are limited as in idiopathic recurrent miscarriage. The mainstay of management of these patients is empirically based upon tender loving care and emotional support.

In the absence of predicted success rates with idiopathic recurrent miscarriage, the clinician is at a disadvantage in the miscarriage clinic setting. The most commonly posed question focuses on the chance of future pregnancy success. Previous population studies are small, and few have documented sufficient patient numbers to generate confidence with clinical prediction of future pregnancy outcome, in terms of success or failure. The effect of emotional support, supplemented by ultrasound in early pregnancy gives 'success rates' of between 70% and 80% (Stray-Pederson *et al*, 1984; Liddell *et al*, 1991; Clifford *et al*, 1997).

As important as an overall success rate is the significance of each gestational milestone attained in the first trimester, which has not been determined by these studies. In particular, the appearance of fetal heart activity is profoundly important to the couple in determining the viability of the pregnancy. At what stage the couple can feel more confident about the outcome can only be answered by regular, longitudinal ultrasound assessment.

In a large prospective study, the authors have attempted to identify important gestational milestones for women presenting with idiopathic recurrent miscarriage and used the data analysis to predict future pregnancy success based on gestational age, maternal age and miscarriage history.

How was the prospective study designed?

All women attending a dedicated miscarriage clinic in a university teaching hospital were entered on a live miscarriage database over a ten-year period ('live' as it is constantly updated). Patient information was entered onto a spreadsheet database, with the findings checked by a second doctor. The majority of patients (76%) attending the clinic had a history of at least three consecutive miscarriages. Due to patient demand for investigation, some patients were seen in the clinic with a history of two consecutive miscarriages (24%).

Following preconceptual presentation to the clinic, an accurate patient history was taken and investigations performed to exclude known associations of recurrent pregnancy loss, such as antiphosholipid syndrome, oligomenorrhoea, cervical weakness and other rarer causes, for example, abnormal parental chromosome karyotype, as previously described (Drakeley *et al*, 1998). Patients with identified causes for their pregnancy loss or those that had a history of second-trimester loss were then excluded from the study sample leaving the 'idiopathic' recurrent miscarriage patients. A separate database was then set up for these patients and all results of the investigations performed were recorded, including number of previous miscarriages and live births. Further differentiation of the group was made into primary losers (those with no previous live births) and secondary losers (those with live births).

Following early presentation to the clinic, usually between four to six weeks in a subsequent pregnancy, all patients followed a standardised clinic protocol. This included fetal viability ultra-sonography on a fortnightly basis until twelve weeks' gestation. Thereafter, patients were followed up in the Pregnancy Support Antenatal Clinic by the same team until delivery. The gestation at which cardiac activity was initially seen was recorded on the database along with the outcome of the pregnancy. A successful outcome was regarded as survival beyond twenty-four weeks. A record was made of the gestation at which cardiac activity was lost.

Ectopic and termination of pregnancy in the subsequent pregnancy were excluded from the study sample.

Using the results from the database, a Kaplan-Meier survival curve was constructed to show time-dependent pregnancy success, in terms of gestational age commencing at four weeks amenorrhoea. Logistic regression analysis was subsequently employed, using the model outlined below, to examine the individual impact of age and miscarriage history on achieving a successful pregnancy outcome.

Formula for logistic regression model:

$$\text{Log } (p/1\text{-}p) = 2.00 - 0.828 \text{ (age–mean [age])} - 0.2467$$
(number of previous first-trimester miscarriages)

What did the results show?

Onto the live database, 716 consecutive patients were entered with a history of recurrent miscarriage and 325 of these were identified as having 'idiopathic recurrent miscarriage'. Twenty-three patients were lost to follow-up. Following postal contact, seventy-six patients reported no further pregnancy.

Of the identified group of 325 patients, 226 (70%) subsequently achieved a further pregnancy, of which two were found to be ectopic pregnancies and two patients had termination of pregnancy. The majority of patients presented to the dedicated clinic by eight weeks gestation (90%) and by ten weeks 98% had presented.

The mean age of the study sample was thirty-two years (range: seventeen to forty-five years) and the mean number of previous miscarriages was three (range: two to ten) (*Table 11.1*).

Of the 222 patients achieving a further pregnancy, 167 (75%) had a successful outcome with survival beyond twenty-four weeks (*Figure 11.1*). There was no statistically significant difference in outcome between the two groups of patients of primary (77%) and secondary losers (74%).

Table 11.1: Previous miscarriage history

Number of previous miscarriages	Patient number (%)
2	79(25)
3	157(48)
4	43(13)
5	25(8)
>5	31(6)

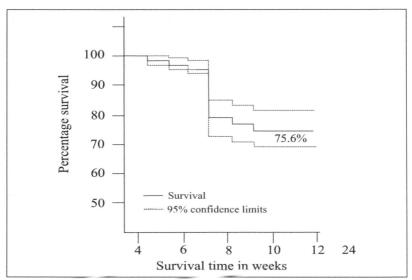

Figure 11.1: Fetal survival in women with a history of idiopathic recurrent miscarriage (n=222)

Within the group of 222 patients, fifty-five (25%) suffered further miscarriages, with fifty-four in the first trimester and one in the second trimester. Of these fifty-five miscarriages, 6/222 occurred following detection of fetal cardiac activity (3%) (fetal loss). Where no cardiac activity was ever identified with serial ultrasound, the miscarriages were classified as embryo loss in 22% of total group and constituted the great majority of loss type in early pregnancy (*Table 11.2*) (Bricker and Farquharson, 2000).

Table 11.2: Type of pregnancy loss classification

Type of loss	Typical gestation (weeks)	Fetal heart activity	Principal diagnostic group	Beta HCG level
Pre-embryo	<6	Never	Idiopathic	Low then fall
Embryo	6–8	Never	Oligomenorrhoea/ idiopathic	Initial rise then fall
Fetal	>8	Lost	Antiphospholipid syndrome	Rise then static or fall

Using the Kaplan-Meier curve (*Figure 11.1*), time-dependent survival is demonstrated in terms of gestational age. It is clear from this survival curve that the most perilous time for women with a history of idiopathic recurrent miscarriage is between six and eight weeks' gestation. Between these gestations, 78% of the total pregnancy losses occurred, of which 89% occurred without the detection of fetal cardiac activity (embryo loss).

The detection of fetal cardiac activity had been identified in 90% of the pregnancies by eight weeks, rising to 98% by ten weeks. As a consequence, by eight weeks' gestation, the chances of a successful outcome in a subsequent pregnancy were 98%, climbing to 99.4% at ten weeks' gestation (*Table 11.3*).

Table 11.3: Important gestational milestones for success and loss prediction

Gestational age (weeks)	Success rate (%)	Miscarriage rate (%)
6	78	22
8	98	2
10	99.4	0.6

The impact of previous miscarriage history and patient age significantly affected the chances of a successful outcome, age being slightly more significant than previous number of miscarriages. (p=0.0329 and p=0.00318 respectively). Women with a history of two previous miscarriages had similar chances of success in a subsequent pregnancy as those that had a history of three previous miscarriages (76% *vs* 79%) (*Table 11.4*).

What is the importance of this work?

The identification of gestational milestones

The appearance of fetal cardiac activity is an important fundamental observation to clinicians and patients. Following detection of fetal cardiac activity, an anticipated fetal loss rate of between 2% and 5% has been quoted by retrospective analysis in normal low risk antenatal populations (Cashner *et al*, 1987; Mackenzie *et al*, 1988). In women with recurrent miscarriage, a small prospective study (n=42) demonstrated a ten-fold increase of loss rates (22%), when the appearance of fetal heart activity was studied longitudinally in the early first trimester (Opsahl and Petit, 1993). By contrast, our prospective study of a larger population showed a fetal loss rate of

3% (6/222) after the initial detection of fetal cardiac activity, perhaps related to a lower than average maternal age than the aforementioned study (*Table 11.4*). Embryo loss and fetal loss rates vary between different population types, for example, our recurrent miscarriage population showed six fetal losses (3%) and forty-eight embryo losses (22%). This contrasts with previous work in unselected populations, where fetal loss is more likely (Goldstein, 1994; Hill *et al*, 1991).

No statistically significant difference was found between the two groups of primary and secondary losers. This observation was also observed in a low risk, prospectively studied antenatal population (Goldstein, 1994). Similarly, in a recurring miscarriage population, there seems to be no obvious benefit of a previous live birth on improving subsequent obstetric performance.

The concept of gestational milestones, has been used to predict pregnancy success at six, eight and ten weeks' gestation. For the entire population there is a 22% loss rate at six weeks' gestation, which dramatically falls to 2% at eight weeks and subsequently at ten weeks' gestation has fallen to 0.6% of the remaining population. The conclusion would be that the most perilous gestation for women with idiopathic recurrent miscarriage is between six and eight weeks' gestation.

Table 11.4: Predicted probability of a successful pregnancy by age and previous miscarriage history. (%) (95% confidence interval <20% in bold)

Age (years)	Number of previous miscarriages			
	2	3	4	5
20	92	90	88	85
	(86,98)	**(83,97)**	**(79,96)**	(74,96)
25	89	86	82	79
	(82,95)	**(79,93)**	**(75,91)**	(68,90)
30	84	80	76	71
	(77,90)	**(74,86)**	**(69,83)**	(61,81)
35	77	73	68	62
	(69,85)	**(66,80)**	**(60,75)**	(51,74)
40	69	64	58	52
	(57,82)	(52,76)	(45,71)	(37,67)
45	60	54	48	42
	(41,79)	(35,72)	(29,67)	(22,62)

Maternal age

Increasing maternal age reduces the chance of a pregnancy success. This has been confirmed in 201 women undergoing ovulation induction fertility treatment (Smith and Buyalos, 1996). These authors clearly showed an increasing rate of pregnancy loss from 2.1% at less than thirty years to 20% in women over forty years of age. Furthermore, the impact of age is considerably profound within large infertility populations undergoing *in vitro* fertilisation (Templeton *et al*, 1996). This study concluded that maternal age is singularly the most important success determinant in predicting pregnancy success in an IVF population.

The profound impact of maternal age on pregnancy outcome is similarly demonstrated in the present study. For example, a woman aged twenty with two previous miscarriages has a 92% (CI 86,98) chance of success in a subsequent pregnancy. This falls dramatically to 60% (CI 41,79) in a woman with a similar loss history who is aged forty-five years (*Table 11.5*) Although the confidence intervals for the success prediction are wide at the extreme ends of the age spectrum, there is little doubt that maternal age has a significant impact on future success in the recurrent miscarriage population.

Recent work on a population wide basis also amplifies the significance of maternal age (Andersen *et al*, 2000). These authors showed that fetal loss is high in women in their late thirties or older, irrespective of reproductive history. Overall, 13.5% of pregnancies in a population of 634,272 women ended with fetal loss. At the age of forty-two years, more than half of such pregnancies resulted in fetal loss. The risk of spontaneous miscarriage (combined fetal and embryo losses) was 8.9% in women aged twenty to twenty-four years and rose dramatically to 74.7% in those aged forty-five years or more.

Table 11.5: Comparison of studies identifying miscarriage rates following detection of fetal cardiac activity

Authors	Type of study	Number of patients	Population type	Fetal loss rate
Brigham et al, 1999	Prospective Longitudinal	325	Selected recurrent miscarriage	3
Qasim et al, 1997	Prospective	116	Infertility	15
Smith et al, 1996	Prospective	201	Infertility Ovulation induction	6.5
Goldstein et al, 1994	Prospective	232	Unselected	2.5
Opsahl et al, 1993	Prospective	23	Unselected recurrent miscarriage	21.7
Cashner et al, 1987	Prospective	489	Unselected from 8–12 weeks	2
Christiaens et al, 1984	Prospective	274	Unselected after 10 weeks	3.3
Gilmore et al, 1985	Prospective	1960	Unselected after 10 weeks	2.1
Hill et al, 1991	Prospective	347	Unselected	6.1
Lind et al, 1986	Prospective	932	Unselected	2.3
Liu et al, 1987	Prospective	1068	Unselected	1.5
Wilson et al, 1986	Prospective	796	Unselected	2.1

Pregnancy support

The provision of tender loving care and emotional support on loss rates in recurrent miscarriage populations has been evaluated recently. The first large population study, utilising tender loving care and emotional support in the first trimester, showed an 80% success rate in patients with idiopathic recurrent miscarriage (Stray-Pederson *et al*, 1983). This study, however, identified eighty-five out of 195 couples as having 'idiopathic recurrent miscarriage' and the population were quasi-randomised, based purely upon geographical location. A separate study, in the absence of tender loving care, showed an 80% success, when studied in a smaller population (n=24) with similar characteristics (Vlaanderen and Treffers, 1987). A more recent study reported an 86% success rate with tender loving care (n=33), as opposed to only 33% in the absence of emotional support (n=9) in an unrandomised population (Liddell *et al*, 1991).

Both these recent studies are restricted by small numbers, in contrast to the present study of 222 consecutive pregnancies, from which a 75% success rate has been obtained with the provision of tender loving care and ultrasound in early pregnancy.

Patient empowerment

Women with a history of idiopathic recurrent miscarriage, understandably, exhibit a marked stress reaction following early diagnosis of a subsequent pregnancy. Ultrasound reassurance and emotional support in a specialised miscarriage clinic may address this problem and go some way to alleviating this stress. The present large population study, as well as determining success rates for the group as a whole, has also identified important gestational milestones for success prediction. These milestones can empower patients to gain increasing reassurance of a potential successful pregnancy outcome, as advancing gestation is reached. Clinicians can also gain confidence from this data to predict the future chances of pregnancy success in women with a history of idiopathic recurring miscarriage.

The authors would like to thank Paul Monaghan and Dr Simon Fear (Department of Statistics) for all their assistance with the data analysis in this study, and in particular to Claire Conlon for help and support with data collection and verification.

References

Andersen AM, Wohlfarht J, Christens P, Olsen J (2000) Maternal age and fetal loss: population based register linkage study. *Br Med J* **320**: 1708–12

Bricker L, Farquharson RG (2000) Recurring Miscarriage. *The Obstetrician and Gynaecologist* **2**(4): 17–23

Brigham S, Conlon C, Farquharson RG (1999) A longitudinal study of pregnancy outcome following idiopathic recurring miscarriage. *Hum Reprod* **14**: 2868–71

Cashner KA, Christopher CR, Dysert GA (1987) Spontaneous fetal loss after demonstration of a live fetus in the first trimester. *Obstet Gynaecol* **70**: 827–30

Christiaens GC, Stoutenbeek PH (1984) Spontaneous abortion in proven intact pregnancies. *Lancet* **2**: 571

Clifford K, Rai R, Regan L (1997) Future pregnancy outcome in unexplained recurrent first trimester miscarriage. *Hum Reprod* **12**: 387–9

Drakeley AJ, Quenby S, Farquharson RG (1998) Mid trimester loss — appraisal of a screening protocol. *Hum Reprod* **13**(7): 1975–80

Everett C (1997) Incidence and outcome of bleeding before the 20th week of pregnancy: prospective study from general practice. *Br Med J* **315**: 32–4

Gilmore DH, McNay MB (1985) Spontaneous fetal loss rate in early pregnancy. *Lancet* **1**: 107

Goldstein SR (1994) Embryonic death in early pregnancy: A new look at the first trimester. *Obstet Gynaecol* **84**: 294–7

Hill LM, Guzick D, Fries J, Hixon J (1991) Fetal loss rate after ultrasonically documented cardiac activity between 6 and 14 weeks menstrual age. *J Clin Ultrasound* **19**: 221–3

Li TC (1998) Recurrent miscarriage:principles of management. *Hum Reprod* **13**(2): 478–82

Liddell HS, Pattison NS, Zanderigo A (1991) Recurrent miscarriage; outcome after supportive care in early pregnancy. *Aust NZ J Obstet Gynaecol* **31**(4): 320–2

Lind T, McFadyen IR (1986) Human pregnancy failure. *Lancet* **1**. 91

Liu DTY, Jeavons B, Preston C *et al* (1987) A prospective study of spontaneous miscarriage in ultrasonically normal pregnancies and relevance to chorionic villus sampling. *Prenat Diagn* **7**: 223

Lyndon M, Hill MD, Guzick D, Fries J, Hixson J (1991) Fetal loss rates after ultrasonically documented cardiac activity between 6 and 14 weeks menstrual age. *J Clin Ultrasound* **19**: 221–3

Mackenzie WE, Holmes DS, Newton JR (1988) Spontaneous abortion rates in ultrasonographically viable pregnancies. *Obstet Gynaecol* **71**(1): 81–3

Opsahl MS, Petit DC (1993) First trimester sonographic characteristics of patients with recurrent spontaneous abortion. *J Ultrasound Med* **12**: 507–10

Qasim SM, Sachdev R, Trias A, Senkowski K, Kemmann E (1997) The predictive value of first-trimester embryonic heart rates in infertility patients. *Obstet Gynecol* **6**: 934–6

Quenby S, Farquharson RG (1993) Predicting recurring miscarriage — what is important? *Obstet Gynaecol* **82**: 132–8

Smith KE, Buyalos RP (1996) The profound impact of patient age on pregnancy outcome after early detection of fetal cardiac activity. *Fertil Steril* **65**(1): 35–40

Stirrat GM (1990) Recurrent miscarriage; definition and epidemiology. *Lancet* **336**: 673–5

Stray-Pederson B, Stray-Pederson S (1983) Etiological factors and subsequent reproductive performance in 195 couples with a prior history of habitual abortion. *Am J Obstet Gynecol* **148**: 140–6

Templeton A, Morris JK, Parslow W (1996) Factors that affect outcome of in-vitro fertilisation treatment. *Lancet* **348**: 1402–6

Vlaanderen W, Treffers PE (1987) Prognosis of subsequent pregnancies after recurrent spontaneous abortion in first trimester. *Br Med J* **295**: 92–3

Wilson RD, Kendrick V, Wittmann BK *et al* (1986) Spontaneous abortion and pregnancy outcome after normal first-trimester ultrasound examination. *Obstet Gynaecol* **67**: 352

Section III:
The Liverpool experience

12

Endometrium in recurrent miscarriage

Siobhan Quenby

At least 50% of cases of recurrent miscarriage have no known aetiology (Quenby and Farquharson, 1993) after couples suffering this condition have been examined by a standard battery of tests on their venous blood (Christiansen, 1996). It is possible that there is an underlying endometrial factor in recurrent miscarriage that leads to a mal-implantation of the pregnancy that ends in miscarriage. This chapter will review the published literature regarding the existence and significance of endometrial factors in recurrent miscarriage.

Luteal phase defect

Luteal phase deficiency (LPD) is a controversial entity thought to result from abnormal ovarian function with inadequate progesterone production or an inadequate progesterone effect on the endometrium (Lee, 1987). Endometrial biopsy is the most widely accepted diagnostic method; a biopsy taken in the luteal phase of the cycle is histologically dated and compared with the onset of the next menses (Noyes *et al*, 1950). A lag of greater than two to three days is considered suspect. LPD has been reported in 23% to 60% of women with recurrent miscarriage (Fritz, 1988). Luteal phase insufficiency has been proposed as a causative factor for recurrent pregnancy loss (Andrews, 1979; Li and Cooke, 1994; Serle *et al*, 1994). LPD has been treated with luteal phase progesterone supplementation (Fritz, 1988), however there has been no well-designed randomised controlled trial to show any benefit from this treatment.

Endometrial proteins

Other evidence for a role of delayed endometrial maturation in recurrent miscarriage comes from the low CA125 and placental protein 14 (PP14) concentrations found in uterine flushings from women with recurrent miscarriage. These were found in women with histologically normal and delayed endometrium (Dalton *et al*, 1995). Furthermore, the low CA125 and PP14 predicted a poor pregnancy outcome (Dalton *et al*, 1998). Another endometrial protein MUC1 was found to be lower in the endometrium of women suffering from recurrent miscarriage than controls (Aplin *et al*, 1996). These data suggest that epithelial function may be compromised in some cases of recurrent miscarriage. This epithelial compromise could either produce insufficient secretory product to allow adequate implantation, or it could mean that there is inhibition of a factor that protects the endometrium from 'poor quality' embryos. If this were the case, then women suffering recurrent miscarriage would allow pregnancies that are destined to fail to recurrently implant and thus, couples present clinically as recurrent miscarriage.

Leucocytes in the endometrium

Leucocytes are an important constituent of human endometrium, accounting for 10% of stromal cells in the proliferative phase. Immediately prior to implantation in the secretory phase, 20% of endometrial cells are leucocytes and, in early pregnancy, leucocytes comprise 30% of decidual cells (Bulmer *et al*, 1991). The leucocyte population in the endometrium consists of T cells, macrophages, and large granular lymphocytes.

The largest leucocyte population in the human endometrium is the large granulated lymphocytes (LGL) which express the natural killer (NK) cell antigen CD56. In contrast to peripheral blood NK cells, LGL do not express the low affinity Fcγ receptor CD16, or the CD57 molecule. Around the time of implantation, LGL comprise 70–80% of the leucocyte population in the endometrium and numbers increase still further if conception occurs (King *et al*, 1989; Starkey, 1992). The LGL appear to be critical in early pregnancy placentation. Unexplained infertility patients were found to have fewer CD56+ cells than fertile controls (Klentzeris *et al*, 1994). Therefore, women suffering recurrent early pregnancy loss may have had an impaired CD56+ leucocyte response in the decidua (Hill *et al*, 1995). Women with recurrent miscarriage had an increased proportion of CD16+ CD56^{dim} compared to the normal population where CD16- CD56^{bright} LGL were more prevalent in their endometrium (Lachapelle *et al*, 1996). However, using immuno-histochemistry more CD56+ LGL were found in the pre-implantation endometrium of the recurrent miscarriage patients than in the controls (Quenby *et al*, 1999; Clifford *et al*, 1999). Furthermore, there were more CD56+ leucocytes in the endometrium of patients that went on to have miscarriages than in those who had live births (Quenby *et al*, 1999). Therefore, either the CD56+ cells are hostile on the invading trophoblast, or they facilitate invasion so that pregnancies that are destined to fail, recurrently implant and thus present clinically, as recurrent miscarriage. There is data supporting the latter possibility as more CD56+ cells were found in the decidua from chromosomally abnormal miscarriages than chromosomally normal miscarriages (Yamamoto *et al*, 1999).

More CD57+ cells were detected in the endometrium from women suffering recurrent miscarriage than control and those women with CD57+ cells were more likely to miscarry in subsequent pregnancies (Quenby *et al*, 1999). Women suffering spontaneous losses (not RPL) had an increase in numbers of CD57 'Classical' NK cells (Vassiliadou and Bulmer, 1996a). However, it is difficult to characterise leucocyte populations after recurrent miscarriage, as it is difficult to distinguish causes of miscarriage from post miscarriage inflammatory responses (Bulmer, 1996).

T cells, account for 45% of leucocytes in the proliferative phase of the cycle. Their numbers remain constant throughout the menstrual cycle, although they decrease in proportion relative to other types of leucocyte by the secretory phase of the cycle (Bulmer, 1996). An increased CD4:CD8 ratio was found In one study (Lachapelle *et al*, 1996) but not in others (Quenby *et al*, 1999). Other studies have shown that reduced numbers of T cells were found in normal first-trimester decidua compared to normal endometrium (Vassiliadou and Bulmer, 1996b), however, similar numbers of T cells were found in normal first-trimester decidua compared to that from spontaneous abortion (Vassiliadou and Bulmer, 1998). As the majority of spontaneous abortions are due to fetal chromosomal abnormalities, extrapolation of data from spontaneous abortions may not apply to recurrent miscarriage.

Macrophages account for a substantial proportion of the leucocyte population in human endometrium throughout the menstrual cycle. Endometrial macrophages have been characterised by their consistent expression of CD14, CD68 and MHC class II (Bulmer, 1996). Pre-implantation endometrium from women suffering recurrent miscarriage was also found to have more macrophages than control endometrium (Quenby *et al*, 1999). Endometrial macrophages increase in number during the luteal phase of the cycle and increase further in early pregnancy decidua, suggesting that they have a role in placentation (Bulmer *et al*, 1991; Hunt and Robertson, 1996). Although the exact function of these endometrial macrophages is unknown, several roles have been suggested. They may act as antigen presenting cells which are then able to activate T cells, as they strongly express MHC class II antigens necessary for antigen presentation (Bulmer, 1996). Decidual macrophages may also have a phagocytic role, as trophoblast invasion into the decidua in normal pregnancy could produce debris requiring removal by phagocytosis (Bulmer, 1996). There is also evidence of a role for macrophages in miscarriage from a murine model of miscarriage, where embryo loss was found to be associated with activated macrophages (Gendron *et al*, 1990). In humans, a small increase in the number of CD68 labelled macrophages was found in the decidua from spontaneous abortions compared to normal controls (Vassiliadou and Bulmer, 1996a). Macrophages have been proposed as immunosuppressive cells in human early pregnancy decidua. This immunoregulatory activity has been reported to be mediated by the secretion of prostaglandin E_2 by decidual macrophages and may block the function of lymphoid cells in the decidua, with potential lytic activity against placental trophoblast (Parhar *et al*, 1989). However, the importance of local immunoregulatory cells in pregnancy has yet to be established. Macrophages are also capable of producing a range of cytokines including M-CSF, G-CSF, and TNF-α. In common with T cells and LGL, decidual macrophage cytokine production in pregnancy could play a role in the control of placental growth (Bulmer, 1996). CD56+, CD16- cells have been found to act synergistically with endometrial macrophages to enhance the release of IFN-γ (Marzusch *et al*, 1997). NK cells can be activated by the cytokines IL-2, TNF-α and IFN-γ, thus they could act together with other activated decidual cell populations to attack trophoblast populations, resulting in subsequent pregnancy loss (Vassiliadou and Bulmer, 1996a).

Endometrial cytokines

Recent attention has focused on elucidating the immunobiological roles of cytokines in normal human pregnancy following the accumulated reports of complex cytokine activity within uteroplacental tissues (reviewed in Robertson *et al*, 1994; Lim *et al*, 1996; Lim *et al*, 1998). T helper (Th) cells can differentiate into subsets with distinctive patterns of cytokine release. It has been proposed that Th1-type responses (eg. the production of IL-2 and IFN-γ) are systemically suppressed in murine pregnancy and that local expression of Th2-type cytokines (eg. IL-4, IL-6, IL-10) in placental tissue might be beneficial for fetal survival (Wegmann *et al*, 1993). Whether an analogous situation exists in human pregnancy is unclear as yet (Vince and Johnson, 1996), although partial systemic impairment of Th1 responses is compatible with clinical evidence that a number of infectious diseases caused by intracellular pathogens can sometimes be exacerbated in pregnancy, eg. CMV and malaria (Hart, 1988). Furthermore, rheumatoid arthritis, characterised by a Th1 response, often undergoes remission during pregnancy (Da Silva and Spector, 1992).

Pre-implantation endometrium was found to have a pre-dominance of Th2 cytokines (Lim *et al*, 1998; Krasnow *et al*, 1996), and in pregnancy a ten-fold increase in decidual Th2 cytokine secretion occurred (Krasnow *et al*, 1996). Women with RPL were found to have a Th1 rather than the healthy women's Th2 cytokine profile in pre-implantation endometrium, however, this profile did not predict pregnancy outcome (Lim *et al*, 2000). Furthermore, decidual T cells from women with recurrent miscarriage produced less Th2 cytokines than T cells from normal pregnancies (Piccinni *et al*, 1998). TNF-α is a regulatory cytokine, which may be produced in Th1 or Th2 responses and is known to have different effects depending on gestational age. More TNF-α was found in the decidua miscarried from RPL women (Vives *et al*, 1999) but less in the trophoblast (Lea *et al*, 1997). Leukaemia inhibitory factor (LIF) is a cytokine required for blastocyst implantation in mice. Less LIF was produced by decidual T cells from women with recurrent miscarriage from normal pregnancies (Piccinni *et al*, 1998).

Infection

The role of endometritis in recurrent miscarriage has been poorly investigated because of the difficulties in accessing the tissue. More CD16+ granulocytes were found in the pre-implantation endometrium of women suffering recurrent miscarriage than in the controls. These granulocytes were also more prevalent in those women who subsequently miscarried compared to those who had a successful pregnancy outcome (Quenby *et al*, 1999). One possibility is that this is indicative of a chronic/latent infection.

U. Urealyticum was found to be more prevalent in the endometrium of women suffering recurrent miscarriage than controls (Naessens *et al*, 1987). Bacterial vaginosis has been associated with both first- (Ralph *et al*, 1999) and second-trimester miscarriages (Llahi-Camp *et al*, 1996; Drakeley *et al*, 1998). Bacterial vaginosis has also been associated with a plasma cell infiltrate into the endometrium (Korn *et al*, 1995). Therefore, it is possible that leucocyte changes that have been found in the endometrium of recurrent miscarriage patients are in fact due to latent endometrial infection.

However, no well-designed randomised controlled trials have found that antibiotics prevented recurrent miscarriage.

Summary

Various studies have suggested an endometrial factor in recurrent miscarriage. This data is strong in that not only is the endometrium from women suffering recurrent miscarriage different from control endometrium, the differences also predict a poor pregnancy outcome in the pregnancy following the endometrial investigation. However, it is unclear whether the endometrium of recurrent miscarriers is hostile to pregnancy implantation rather than more receptive, leading to the implantation of abnormal conspectuses which subsequently miscarry.

References

Andrews WC (1979) Luteal phase defects. *Fertil Steril* **32**: 501–9

Aplin JD, Hey NA, Li TC (1996) MUC1 as a cell surface and secretory component of endometrial epithelium: Reduced levels in recurrent miscarriage. *Am J Reprod Immunol* **35**: 261–6

Bulmer JN, Longfellow M, Ritson A (1991) Leucocytes and resident blood cells in endometrium. *Ann NY Acad Sci* **622**: 57–68

Bulmer JN (1996) Cellular constituents of human endometrium in the menstrual cycle and early pregnancy. In: Bronson RA, Alexander NJ, Anderson D, Branch WD, Kutteh WH, eds. *Reproductive Immunology*. Blackwell Science, Oxford: 212–39

Christiansen OB (1996) A fresh look at the causes and treatments of recurrent miscarriage, especially its immunological aspects. *Hum Reprod Update* **2**: 271–9

Clifford K, Flanagan AM, Regan L (1999) Endometrial CD56+ natural killer cells in women with recurrent miscarriage: a histomorphometric study. *Hum Reprod* **14**: 2727–30

Da Silva JA, Spector TD (1992) Rheumatoid arthritis in pregnancy. *Clin Rheumatol* **11**: 189–202

Dalton CF, Laird SM, Searle E *et al* (1995) The measurement of CA125 and placental protein 14 in uterine flushings in women with recurrent miscarriage: relation to endometrial morphology *Hum Reprod* **10**: 2680 4

Dalton CF, Laird SM, Estdale SE *et al* (1998) Endometrial protein PP14 and CA125 in recurrent miscarriage patients; correlation with pregnancy outcome. *Hum Reprod* **11**: 3197–3202

Drakeley AJ, Quenby S, Farquharson RG (1998) Mid-trimester loss-appraisal of a screening protocol. *Hum Reprod* **13**: 1975–80

Fritz MA (1988) Inadequate luteal function and recurrent abortion. *Semin Reprod Endocrinol* **6**: 129–43

Gendron RL, Nestel FP, Lapp WS, Baines MG (1990) LPS-induced fetal resorption in mice is associated with the intrauterine production of TNF-α. *J Reprod Fertil* **90**: 395–402

Hill JA, Melling GC, Johnson PM (1995) Immunohistochemical studies of human uteroplacental tissues from first trimester spontaneous abortion. *Am J Obstet Gynecol* **173**: 90–6

Hunt JS, Robertson SA (1996) Uterine macrophages and environmental programming for pregnancy success. *J Reprod Immunol* **32**: 1–25

King A, Wellings V, Gardner L, Loke YW (1989) Immunohistochemical distribution of the unusual large granular lymphocytes in human endometrium throughout the menstrual cycle. *Hum Immunol* **24**: 66–73

Klentzeris LD, Bulmer JN, Warren MA *et al* (1994) Lymphoid tissue in the endometrium of women with unexplained infertility: morphometric and immunohistochemical aspects. *Hum Reprod* **9**: 646–52

Kodama T, Hara T, Okamoto E *et al* (1998) Characteristic changes of large granular lymphocytes that strongly express CD56 in endometrium during the menstrual cycle and early pregnancy. *Hum Reprod* **13**: 1036–43

Korn AP, Bolan G, Padian N *et al* (1995) Plasma cell endometritis in women with symptomatic bacterial vaginosis. *Obstet Gynecol* **85**: 387–90

Krasnow JS, Tollerud DJ, Naus G, DeLoia JA (1996) Endometrial Th2 cytokine expression throughout the menstrual cycle and early pregnancy. *Hum Reprod* **11**: 1747–54

Lachapelle M-H, Mirion P, Hemmings R, Roy DC (1996) Endometrial T, B, and NK cells in patients with recurrent spontaneous abortion. *J Immunol* **156**: 4027–34

Lea RG, Tulppala M, Critchley HO (1997) Deficient syncytiotrophoblast tumour necrosis factor-alpha characterizes failing first trimester pregnancies in a sub-group of recurrent miscarriage patients. *Hum Reprod* **12**: 1313–20

Lee CS (1987) Luteal phase defects. *Obstet Gynecol Surv* **42**: 267

Li TC, Cooke ID (1994) Evaluation of the luteal phase. *Hum Reprod* **6**: 484–99

Li TC (1998) Guides for practitioners recurrent miscarriage: principles of management. *Hum Reprod* **13**: 478–82

Lim KJH, Odukoya OA, Li TC *et al* (1996) Cytokines and immuno-endocrine factors in recurrent miscarriage. *Hum Reprod Update* **2**: 468–9

Lim KJH, Odukoya OA, Ajjan RA *et al* (1998) Profile of cytokine mRNA expression in peri-implantation human endometrium. *Mol Hum Reprod* **4**: 77–81

Lim KJH, Odukoya OA, Ajjan RA *et al* (2000) The role of T-helper cytokines in human reproduction. *Fertil Steril* **73**: 136–42

Llahi-Camp JM, Rai R, Ison C, Regan L, Taylor-Robinson D (1996) Association of bacterial vaginosis with a history of second trimester miscarriage. *Hum Reprod* **11**: 1575–8

Marzusch K, Buchholz F, Ruck P *et al* (1997) Interleukin-12 and interleukin-2-stimulated release of interferon-γ by uterine CD56++ large granular lymphoytes is amplified by decidual macrophages. *Hum Reprod* **12**: 921–4

Naessens A, Foulon W, Cammu H *et al* (1987) Epidemiology and pathogenesis of ureaplasma urealyticum in spontaneous miscarriage and early preterm labour. *Acta Obstet Gynaecol Scand* **66**: 513–16

Noyes R, Hertig A, Rock J (1950) Dating the endometrial biopsy. *Fertil Steril* **1**: 3–25

Parhar RS, Yagel S, Lala PK (1989) PGE2-mediated immunosuppression by first trimester human decidual cells blocks activation of maternal leukocytes in decidua with potential anti-trophoblast activity. *Cell Immunol* **120**: 61–74

Piccinni MP, Beloni L, Livi C *et al* (1998) Defective production of both leukemia inhibitory factor and type 2 T-helper cytokines by decidual T cells in unexplained recurrent abortions. *Nat Med* **4**: 1020–4

Quenby S, Farquharson R (1993) Predicting recurring miscarriage: What is important? *Obstet Gynecol* **82**: 132–8

Quenby S, Bates M, Doig T *et al* (1999) Pre-implantation endometrial leucocytes in women with recurrent miscarriages. *Hum Reprod* **14**: 737–41

Ralph SG, Rutherford AJ, Wilson JD (1999) Influence of bacterial vaginosis on conception and miscarriage in the first trimester: cohort study. *Br Med J* **319**: 220–3

Robertson SA, Seamark RF, Guilbert LJ, Wegmann TG (1994) The role of cytokines in gestation. *Crit Rev Immunol* **14**: 239–92

Serle E, Aplin JD, Li TC (1994) Endometrial differentiation in peri-implantation phase of women with recurrent miscarriage: a morphological and immunohistochemical study. *Fertil Steril* **62**: 989–96

Starkey PM (1992) Natural killer cells/large granular lymphocytes in pregnancy. In: Lewis CE, McGee JOD, eds. *The Natural Killer Cell*. IRL Press, Oxford: 205–40

Vassiliadou N, Bulmer JN (1996a) Immunohistochemical evidence for increased numbers of classical CD57+ natural killer cells in the endometrium of women suffering spontaneous early-pregnancy loss. *Hum Reprod* **11**: 1569–74

Vassiliadou N, Bulmer JN (1996b) Quantitative analysis of T lymphocytes subsets in pregnant and non-pregnant human endometrium. *Biol Reprod* **55**: 1017–1922

Vassiliadou N, Bulmer JN (1998) Characterization of endometrial T lymphocyte subpopulations in spontaneous early loss. *Hum Reprod* **13**: 44–7

Vince GS, Johnson PM (1997) Is there a Th2 bias in human pregnancy? *J Reprod Immunol* **32**: 101–4

Vives A, Balasch J, Yague J *et al* (1999) Type-1 and type-2 cytokines in human decidual tissue and trophoblasts from normal and abnormal pregnancies detected by reverse transcriptase polymerase chain reaction (RT-PCR). *Am J Reprod Immunol* **42**: 361–8

Wegmann TG, Lim H, Guilbert L, Mosmann TR (1993) Bidirectional cytokine interactions in the maternal-fetal relationship: is successful pregnancy a TL2 phenomenon. *Immunol Today* **14**: 353–6

Woods GS, Warner NL, Warnke RA (1983) Anti-Leu-3/T4 antibodies react with cells of monocyte/macrophage and Langerhans lineage. *J Immunol* **131**: 212–6

Yamamoto T, Takahashi Y, Kase N *et al* (1999) Role of decidual natural killer NK cells in patients with missed abortion: differences between cases with normal and abnormal chromosome. *Clin Exp Immunol* **116**: 449–52

13

Oligomenorrhoea and recurring miscarriage

Siobhan Quenby, Roy G Farquharson

Introduction

An hormonal cause for recurring miscarriage is an attractive concept for several reasons. Progesterone is known to be essential for the maintenance of early pregnancy (Csapo and Pulkkien, 1973). Progesterone is secreted by the corpus luteum initially but by fourteen weeks' gestation, this function is overtaken by the fetoplacental unit. This change in site of production coincides with the majority of clinically recognised miscarriages, thereby casting doubt on the sufficiency of steroid production, and hormonal support of pregnancy at a crucial phase.

Research into patient types susceptible to pregnancy loss with hormonal cause led to the identification of oligomenorrhoea (infrequent periods >35 days apart) as a separate risk factor The presence of oligomenorrhoea and an alteration in the hormonal milieu has been reported in miscarriage groups (Quenby and Farquharson, 1993; Hasegawa *et al*, 1996)

Luteinising hormone (LH) and polycystic ovaries have been implicated in miscarriage. Polycystic ovary syndrome (PCOS) is one of the most common endocrine disorders presenting during the reproductive period of a woman's life. It is not surprising that miscarriage, the commonest complication of pregnancy, has been associated with PCOS for several years. Whether such association is causal or casual has become increasingly difficult to decide. It is also interesting to note that the exact aetiology and pathogenesis of both these common disorders continues to elude both scientists and clinicians.

PCOS — A diagnosis in evolution

Ever since the syndrome was first described by Stein and Leventhal in 1935, the understanding of this heterogenous disorder has changed continuously. Early descriptions of the syndrome were based on ovarian morphology (Stein and Leventhal, 1935). Later on, but before the advent of high resolution ultrasonography, PCOS was defined mainly on the basis of a combination of clinical and biochemical features. Recent availability of modern high resolution diagnostic ultrasonography has, again, tipped the balance towards a more morphologically based diagnosis. Ovarian morphology, using the criteria of ten or more cysts, 2–8mm in diameter, arranged around an echodense stroma (Adams *et al*, 1985), appears to be the most sensitive marker of polycystic ovaries (PCO). Some women, in whom polycystic ovaries have been detected by ultrasound, remain completely asymptomatic, although symptoms may develop later, for example, after an increase in body mass index. It is well known that approximately 20% of apparently normal women may have polycystic ovaries (Polson *et al*, 1988).

The current belief is that PCOS is a spectrum of heterogenous disorders with signs such as obesity, hyperandrogenism, disturbance of menstrual cycle and infertility, which may present singly or in combination. In view of such a heterogenous syndrome, it is likely that PCOS has multiple causes and represents a complex disorder, in which genetic and environmental factors each play an important part (Franks, 1997). Genetically determined disorders of folliculogenesis and follicular function may be the cause of abnormal steroidogenesis with hyperandrogenism in cases of PCOS

Hypersecretion of LH

In the majority of cases, exact cause of recurrent miscarriage (RM) remains undiagnosed. Until very recently, it was thought that PCOS, predisposed to recurrent miscarriage and hypersecretion of LH, was the main incriminating factor. As a result of studies by several authors, this seemingly inseparable relationship has been breached. It is now apparent that subfertility, rather than miscarriage, is a more likely sequelae to PCOS and high LH levels, and that hypersecretion of LH is by no means universal to all cases with PCO. Forty percent of women with PCO will have an abnormal follicular phase luteinising hormone (LH) level of more than 10 IU/L. The incidence of subfertility among such women is 37%, compared with 21% of women with PCO and normal follicular phase LH levels (Conway *et al*, 1989). Sagle *et al* (1988) investigated the association between polycystic ovaries and recurrent miscarriage in women with spontaneous ovulatory cycles. The prevalence of ultrasonographic-determined PCO in women who had recurrent miscarriages and normal LH levels, was found to be high (82%). A diagnosis of PCOS could not be substantiated by biochemical criteria among 203 patients attending a miscarriage clinic (Quenby *et al*, 1993). In this study, oligomenorrhoea was identified to be the most critical risk factor associated with recurrent miscarriage. This apparent difference in the two studies could have occurred due to the variable methods of diagnosis of PCO. Both studies confirm that the serum LH and mid-luteal urinary pregnandiol-3-glucuronide concentrations were normal in all of the women with recurrent miscarriage. As a result, all authors consider abnormal endometrial maturation as a causal effect, especially the demonstration of a significantly low luteal phase oestradiol level in the recurring miscarriage group (Quenby and Farquharson, 1993).

At the beginning of the 1990s, evidence from some studies suggested that hypersecretion of LH may play an important role, before conception, in miscarriage. In a prospective study of 193 women with regular spontaneous menstrual cycles, forty-six women were found to have a high pre-pregnancy follicular phase serum LH value (>10 IU/L) and, of these, 65% of the pregnancies ended in miscarriage, whereas only 12% of pregnancies in the normal LH group did so (Regan *et al*, 1990). To find out the relationship of the amount of PCO, LH levels and recurring miscarriage, the same author (Clifford *et al*, 1994) investigated 500 women with a history of recurrent miscarriage. Fifty-six percent of these cases had sono-graphic features of PCO and 58% of this later group had hypersecretion of LH, as demonstrated by early morning urinary LH analysis. In essence, only 25% of the total number of women were found to hypersecrete LH.

By contrast, the association of PCO and miscarriage was questioned by a study done by Farquhar *et al*, 1994. They found no detectable effect of PCO on parity or miscarriage. In addition, no association was found between high follicular LH levels and poor reproductive performance (Li *et al*, 1993). No difference between mid-follicular and mid-luteal serum LH and FSH levels in a group of women with recurrent early pregnancy loss, compared to a group of multiparous controls, could be demonstrated (Watson *et al*, 1993).

These conflicting findings by several authors prompted further investigations to study the treatment effect of suppression of LH secretion on miscarriage rate. A randomised controlled trial (Clifford,

1996) proved that the outcome of pregnancy was not improved by pre-pregnancy suppression of high LH concentrations in ovulatory women with recurrent miscarriage and hypersecretion of LH. These authors concluded that hypersecretion of LH did not seem to be causally related to early pregnancy loss and that the outcome of pregnancy, without pituitary suppression, was uncompromised.

To prove that the commonly perceived hormonal derangement in women with PCOS, ie. hypersecretion of LH and hyper-androgenism, is by no means universal among women having PCO, results of another group of investigators are worth reviewing. These authors checked mid-follicular phase LH, FSH, testosterone, androstenedione, unbound testosterone and DHEAS in fifty-five women, which included women with PCO and ovulatory women with PCO, as well as normal ovaries. Both groups of ovulatory women had values which were similar and significantly lower than those of women with PCOS. Unfortunately, oestradiol levels were not checked in this study (Carmina *et al*, 1997).

Miscarriage: the endometrial perspective

The LH storm has subsided and, with it, has faded the argument for premature resumption of meiosis in the ovum, but the search for a cause for recurrent miscarriage continues. Quite naturally, the focus has shifted from LH to other hormones, mainly sex steroids. It is envisaged that abnormal sex steroid levels can cause inadequate endometrial preparation during implantation leading to miscarriage.

Oestrogen and progesterone decidualise the endometrium and, therefore, the serum level of these hormones may have important implications on appropriate implantation of blastocyst and adequate maintenance of pregnancy. Liu *et al* (1991) measured serum oestradiol and beta-HCG levels in a bid to predict pregnancy outcome in eighty-seven patients with pregnancies following IVF or ET. Prolonged HCG doubling time and reduced corpus luteum oestradiol secretion were signs of miscarriage. However, the predictability for spontaneous abortion by late luteal oestradiol pattern (63.9%) was significantly higher than that of HCG doubling time (37.8) (p< 0.01). Furthermore, a different group of investigators found that serum oestradiol levels could help differentiate conception cycles from non-conception cycles in an IVF programme (Hutchinson-Williams *et al*, 1989). To further the case for a low oestradiol effect (Quenby and

Farquharson, 1993) investigated a group of women attending their miscarriage clinic and noted that an isolated deficiency of luteal phase oestradiol secretion was a significant factor for miscarriage in a subsequent pregnancy.

Oligomenorrhoea: marker for miscarriage?

Oligomenorrhoea carries the highest risk load for a subsequent miscarriage (Quenby et al, 1993). The paper emphasises that an endocrine dysfunction is an effect of oligomenorrhoea and plays a key role in idiopathic pregnancy loss. Oligomenorrhoea is grossly over-represented in the recurring miscarriage population (19%), which is in sharp contrast to the incidence of oligomenorrhoea (0.9%) in the general population (Munster et al, 1992).

Recent evidence of the strong association between oligo-menorrhoea and subsequent miscarriage has been reported. Hasegawa et al (1996) clearly demonstrated that, in a population of 119 consecutive women with spontaneous first-trimester miscarriage, the incidence of oligomenorrhoea was again over-represented at 11%. In the oligomenorrhoeic women, a normal fetal karyotype was shown in 34%, versus 12.5% (p < 0.01) in the women with normal menstrual cycles. Further analysis revealed that for those women with anembryonic pregnancy and normal karyotype, the incidence of oligomenorrhoea was 57%, suggesting that it is not necessarily a high abnormal chromosome rate that provokes miscarriage, but that oligomenorrhoea is clearly a highly loaded risk factor.

Early pregnancy support with human chorionic gonadotrophin (HCG)

In women with oligomenorrhoea and recurring miscarriage, there is an excess of fetal wastage and miscarriage. In those women with recurring miscarriage and normal monthly menstrual cycles, there is no evidence that HCG support is beneficial (Harrison, 1992; Quenby and Farquharson, 1994). There is little doubt that in women with oligomenorrhoea and recurring miscarriage, HCG support, from weeks six to fourteen weeks of pregnancy, can be beneficial (Quenby and Farquharson, 1994). Although this initial randomised double-blind controlled trial contains small numbers of oligomenorrhoeic women, analysis of a large database continues to show an excess of fetal wastage and miscarriage in those women who do not receive HCG in early pregnancy (n=91 patients) (*Figure13.1a, b*). The excess miscarriage rate of approximately 10% (30% no HCG versus 20% with HCG) still persists. There is a need for a large prospective randomised controlled trial of HCG versus placebo in early pregnancy support. An assertive power calculation demands that 300 women in each arm of the trial would be necessary to find a significant improvement with HCG. As a result, the trial would need to be multi-centred and is logistically possible, but financially demanding. At the present time, HCG support should be offered to those women with recurring miscarriage and oligomenorrhoea who seek a potentially beneficial treatment in the early anxious stages of a subsequent pregnancy.

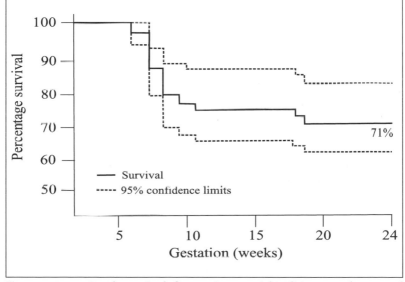

Figure 13.1a: Fetal survival for patients with oligomenorrhoea and recurring miscarriage (n=84)

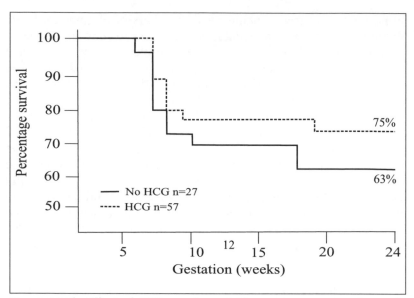

Figure 13.1b: Effect of HCG supplementation on pregnancy outcome in patients with oligomenorrhoea and RM

References

Adams J, Franks S, Polson DW *et al* (1985) Multifollicular ovaries: clinical and endocrine features and response to pulsatile gonadotrophin releasing hormone. *Lancet* **ii**: 1375–8

Carmina E, Wong L, Chang L and Paulson R J *et al* (1997) Endocrine abnormalities in ovulatory women with polycystic ovaries on ultrasound. *Hum Reprod* **12**: 905–9

Csapo AI, Pulkkien MO, Wiest WG (1973) Effects of lutectomy and progesterone replacement therapy in early pregnancy patients. *Am J Obstet Gynecol* **115**: 759–65

Clifford K, Rai R, Watson H, Regan L (1994) An informative protocol for the investigation of recurrent miscarriage: Preliminary experience of 500 consecutive cases. *Hum Reprod* **9/7**: 1328–32

Clifford K, Rai R, Watson H, Franks S, Regan L (1996) Does suppressing luteinising hormone secretion reduce the miscarriage rate? Results of a randomised controlled trial. *Br Med J* **312**: 1508–11

Conway CS, Honour JW, Jacobs HS (1989) Heterogeneity of the polycystic ovary syndrome: clinical, endocrine and ultrasound features in 556 patients. *Clin Endocrinol* **30**: 459–70

Farquhar CM, Birdsall M, Manning P, Mitchell JM, France JT (1994) The prevalence of PCO on ultrasound scanning in a population of randomly selected women. *Aust NZ J Obstet Gynaecol* **34**: 67–72

Franks S (1997) Polycystic ovary syndrome: approaching the millennium. JBFS, 2 (1), *Hum Reprod* **12**(Natl Suppl): 43–5

Harrison RF (1992) Human chorionic gonadotrophin (HCG) in the management of recurrent abortion: results of a multi-centre placebo controlled study. *Eur J Obstet Gynaecol* **47**: 175–9

Hasegawa I, Takakuwa K, Tanaka K (1996) The roles of oligomenorrhoea and fetal chromosomal abnormalities in spontaneous abortion. *Hum Reprod* **11**: 2304–5

Hutchinson-Williams KA, Luenfeld B, Diamond MP *et al* (1989) Human chorionic gonadotrophin, oestradiol and progesterone profiles in conception and non-conception cycles in an in-vitro fertility program. *Fertil Steril* **52**: 441–5

Li TC, Serle E, Warren MA, Cooke ID (1993) Is endometrial development in the peri-implantatic period influenced by high concentrations of luteinising hormone in the follicular phase? *Hum Reprod* **8**: 1021–4

Liu HC, Davis O, Berkeley A, Graf M, Rosenwaks Z (1991) Late luteal oestradiol patterns are a better prognosticator of pregnancy outcome than serial beta-human chorionic gonadotrophin concentrations. *Fertil Steril* **56**: 421

Munster K, Schmidt L, Helm P (1992) Length and variation in the menstrual cycle: a cross-sectional study from a Danish county. *Br J Obstet Gynaecol* **99**: 422–9

Polson DW, Wadsworth J, Adams J, Franks S (1988) Polycystic ovaries: a common finding in normal women. *Lancet* **II**: 870–2

Quenby SM, Farquharson RG (1993) Predicting recurring miscarriage: What is important? *Obstet Gynaecol* **82**: 132–8

Quenby SM, Farquharson RG (1994) Human chorionic gonadotrophin supplementation in recurring pregnancy loss: A controlled trial. *Fertil Steril* **62**. 708–10

Regan L, Owen EJ, Jacobs HS (1990) Hypersecretion of LH, infertility and miscarriage. *Lancet* **33**: 1141–4

Sagle M, Bishop K, Ridley N *et al* (1988) Recurrent early miscarriage and polycystic ovaries. *Br Med J* **297**: 1027–8

Stein IF, Leventhal ML (1935) Amenorrhoea associated with bilateral polycystic ovaries. *Am J Obstet Gynaecol* **29**: 181–91

Watson H, Kiddy DS, Hamilton-Fairley D, Scanlon MJ, Barnard C, Collins WP, Bonney RC, Franks S (1993) Hypersecretion of LH and ovarian steroids in women with recurrent early miscarriage. *Hum Reprod* **8**: 829–33

Yoshino K, Takahashi K, Eda Y, Nishigaki A, Kitao M (1992) Polycystic ovaries with normal menstruation and with oligomenorrhoea. *J Obstet Gynaecol* **12**: 202–4

14

Type of pregnancy loss in recurrent miscarriage

Leanne Bricker, Roy G Farquharson

Introduction

Recurrent pregnancy loss (RPL) can be defined as more than two consecutive pregnancy losses at less than twenty-four weeks' gestation and occurs in 1–2% of fertile women. When clinical pregnancy is established, the risk of spontaneous pregnancy loss is about 12–14% (Miller *et al*, 1980; Edmonds *et al*, 1982), and therefore the incidence of RPL by chance alone, would be in the order of 0.35%. This discrepancy implies that in some cases there is an underlying pathological explanation. Following investigation of RPL about 50 % of cases have no cause or association found and are classified as idiopathic (Stirrat, 1990; Quenby and Farquharson, 1993). It is generally accepted that within the idiopathic group there is considerable hetcrogeneity and it is unlikely that one single pathological mechanism can be attributed to their RPL. Known causes or associations of RPL fall into four categories:

- endocrine
- immunological
- anatomical
- genetic.

However, there is much debate about cause and association, as the exact pathophysiological mechanisms have not been elucidated. Current research is directed at theories related to implantation, trophoblast invasion and placentation, as well as factors which may be embryopathic.

Historically, clinicians have grouped all pregnancy losses that occur at gestations prior to theoretical viability under the umbrella of 'abortion'. More recently, among researchers in the field of RPL, it has been recognised that the classification of pregnancy loss is more complex, as the developing pregnancy undergoes various important stages, and differing pathology at the time of pregnancy loss is exhibited at these different stages. There has been a plea to classify pregnancy losses according to the gestation at which they occur and detail the event, for example, intrauterine fetal death. In this way, possible pathophysiological mechanisms may be postulated and studied.

The objective of this study was to determine whether the pregnancy loss patterns in women with RPL differ according to causal or associated conditions, thus suggesting differing disease processes. If different conditions associated with RPL have specific, although as yet unexplained, mechanisms, one would expect the patterns of pregnancy loss to be different. This information is useful for the ongoing primary scientific research into RPL as laboratory findings are often correlated with subsequent pregnancy outcome. In addition, women who present themselves for investigation and management of RPL are generally highly motivated, and seek an understandable explanation. In fact, often the finding of no association causes much disappointment despite the fact that a subsequent pregnancy is more likely to be successful. Developing a knowledge base of gestational milestones for these women is very useful as an integral part of the supportive care provided by clinicians in recurrent miscarriage clinics.

Methods

The setting for this study was the Recurrent Miscarriage Clinic at Liverpool Women's Hospital, a teaching hospital of the University of Liverpool. Between 1988–1998, 850 women with a history of two or more pregnancy losses were referred to the clinic. Although the textbook definition of RPL is >2 pregnancy losses, we do accept referrals of women who have had two previous pregnancy losses, particularly if one or both have been second-trimester losses or intrauterine deaths. Women are seen initially before a subsequent pregnancy, and at this preconceptual visit a thorough clinical history and investigation protocol is undertaken to exclude known associations with RPL, such as antiphospholipid syndrome (APS) and oligomenorrhoea (menstrual cycle length of over thirty-five days). The full investigation protocol has been previously described (Drakeley *et al*, 1998). At the second clinic appointment results and a plan of management for the next pregnancy are discussed. At this time a repeat APS screen is undertaken. All women are advised to take preconceptual folic acid supplements.

In a subsequent pregnancy, women are seen within a week of missing a period, and scanned twice weekly thereafter, until twelve to fourteen weeks' gestation. Thereafter, follow-up occurs in the Pregnancy Support Antenatal Clinic. Transabdominal and/or transvaginal ultrasonography (using 3.5 MHz and 7.5 -5 MHz transducers respectively) are employed depending on the individual situation, to ensure optimal visualisation of the pregnancy and the pelvis. Management options include supportive care if idiopathic RPL, aspirin or a combination of heparin and aspirin if APS, HCG supplementation if oligomenorrhoeic, and transcervical or transabdominal cerclage if indicated for cervical weakness. There is a dedicated miscarriage nurse who is available for advice during working hours, and after hours women are referred or have direct access to the gynaecological emergency room.

Data is entered onto a live database in an ongoing fashion, and includes demographic details, relevant past history (medical, surgical, obstetric and gynaecological), results of investigations, details and outcome of the subsequent pregnancy. In the case of a subsequent miscarriage, the gestation at miscarriage and details of whether fetal cardiac activity was ever identified is recorded. If miscarriage occurs before fetal cardiac activity is identified, the pregnancy loss is defined as embryonic loss. If pregnancy loss occurs after fetal cardiac activity is identified, the pregnancy loss is defined as fetal loss.

For the purposes of this study women were included if their previous pregnancy losses were in the first trimester, and they had idiopathic RPL, APS, or oligomenorrhoea. Women who had tested positive for APS on one occasion only were also analysed, but in a separate group ('possible' APS), as we wanted to assess whether clinical outcome differed from the other groups. Women with a history of one or more mid-trimester losses, or who had a combination of diagnoses (eg. APS and oligomenorrhoea) or who had a confirmed genetic abnormality were excluded from the study.

Maternal age has been shown to be an independent factor in predicting pregnancy outcome. Subgroup analysis was therefore undertaken for women aged under thirty-five and women aged thirty-five and over. This age was chosen as it is the age at which the risk of aneuploidy in pregnancy rises significantly.

Results

Over the ten-year period studied, 850 women with a history of RPL were seen, investigated and entered onto the database. In 357 (42%) women no cause or association could be found and they were classified idiopathic RPL. Seventy-three (8.6%) had oligomenorrhoea (defined as a cycle ≥35 days), eighty-six (10.1%) true APS and ninety-three (10.9%) tested positive for APS on one occasion ('possible' APS). These 609 women were included in the study. The remaining 241 women were classified as mid-trimester loss (14.6%), multiple pathology (12.9%) and genetic abnormality (0.8%), and were excluded from the study (*Table 14.1*).

Table 14.1: Diagnostic group classification		
'Diagnostic' group	**Number of women**	**%**
Idiopathic	357	42.0
Oligomenorrhoea	73	8.6
Antiphospholipid syndrome (APS)	86	10.1
'Possible' APS	93	10.9
Mid-trimester loss	124	14.6
Multiple pathology	110	12.9
Genetic abnormality	7	0.8
Total	**850**	

Of the 609 women the median age was thirty-two years (range 18–45) and the median number of previous pregnancy losses was three (range 2–14). One hundred and eighty-one (30%) had a history of two previous miscarriages, and in this subgroup the median age was thirty-two (range 19–44). The number of primary losers (ie. no previous pregnancy survival > 24 weeks gestation) was 324 (53%). Between the diagnostic groups these demographic details showed similarity (*Table 14.2*).

In the study group of 609, 452 women became pregnant, of which 114 had a further miscarriage (25%). The remaining 157 women had not conceived again, verified by direct patient contact or GP contact. *Table 14.3* shows the pregnancies, pregnancy losses and types of pregnancy losses overall and for each diagnostic group. Pregnancies, pregnancy losses and types of pregnancy losses overall and for each diagnostic group are shown for the subgroups women aged thirty-five and over, and women aged under thirty-five in *Tables 14.4* and *14.5* respectively.

Table 14.2: Demographic characteristics of each diagnostic group

Characteristic	Overall N=609	Idiopathic N=357	Oliogomenorr- hoea N=73	APS N=86	Possible APS N=93
Median age (range)	32 (18–45)	32 (18–45)	31 (18–41)	33 (21–43)	33 (19–43)
Median no. previous miscarriages (range)	3 (2–14)	3 (2–10)	3 (2–14)	3 2–11)	3 (2–12)
<3 previous miscarriages (%)	181 (30)	108 (30)	19 (26)	29 (30)	25 (27)
Number primary losers (%)	324 (53)	195 (55)	41 (56)	42 (49)	46 (50)

Table 14.3: Pregnancies, pregnancy outcomes, and types of pregnancy loss overall and for each diagnostic group

	Overall	Diagnostic groups			
		Idiopathic	Oligomenorr- hoea	APS	Possible APS
Number of women	609	357	73	86	93
Number of pregnancies	452	254	55	78	65
Number of pregnancy losses	114	66	12	22	14
Pregnancy loss rate (%)	25.2	26.0	21.8	28.2	21.5
Number of embryonic losses	92	55	11	16	10
Embryonic loss rate (%)[a]	20.4	21.6	20	20.5	15.4
Number of fetal losses	22	11	1	6	4
Fetal loss rate (%)[b]	6.1	5.5	2.3	9.7	7.3

[a]numerator = number of embryonic losses; denominator = number of pregnancies
[b]numerator = number of fetal losses; denominator = number of pregnancies — number of embryonic losses

Fisher's exact test for feta loss rates:
Ideopathic *vs* Oligomenorrhoea p = 0.68 (NS) and Idiopathic *vs* APS p = 0.35 (NS)

Table 14.4: Pregnancies, pregnancy outcomes, and types of pregnancy loss overall and for each diagnostic group in women aged thirty-five and over

	Overall	Diagnostic groups			
		Idiopathic	Oligomenorr-hoea	APS	Possible APS
Number of women	212	132	12	28	40
Number of pregnancies	139	77	10	24	28
Number of pregnancy losses	50	29	3	10	8
Pregnancy loss rate (%)	36.0	37.7	30.0	41.7	28.6
Number of embryonic losses	38	23	2	8	5
Embryonic loss rate (%)[a]	27.3	29.9	17.9	20.0	33.3
Number of fetal losses	12	6	1	2	3
Fetal loss rate (%)[b]	11.9	11.1	12.5	12.5	13.0

[a]numerator = number of embryonic losses; denominator = number of pregnancies
[b]numerator = number of fetal losses; denominator = number of pregnancies — number of embryonic losses

Table 14.5: Pregnancies, pregnancy outcomes, and types of pregnancy loss overall and for each diagnostic group in women aged under thirty-five

	Overall	Diagnostic groups			
		Idiopathic	Oligomenorr-hoea	APS	Possible APS
Number of women	397	225	61	58	53
Number of pregnancies	313	177	45	54	37
Number of pregnancy losses	64	37	9	12	6
Pregnancy loss rate (%)	20.4	20.9	20.0	22.2	16.2
Number of embryonic losses	54	32	9	8	5
Embryonic loss rate (%)[a]	17.3	18.1	20.0	14.8	13.5
Number of fetal losses	10	5	0	4	1
Fetal loss rate (%)[b]	3.9	3.4	0	8.7	3.1

[a]numerator = number of embryonic losses; denominator = number of pregnancies
[b]numerator = number of fetal losses; denominator = number of pregnancies — number of embryonic losses

Discussion

In normal pregnancy the presence of fetal cardiac activity on ultrasound scan is generally reassuring, as the risk of spontaneous loss is lower following this gestational milestone (Brigham *et al*, 1999). In recent years, with the advancing ultrasonographic technology including the advent of transvaginal probes, fetal cardiac activity can be confirmed at earlier gestations (Goldstein *et al*, 1988). Embryologically the fetal heart is established and beating at twenty-two days postconception, and the embryonic period is defined as the first fifty-six days after conception (5–9+6 weeks' gestation), followed by the fetal period (from ten weeks' gestation). The embryonic period is characterised by morphogenesis (development of shape) and organogenesis (formation of organs), and the fetal period by growth and differentiation of already formed structures (Moore, 1982). Theoretically, on a transvaginal scan a fetal pole and yolk sac should be seen if the gestation sac diameter is >20mm and fetal cardiac activity should be visualised if the CRL is >5mm, ie. after six weeks' gestation (RCR/RCOG, 1995). On transabdominal scan these features may only be seen a week later.

This study demonstrates the value of serial ultrasound examination in discriminating type of pregnancy loss. To our knowledge, this is the first study to report both embryonic and fetal loss rates in a recurrent miscarriage population, presented according to diagnostic groups. Several studies have been published which evaluate pregnancy loss rates after ultrasonographic documentation of fetal cardiac activity (fetal loss rates) (*Table 14.6*). However, marked differences in study design make comparisons difficult. These differences include the type of population studied, indication for ultrasound, type of ultrasound scan performed, whether ultrasound was single or serial and gestation at which first ultrasound was performed. In some, details of the aforementioned factors are unclear, further compounding the difficulty in comparisons. In addition, ultrasound is a relatively new technology with rapid advances which constantly expand clinical application, making earlier studies less relevant in the present clinical setting. This is particularly important when considering first-trimester ultrasound assessment because, as mentioned before, the introduction of transvaginal ultrasonography in the late 1980s has greatly improved early pregnancy assessment.

We have demonstrated that the overall pregnancy loss rate is 25.2% and that for each diagnostic group, the rates are similar (21.5–28.2%) (*Table 14.3*). Embryo loss is far more common than fetal loss (embryo:fetal loss ratio = 4:1), and the observed number of fetal losses is small. The overall embryonic loss rate is 20.4% and is similar between diagnostic groups (15.4–21.6%). The fetal loss rate, however, differs according to diagnostic groups and this emerging pattern, though not statistically significant, is consistent with differing pathophysiological mechanisms. The fetal loss rate of 5.5% in idiopathic RPL is similar to that described in other populations. The 10% fetal loss rate in recurrent miscarriage associated with APS is almost twice that described in normal populations and, therefore, for these women, once fetal cardiac activity is documented a guarded prognosis should be given. Antiphospholipid syndrome (APS) is associated with pregnancy complications and pregnancy loss in all three trimesters of pregnancy (Branch *et al*, 1992). By definition, pregnancy loss forms a part of the diagnostic criteria. To make the diagnosis of APS requires:

- a clinical history of RPL, or
- pregnancy complications due to placental insufficiency, or
- thrombosis, or
- thrombocytopenia, and
- positive tests for antiphospholipid antibodies (anticardiolipin antibodies and/or lupus anticoagulant) on at least two occasions six weeks apart (Wilson *et al*, 1999).

APS activity is most likely to be detected in the first trimester of pregnancy (Topping *et al*, 1999) and despite repeat testing some women test positive on only one occasion, thus defying the diagnostic criteria. We have also shown that these women ('possible' APS) have a higher fetal loss rate (7.3%) than those women who have never tested positive. The significance of this is not known and further evaluation of this group of women is required.

Preconceptual hypersecretion of luteinising hormone (LH) associated with polycystic ovarian disease (PCOD) was thought to be associated with an increased risk of pregnancy loss (Regan *et al*, 1990). However, studies aimed at suppressing LH failed to show an improvement in pregnancy outcome (Clifford *et al*, 1996). By contrast, oligomenorrhoea has been shown to be an independent adverse risk factor for pregnancy loss in a RPL population and this group of women have lower luteal phase oestradiol levels suggesting poor endometrial receptivity (Quenby and Farquharson, 1993).

Table 14.6: Studies reporting pregnancy loss rates (published from 1990 onward)

Author	Type of study	Population studied	Median age (range)	Type of scan	No. of scans	Embryonic loss rate (%)	Fetal loss rate (%)
Rosen et al, 1990	Prospective	?316 pregnancies	?	TV	?serial	7.3	?
Hill et al, 1991	Retrospective	347 unselected, viable pregnancy at scan for bleeding, gestational dating or other (for example, suspected pelvic mass)	25(15–44)	?	single	?	4.4*
Molo et al, 1993	Prospective	160 women with positive pregnancy test and history of infertility	?	TV	serial	?	7
Opsahl and Pettit, 1993	Retrospective	23 pregnancies with documented fetal cardiac activity — history of recurrent spontaneous abortion	?	?	?	?	21.7
		167 pregnancies with documented fetal cardiac activity — history of infertility	?	?	?	?	7.2
Van Leeuwen et al, 1993	Prospective	101 pregnancies in 67 women with recurrent miscarriage (diagnosis not reported)	?	?	?	?	17
Goldstein, 1994	Prospective	232 women attending a private clinic with positive pregnancy test	32(21–43)	TV	single	7.8	6.1
Laufer et al, 1994	Retrospective	248 pregnancies in 185 women with unexplained multiple spontaneous abortion	34(21–44)	?	single	?	22.7
		63 randomly selected controls (fetal cardiac activity documented in early pregnancy)	32(24–40)	?	single	?	3.3
Smith and Buyalos, 1996	Retrospective	201 pregnancies with documented fetal cardiac activity in women with history of infertility	?(20–43)	TV	single	?	6.5
Qasim et al, 1997	Prospective	116 pregnancies with documented fetal cardiac activity in women with history of infertility	34(24–43)	TA +/TV	single	?	15
Keenan et al, 1998	Retrospective	231 clinical pregnancies with documented fetal cardiac activity in women with a history of infertility	?	TV	single	?	9.6

*this figure includes pregnancies without antecedent vaginal bleeding   TV = transvaginal   TA = transabdominal

In recurrent miscarriage associated with oligomenorrhoea, the presence of a live fetus is encouraging, with the risk of fetal loss at 2.3%.

Table 14.6 summarises studies published from 1990 onwards which have reported pregnancy loss rates. In unselected populations with no history of infertility or RPL, fetal loss rates are 3.3–6.1%. The reported fetal loss rates in infertile populations vary widely, ranging from 7–15%. Three studies evaluating pregnancy loss after ultrasonographic documentation of fetal cardiac activity in women with a history of RPL (Opsahl and Pettit, 1993; Van Leeuwen *et al*, 1993; Laufer *et al*, 1994) report fetal loss rates of 17–22.7%. The first two studies do not report the diagnostic work-up of these women and may represent an unknown and complex case mix, a feature that we allowed for by removal of mid-trimester loss and dual pathology groups.

It is difficult to explain why the fetal loss rate in our population of women with a history of RPL is relatively lower than other reported recurrent miscarriage populations. It may be attributable to the effect of the various treatments we offer and perhaps, more importantly, the intensive supportive care given throughout pregnancy. There is evidence in the literature to support the effectiveness of 'tender loving care' on successful pregnancy outcome (Stray-Pederson and Stray-Pederson, 1983; Liddell *et al*, 1991). Of course, the fact that the women included in our study received various treatment regimens may introduce bias, but if anything, one would expect higher pregnancy loss rates and larger differences in the types of pregnancy loss between diagnostic groups had the pregnancies been untreated. It would have been unethical to withhold treatment for the purposes of the study. The results of this study should be applied to women undergoing treatment and as most women attending recurrent miscarriage services receive some form of treatment, especially if they have antiphospholipid antibodies, our data is pragmatic.

The differential fetal loss pattern according to diagnostic group is not evident in women aged ≥35, where the fetal loss rate is uniformly high in all the groups (11.1–13.0%) (*Table 14.6*). Smith and Buyalos (1996) demonstrated a similar finding in an infertile population. However, in the subgroup of women aged < 35, there is still a difference in fetal loss rates (idiopathic 3.4%; APS 8.7% and oligomenorrhoea 0%) (*Table 14.5*).

In a retrospective analysis of products of conception from 224 pregnancies, Stern *et al* (1996) reported no difference in the frequency of abnormal karyotype in pregnancy losses from women with RPL compared with women with no history of RPL (57%

abnormal karyotypes in both groups). In a more robust, large, prospective study of 1309 pregnancies, Ogasawara *et al* (2000) showed that an overall loss rate of 35% can be expected in RPL groups, irrespective of associated pathology. In their study of 458 pregnancy losses, 234 (51%) were karyotyped, of which 120 (51%) had an abnormal karyotype. By contrast, of 114 sporadic losses in a general population, 77% had an abnormal karyotype, and this difference was significant. Of interest was the finding that the frequency of normal karyotypes significantly increased with the number of previous pregnancy losses and this further confirms the likelihood of underlying pathophysiology in RPL apart from abnormal karyotype. Unfortunately, for pragmatic and financial reasons, over the ten-year period of our study we have not routinely undertaken cytogenetic analysis of the products of conception in our population.

This data is valuable in both the research and clinical setting. In the research setting, clinical outcome is often correlated with *in vitro* laboratory experiments on tissue samples from women with RPL (for example, endometrial and serum studies), which are undertaken in an attempt to identify the pathophysiology of early pregnancy failure. More detailed information about the type of pregnancy loss is useful in interpreting the findings. While numerous studies have reported fetal loss rates in different populations on the basis of ultrasound viability, none have correlated these findings with karyotypic characterisation of the pregnancies. As pregnancy losses accumulate, abnormal karyotypes remain constant and loss of normal karyotypes increases (Ogasawara *et al*, 2000). We suspect that embryonic losses are more likely to be karyotypically abnormal and fetal losses more likely to be karyotypically normal. Future research is needed to evaluate types of pregnancy losses in an RPL population divided into clinical subgroups, and correlate these findings with cytogenetic analysis of products of conception to elucidate whether different types of pregnancy losses are characterised by chromosomally normal or abnormal conceptuses.

In the clinical setting, women with a history of RPL experience intense stress and anxiety following conception in a subsequent pregnancy. Emotional support and regular pregnancy assessment with ultrasound forms the mainstay of the miscarriage clinic service. Providing accurate and realistic information about the chances of success in an ongoing pregnancy is essential in this process and it is clear that success prediction will depend on which diagnostic group the woman fits into. For example, once the fetal heart is identified, a more guarded prognosis is required in the presence of antiphospholipid syndrome as compared to oligomenorrhoea and idiopathic RPL. In addition, this data is useful when assessing the clinical outcome of treatment intervention trials before implementation of evidence-based practice.

The authors would like to thank Kelly Wood and Jo Teare for their maintenance of the Miscarriage Clinic database, Ann-Maria Hughes, the Miscarriage Clinic nurse, and the women of Liverpool and beyond who attend the Miscarriage Clinic.

References

Branch DW, Silver RM, Blackwell JL, Reading JC, Scott JR (1992) Outcome of treated pregnancies in women with antiphospholipid syndrome: an update of the Utah experience. *Obstet Gynecol* **80**: 614–20

Brigham SA, Conlon C, Farquharson RG (1999) A longitudinal study of pregnancy outcome following idiopathic recurrent miscarriage. *Hum Reprod* **14**: 2868–71

Clifford K, Rai R,Watson H *et al* (1996) Does suppressing luteinising hormone secretion reduce the miscarriage rate? Results of a randomised trial. *Br Med J* **312**: 1508–11

Drakeley AJ, Quenby S, Farquharson RG (1998) Mid-trimester loss — appraisal of a screening protocol. *Hum Reprod* **13**: 1975–80

Edmonds DK, LindsayKS, Miller JF, Williamson E, Woods PJ (1982) Early embryonic mortality in women. *Fertil Steril* **38**(4): 447–53

Goldstein SR, Snyder JR, Watson C *et al* (1988) Very early pregnancy detection with endovaginal ultrasound. *Obstet Gynecol* **72**: 200

Goldstein SR (1994) Embryonic death in early pregnancy: a new look at the first trimester. *Obstet Gynecol* **84**: 294–7

Hill LM, Guzick D, Fries J, Hixson J (1991) Fetal Loss rate after ultrasonically documented cardiac activity between 6 and 14 weeks, menstrual age. *J Clin Ultrasound* **19**: 221–3

Keenan JA, Rizvi S, Caudle M (1998) Fetal loss after early detection of heart motion in infertility patients: Prognostic factors. *J Reprod Med Obstet Gynecol* **43**(suppl): 199–202

Laufer MR, Ecker JL, Hill JA (1994) Pregnancy outcome following ultrasound-detected fetal cardiac activity in women with a history of multiple spontaneous abortions. *J Soc Gynecol Invest* **1**(2): 138–42

Liddell HS, Pattison NS, Zanderigo A (1991) Recurrent miscarriage: outcome after supportive care in early pregnancy. *Aust N Z J Obstet Gynaecol* **31**: 320–2

Miller JF, Williamson E, Glue J, Gordon YB, Grudzinskas JG, Sykes A (1980) Fetal loss after implantation: A prospective study. *Lancet* **ii**: 554–6

Molo MW, Kelly M, Balos R, Mullaney K, Radwanska E (1993) Incidence of fetal loss in infertility patients after detection of fetal heart activity with early transvaginal scan. *J Reprod Med* **38**(10): 804–6

Moore KL (1982) *The Developing Human.* 3rd edn. WB Saunders Company, Philadelphia: 70–109

Ogasawara M, Aoki K, Okada S, Suzumori K (2000) Embryonic karyotype of abortuses in relation to the number of previous miscarriages. *Fertil Steril* **73**(2): 300–4

Opsahl MS, Pettit DC (1993) First trimester sonographic characteristics of patients with recurrent spontaneous abortion. *J Ultrasound Med* **12**: 507–10

Qasim SM, Sachdev R, Trias A *et al* (1997) The predictive value of first-trimester embryonic heart rates in infertility patients. *Obstet Gynecol* **6**: 934–6

Quenby S, Farquharson RG (1993) Predicting recurring miscarriage — what is important? *Obstet Gynecol* **82**: 132–8

Regan L, Owen EJ, Jacobs HS (1990) Hypersecretion of LH: Infertility and miscarriage. *Lancet* **iii**: 1141–4

Rosen GF, Silva PD, Patrizio P, Asch RH, Yee B (1990) Predicting pregnancy outcome by the observation of a gestational sac or of early fetal cardiac motion with transvaginal ultrasonography. *Fertil Steril* **54**(2): 260–4

Smith KE, Buyalos RP (1996) The profound impact of patient age on pregnancy outcome after early detection of fetal cardiac activity. *Fertil Steril* **65**: 35–40

Standing Joint Committee of the Royal College of Radiologists and the Royal College of Obstetricians and Gynaecologists (1995) *Guidance and Ultrasound Procedures in Early Pregnancy.* HMSO, London

Stern JJ, Dorfmann AD, Gutierrez-Najar AJ *et al* (1996) Frequency of abnormal karyotypes among abortuses from women with and without a history of recurrent spontaneous abortion. *Fertil Steril* **65**: 250–3

Stirrat GM (1990) Recurrent miscarriage; definition and epidemiology. *Lancet* **348**: 1402–6

Stray-Pederson B, Stray-Pederson S (1983) Etiologic factors and subsequent reproductive performance in 195 couples with a prior history of habitual abortion. *Am J Obstet Gynecol* **148**: 140–6

Topping J, Quenby S, Farquharson RG, Malia R, Greaves M (1999) Marked variation in antiphospholipid antibodies during pregnancy: Relationships to pregnancy outcome. *Hum Reprod* **14**: 224–8

Van Leeuwen I, Ware Branch D, Scott JR (1993) First-trimester ultrasonography findings in women with a history of recurrent pregnancy loss. *Am J Obstet Gynecol* **168**(11): 111–4

Wilson WA, Gharavi AE, Kolke T, Lockshin MD, Branch DW, Plette JC (1999) International consensus statement on preliminary classification criteria for definite antiphospholipid syndrome: Report of an internal workshop. *Arthritis Rheum* **42**: 1309–11

15

Mid-trimester loss

Andrew J Drakeley, Roy G Farquharson

Introduction

The mid- or second-trimester is defined as being between twelve and twenty-four weeks of gestation. This is an intriguing time of pregnancy as so much has happened, eg. embryo genesis, fetal heart function and yet independent viability is still an elusive milestone away. Recurrent miscarriage is historically defined as being three consecutive pregnancy losses. Overall loss of pregnancy from conception is 30%, of which at least 50% can be attributed to chromosomal abnormalities in a sporadic miscarriage population. The miscarriage rate after eight weeks is reduced to less than 5% if a live fetus is identified by ultrasonography (Cashner *et al*, 1987; Brigham *et al*, 1999). For mid-trimester loss, there is likely to be an overlap with the causes of first-trimester miscarriage, but the proportions may be different (Flint and Gibb, 1996).

Investigation

In modern practice, investigation involves adherence to a strict protocol to exclude conditions and diseases that are known to contribute to second-trimester miscarriage. Importantly, pathology may be present either in isolation (40%) or combined (10%) or absent in 50% despite intensive investigation. Couples attending miscarriage clinics are a very heterogeneous group, displaying widely varying presentation. Multiple pathology must always be considered in a woman with repeated second-trimester miscarriages (Drakeley *et al*, 1998).

History questions

- Time order of event sequence essential, eg. bleeding, pain, ruptured membranes, cervical dilatation.
- Detail each miscarriage in chronological order.
- Gestation that miscarriage was diagnosed?
- Was a fetal heart observed on ultrasound scan, if so, until what gestation?
- Was the miscarriage painful (like labour pains) or painless?
- Was evacuation of the uterus required or repeated?
- Was cytogenetic placental/fetal testing ever done to investigate cause?
- Is there a family history of thrombophilias, eg. mother or sister?

Initial investigations

- Antiphospholipid/thrombophilia screen.
- Pelvic and renal ultrasound scan (Müllerian).
- Vaginal and cervical swabs (BV, chlamydia).
- Hysteroscopy and cervical resistance studies.

Differential diagnosis

- Idiopathic.
- Antiphospholipid syndrome.
- Cervical weakness/incompetence.
- Uterine anomaly.
- Infection.

Idiopathic

Within the mid-trimester loss group, approximately half are deemed 'idiopathic' (*Figure 15.1*). Whether this implies that investigation was in some way incomplete or inaccurate is unclear. However, it is known from an early loss group that 60–70% of cases remain unexplained (Stirrat, 1990). Few studies can claim complete cyto-genetic analysis of lost pregnancies (Ogasawara *et al*, 2000), which would be the ideal form of complete assessment.

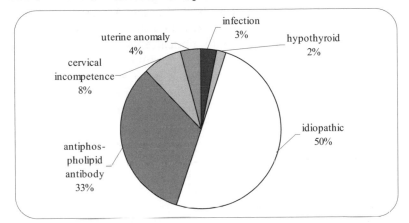

Figure 15.1: Causes of mid-trimester loss

Antiphospholipid syndrome and thrombophilias

The antiphospholipid antibody syndrome, comprising lupus anti-coagulant (LA) and anticardiolipin antibodies (aCL) are known to bind to negatively charged phospholipids and are regarded as markers of thrombosis (Birdstall and Pattison, 1993). Various theories exist as to how they cause miscarriage: binding to platelet membrane, activating release of thromboxane and subsequent platelet aggregation and thrombosis; binding to endothelial cells, inhibiting prostacyclin production or involvement with other clotting factors. It is likely that APS is a family of autoantibodies. A high index of suspicion is needed in any patient with an unexplained intrauterine death (Lubbe *et al*, 1984), especially if associated with thrombocytopenia and arterial or venous thromboses.

APS is associated with miscarriage in any trimester. Rai *et al* (1995a) reported that in a small group of nineteen patients most of their patients with APS lost in the first trimester. Of those that miscarried, a fetal heartbeat was identified in 86% of cases. Branch *et al* (1985) found that their patients with APS mostly lost in the second or early third trimester. Prevalence rates of 42% have previously been reported (Unander *et al*, 1987). The mainstay of treatment has been the use of anticoagulants in the form of either low dose aspirin or unfractionated/low molecular weight heparin.

The distribution of diagnostic APS parameters (*Table 15.1)* in our mid-trimester loss group shows an interesting pattern (Drakeley *et al*, 1998). The dRVVT is regarded as the gold standard investigation and was the only positive test in 38% of cases. Anticardiolipin anti-body was positive for IgM in 21% for IgG in 8%. The dRVVT was also found in combination with anticardiolipin antibodies (dual parameter positive) in 29% of cases (LA+ IgG/IgM). Another series on APS found that LA alone was found in 63.9% of cases of APS; IgM alone in 8.2% and all three parameters testing positive in 1.6% of patients (Rai *et al*, 1995b). APS is an important condition to test for as the treatment is inexpensive and effective.

Following diagnosis, there is general consensus regarding treatment intervention that 75mg of aspirin is beneficial, with or without heparin at low or normal molecular weight. Two publications by Kutteh (1996) looked at treated pregnant patients with APS, comparing low dose aspirin alone versus low dose aspirin and heparin. Both papers showed a statistically significant improvement in live birth rate for the patients treated with low dose aspirin and heparin. Both single centre studies report prospective trials but are not comparable in study design for inclusion criteria. The trial reported by Kutteh does not use prospective random assignment to treatment and excludes patients with LA. This would exclude half the patients seen in our clinic and in the Rai trial (1995a, b) over half of the patients were positive for LA, although low threshold entry criteria were used for aCL, ie. IgG >5 GPL, IgM >3 MPL. In a selected group of mid-trimester cases (Rai *et al*, 2000), low dose aspirin seems to confer benefit in the prevention of recurrence but further clear evidence by randomised controlled trial needs to be performed before empirical treatment can become evidence-based practice.

Table 15.1: Distribution of antiphospholipid diagnostic parameters		
Antiphospholipid parameter	**Incidence**	**%**
dRVVT	20	38
Anticardiolipin IgM	11	21
Anticardiolipin IgG	4	8
dRVVT and IgM	6	11
dRVVT and IgG	5	10
dRVVT and IgM and IgG	4	8
IgM and IgG	2	4
Total	n=52	100

Cervical weakness (incompetence)

Before the diagnosis of cervical incompetence is confirmed, strict criteria are observed, as resultant management is invasive and not without adverse sequelae. There is no agreed definition of cervical weakness as stated by the *Euro-Team Early Pregnancy Protocol* (Berry *et al*, 1995). One definition used includes painless dilatation of the cervix resulting in ruptured membranes and second-trimester miscarriage after twelve weeks, or early preterm delivery and also the passage, without resistance, of size nine Hegar dilator through the cervix in the non-pregnant state (Drakeley *et al*, 1998). The overuse of prophylactic cerclage is a manifestation of our inability to diagnose cervical incompetence with any degree of reliability on the basis of historical criteria alone (Rust *et al*, 2000).

Cervical cerclage

Shirodkar (1960) and McDonald (1957) described the two classical techniques of vaginal cervical cerclage. In Shirodkar's technique, the bladder is reflected to enable a suture to be placed as close to the internal cervical os as possible per vaginum. Bladder reflection is not required for McDonald's description. The MRC/RCOG trial on cervical cerclage (1993) studied more than 1200 patients and concluded that cerclage is beneficial to patients with three or more pregnancies ending before thirty-seven weeks' gestation (mid-trimester losses). There was also a higher rate of medical intervention; puerperal pyrexia; use of B-sympathomimetics; hospital admissions; induction of labour and Caesarean section. Rust *et al* (2000) randomly assigned sixty-one women to either cervical cerclage or no cerclage on presentation with ultrasonographically detected second-trimester preterm dilatation of the internal os, but were unable to demonstrate improved perinatal outcome with cerclage. They proposed a hypothesis that ultrasonographic dilatation of the internal os, prolapse of the membranes into the endocervical canal and shortening of the distal cervix during the second trimester share a final common pathway of multiple pathophysiologic processes, such as infection, immunologically mediated inflammatory stimuli and subclinical abruptio placentae.

Preliminary results of the Dutch CIPRACT (cervical

incompetence prevention randomised cerclage trial) have not shown significant differences between the prophylactic cerclage group and the observational group in terms of preterm delivery rate <34 weeks' gestation and the neonatal survival rate. In this study, patients are initially randomised to cerclage or no cerclage using ultrasound follow-up of cervical length measurement. If, in the no cerclage arm, the cervical length decreases to <25mm, women undergo a second randomisation to either cerclage and bed rest or simply bed rest. Interim results indicate that transvaginal ultrasonographic follow-up examination of the cervix can save the majority of women from unnecessary intervention (Althuisius *et al*, 2000). Clearly, final results are required before any firm conclusions can be drawn.

In a small proportion of cases, transabdominal cervical cerclage is indicated, ie. those with failed elective vaginal cervical suture and very short or scarred cervices (*Chapter 16*). If delivery is by Caesarean section, the suture can be left *in-situ* as these women often want another child (*Chapter 16*).

Uterine anomalies

The urogenital system develops from a common mesodermal ridge (intermediate mesoderm) along the posterior wall of the abdominal cavity and initially, the excretory ducts of both systems enter a common cavity, the cloaca. Duplications of the uterus result from lack of fusion of the paramesonephric ducts, in a localised area or throughout the length of the ducts. In its extreme form, the uterus is entirely double (uterus didelphys); in the least severe form, it is only slightly indented in the middle (uterus arcuatus). One of the more common anomalies is the uterus bicornis, in which the uterus has two horns entering a common vagina. This condition is normal in many mammals below the primates. The uterine septum should normally disappear by the end of the third month of embryonic life (Sadler, 1995).

In 1931, Smith reported one case of double uterus for every 7040 consecutive obstetric patients in New York from 1899 to 1924. Having taken an interest in the finding, Smith's detection rate for years 1925 to 1930 increased the reported incidence by five times. Harger *et al* (1993) reported an incidence of 27% of uterine anomalies in their data set of late miscarriage patients. Strassman (1966) reasoned that when there is only limited uterine space available, a point is reached whereby the semi-uterus is unable to expand further, resulting in miscarriage. Uterine abnormalities can be broadly divided into two main types, those externally divided and those externally unified though with two endometrial cavities. Other explanations for miscarriage have included implantation into an avascular septum (DeCherney *et al*, 1986).

Modes of diagnosis for uterine anomalies have also evolved with time. Hysterosalpingogram used to be the mainstay of investigation, but is painful for the woman. Pelvic ultrasound is highly specific for uterine anomaly and is non-invasive and so suitable for screening purposes (Clifford *et al*, 1994). Magnetic resonance imaging (MRI) has been proposed for the same reason, though is much more expensive (Kirk *et al*, 1993). Hysteroscopy is now widely used (with laparoscopy) for directly visualising septal defects and intrauterine synechiae.

Results from metroplasty studies have claimed good success rates post procedure from 73% to 85% (Strassman, 1966; DeCherney *et al*, 1986; Kirk *et al*, 1993). As for cervical cerclage, invasive intervention is only beneficial in highly selected patients. Successful hysteroscopic myomectomy for submucous fibroids up to 2cm diameter have been described (Buttram *et al*, 1981).

The majority of women with uterine abnormality will successfully achieve a pregnancy without intervention, although the incidence of miscarriage, malpresentation and Caesarean section are increased (Heinonen *et al*, 1982; Acien 1993). Pregnancies should always be treated as high risk and supervised accordingly. The evidence for the benefit of hysteroscopic metroplasty in recurrent miscarriage is of poor quality and should be interpreted with caution. This is because there are no reported randomised trials, and eligible groups are heterogeneous and follow-up is incomplete. In women with second-trimester loss and preterm labour, metroplasty may improve pregnancy outcome, but they remain at increased risk of preterm delivery, although the data are again of poor quality (Matts *et al*, 2000). Furthermore, hysteroscopic metroplasty does not improve outcome or 'cure' unexplained infertility.

Fibroids

The role of leiomyomata in miscarriage is also unclear. Proposed theories are that fibroids cause the uterus to become irritable, rapidly growing and degenerating, or that they alter the oxytocinase activity or endometrial stroma or vasculature (Buttram *et al*, 1981).

Infection

The role of infection in the aetiology of miscarriage appears to be in the second trimester rather than the first. Bacterial vaginosis (BV) is known to contribute to late fetal loss (Llahi-Camp *et al*, 1996). The most sensitive and specific method to diagnose BV is by examining a Gram stain of a vaginal smear for clue cells. Ideally, this should be done in the first quarter of the menstrual cycle when levels are highest. Positive diagnosis should be treated with intra-vaginal clindamycin or, alternatively, with a combination of erythromycin and metronidazole. Infrequently, other pathogens will be detected with cervical swabs.

Future implications following a previous mid-trimester loss

Prediction of pregnancy success after a second-trimester miscarriage remains largely unknown as few studies have generated large numbers of adequately investigated groups for robust analysis. Unpublished data from Liverpool following 200 women with recurrent mid-trimester loss (>1 loss after twelve weeks) would suggest that this is related to the number of associated pathologies identified. Multiple pathology patients are fortunately less frequent, and as a result, patient numbers are too small to reach statistical significance (*Table 15.2*). Nonetheless, a distinct trend for increasing failure is seen with increasing pathology.

Table 15.2: Subsequent pregnancy outcome and diagnostic group			
Group	Success rate (%)	Subsequent mid-trimester loss rate (%)	Early embryo loss rate (%)
Idiopathic n=82	78	5	17
Single factor n=59	66	12	22
Multiple factor n=13	62	23	15

References

Acien P (1993) Reproductive performance in women with uterine malformations. *Hum Reprod* **8**: 122–6

Althuisius SM, Dekker GA, van Geijn HP, Bekedam DJ, Hummel P (2000) Cervical incompetence prevention randomized cerclage trial (CIPRACT): study design and preliminary results. *Am J Obstet Gynecol* **183**: 823–9

Berry CW, Brambati B, Eskes TK *et al* (1995) The Euro-team early pregnancy (ETEP) protocol for recurrent miscarriage. *Hum Reprod* **10**(6): 1516–20

Birdstall MA, Pattison NS (1993) Antiphospholipid antibodies in pregnancy: clinical associations. *Br J Hosp Med* **50**(5): 251–60

Branch DW, Scott JR, Kochenour NK, Hershgold E (1985) Obstetric complications associated with the lupus anticoagulant. *N Eng J Med* **313**(21): 1322–6

Brigham S, Conlon C, Farquharson RG (1999) A longitudinal study of pregnancy outcome following idiopathic recurrent miscarriage. *Hum Reprod* **14**: 2868–71

Buttram VC, Reiter RC (1981) Uterine leiomyomata: etiology, symptomatology and management. *Fertil Steril* **36**(4): 433–45

Carp HJA, Toder V, Mashiach S, Nebel L, Serr DM (1990) Recurrent miscarriage: a review of current concepts, immune mechanisms and results of treatment. *Obstet Gynaecol Surv* **45**: 657–69

Cashner KA, Christopher CR, Dysert GA (1987) Spontaneous fetal loss after demonstration of a live fetus in the first trimester. *Obstet Gynecol* **70**(6): 827–30

Clifford K, Rai R, Watson H, Regan L (1994) An informative protocol for the investigation of recurrent miscarriage: preliminary experience of 500 consecutive cases. *Hum Reprod* **9**(7): 1328–32

DeCherney AH, Russell JB, Graebe RA, Polan ML (1986) Resectoscopic management of mullerian fusion defects. *Fertil Steril* **45**(5): 726–8

Drakeley AJ, Quenby S, Farquharson RG (1998) Mid-trimester loss — appraisal of a screening protocol. *Hum Reprod* **13**(7): 1975–80

Flint S, Gibb DMF (1996) Recurrent second trimester miscarriage. *Curr Opin Obstet Gynecol* **8**: 449–53

Gibb DMF, Salaria DA (1995) Transabdominal cervico-isthmic cerclage in the management of recurrent second trimester miscarriage and pre-term delivery. *Br J Obstet Gynaecol* **102**: 802–6

Harger JH, Archer DF, Marchese SG, Muracca-Clemens M, Garver KL (1983) Etiology of recurrent pregnancy losses and outcome of subsequent pregnancies. *Obstet Gynaecol* **62**(5): 574–81

Heinonen PK, Saarikoski S, Pysteynen P (1982) Reproductive performance of women with uterine anomalies: an evaluation of 182 cases. *Acta Obstet Gynecol* **62**: 157–62

Kirk EP, Chuong CJ, Coulam CB, Williams TJ (1993) Pregnancy after metroplasty for uterine anomalies. *Fertil Steril* **59**: 1164–8

Kutteh WH (1996) Antiphospholipid antibody — associated recurrent pregnancy loss: treatment with heparin and low-dose aspirin is superior to low-dose aspirin alone. *Am J Obstet Gynecol* **174**: 1584–9

Llahi-Camp JM, Rai R, Ison CR, ReganL, Taylor-Robinson D (1996) Association of bacterial vaginosis with a history of second trimester miscarriage. *Hum Reprod* **11**(7): 1575–8

Lubbe WF, Butler WS, Palmer SJ, Liggins GC (1984) Lupus anticoagulant in pregnancy. *Br J Obstet Gynaecol* **91**: 357–63

Matts SJF, Clark TJ, Khan KS, Gupta JK (2000) Surgical correction of congenital uterine anomalies. *Hosp Med* **61**: 246–9

McDonald IA (1957) Suture of the cervix for inevitable miscarriage. *J Obstet Gynaecol Br Emp* **64**: 346–50

MRC/RCOG working party on cervical cerclage (1993) Final Report of the Medical Research Council/Royal College of Obstetricians and Gynaecologists Multicentre Randomised Trial of Cervical Cerclage. *Br J Obstet Gynaecol* **100**: 516–23

Ogasawara M, Aoki K, Okada S, Suzumori K (2000) Embryonic karyotype of abortuses in relation to number of previous miscarriages. *Fertil Steril* **73**: 300–4

Rai RS, Clifford K, Cohen H, Regan L (1995a) High prospective fetal loss rate in untreated pregnancies of women with recurrent miscarriages and antiphospholipid antibodies. *Hum Reprod* **10**(12): 3301–4

Rai R, Regan L, Clifford K, Pickering W, Dave M, Mackie I, McNally T, Cohen H (1995b) Antiphospholipid antibodies and B2-glycoprotein-I in 500 women with recurrent miscarriage: results of a comprehensive screening approach. *Hum Reprod* **10**(8): 2001–5

Rai R, Backos M, Baxter N, Chilcott I, Regan L (2000) Recurrent miscarriage — an aspirin a day? *Hum Reprod* **15**(10): 2220–3

Rust OA, Atlas RO, Jones KJ, Benham BN, Balducci J (2000) A randomized trial of cerclage versus no cerclage among patients with ultrasonographically detected second-trimester preterm dilatation of the internal os. *Am J Obstet Gynecol* **183**(4): 830–5

Sadler TW, ed (1995) *Langman's Medical Embryology*. 7th edn. Williams & Wilkins: 272, 296–7

Shirodkar VN (1960) *Contributions to Obstetrics and Gynaecology*. Churchill Livingstone, Edinburgh

Smith FR (1931) The significance of incomplete fusion of the Mullerian ducts in pregnancy and parturition, with a report on 35 cases. *Am J Obstet Gynecol* **22**: 714–28

Stirrat GM (1990) Review article: recurrent miscarriage ii: clinical associations, causes and management. *Lancet* **336**: 728–33

Strassmann EO (1966) Fertility and unification of double uterus. *Fertil Steril* **17**(2): 165–76

Stray-Pederson B, Stray-Pederson S (1984) Etiological factors and subsequent reproductive performance in 195 couples with a prior history of habitual abortion. *Am J Obstet Gynecol* **148**(2): 140–6

Unander AM, Norberg R, Hahn L, Arfors L (1987) Anticardiolipin antibodies and complement in ninety-nine women with habitual abortion. *Am J Obstet Gynecol* **156**(1): 114–9

16

Transabdominal cervical cerclage

Joanne Topping, Roy G Farquharson

Introduction

Mid-trimester loss occurs between twelve and twenty-four weeks' gestation and accounts for approximately 3–5% of all pregnancy losses. Following investigation and assessment, true cervical weakness accounts for less than 10% of causes. Cervical weakness has long been known to be a factor in recurring mid-trimester miscarriage (Bricker and Farquharson, 2000; Flint and Gibb, 1996). It can be due to previous damage caused by a cone biopsy, operative dilation of the cervix, or in rare cases due to a congenital defect. Classically, cervical weakness presents in pregnancy as a painless dilatation of the cervix, which can lead to early rupture of membranes and mid-trimester miscarriage. Since the 1950s (MacDonald, 1957) the technique of putting a suture round the cervix has been used in an effort to prevent mid-trimester miscarriage.

Cervical weakness

Although it is relatively easy to understand why cervical weakness is a factor, diagnosis is still difficult. The main drawback to diagnosis and the decision whether to insert a suture is that it is a functional diagnosis, which, in many patients, may only appear in the mid-trimester of pregnancy. Diagnosis is often indicated exclusively by the appearance of repeated mid-trimester miscarriages. However, a history of one mid-trimester miscarriage does not mean immediate repetition. Indeed, 85% of women who have had one and 70% of those who have experienced two mid-trimester losses, can go on to have term deliveries (MRC/RCOG, 1993).

Following mid-trimester miscarriage, careful history analysis and relevant investigations are undertaken to ascertain whether cervical weakness is a cause. These are best performed when the patient is not pregnant. Techniques involve examination under anaesthesia, assessment of cervical length using uterine sound, as well as cervical dilatation with Hegar dilators. Hysteroscopy to exclude uterine anomaly and endometrial denuding from over enthusiastic curettage is recommended as well as cervical and vaginal swabs to diagnose mycoplasma, chlamydia and bacterial vaginosis. More recently, transvaginal ultrasound examination of the cervical length during pregnancy (Flint and Gibb, 1996) has been found to possibly predict an increasing risk of spontaneous preterm delivery with decreasing length of the cervix (Iams *et al*, 1996).

Diagnostic criteria can vary but most use a combination including a history of painless dilatation of the cervix resulting in ruptured membranes and second-trimester miscarriage after twelve weeks. Alternatively, diagnosis can be made after extreme preterm delivery followed by cervical examination in the non-pregnant state which allows the passage of a size nine or larger Hegar dilator without resistance (Drakeley *et al*, 1998). Hysteroscopy also eliminates significant uterine anomaly. It is on the analysis of a clear history with painless cervical dilatation and confirmatory hystero-scopic investigation that the decision to perform future cervical cerclage is made.

Cervical cerclage

In 1955 Shirodkar first described the use of cerclage in the treatment of cervical weakness (Olka and Lesinski, 1967). Since then it has become widely used. Both Shirodkar's method and a method developed in 1957 by MacDonald (MacDonald, 1957) involve inserting a suture of inert material around the cervix using a trans-vaginal route. The MacDonald suture involves passing a purse-string suture around the cervix taking bites at all four quadrants. The Shirodkar technique involves making a transverse incision anteriorly and posteriorly so that a higher stitch placement can be achieved (Olka and Lesinski, 1967).

Originally, cervical cerclage was performed to decrease established cervical dilation that had occurred during pregnancy. The patient would often present with abdominal pain and bulging membranes through a dilated os (MacDonald, 1957) and a cervical cerclage procedure was performed (salvage or emergency cerclage). It was acknowledged by MacDonald in his description of his purse-string suture that during his investigations it emerged that patients in strong labour with intact membranes bulging beyond the os were not suitable for cervical cerclage (MacDonald, 1957). It is now recognised that pregnancy outcome in emergency cervical cerclage is far less successful than when cerclage is applied prophylactically and electively at twelve to fourteen weeks' gestation (Caruso *et al*, 2000).

Original reports (MacDonald, 1957; Olka and Lesinski, 1967; Seppälä and Vara, 1970) reported success rates of cervical cerclage to be between 50% and 82% compared with fetal salvage rates of 7.8% to 26.7% prior to insertion of suture. More recently, a randomised trial of cervical cerclage conducted by the Royal College of Obstetricians and Gynaecologists (MRC/RCOG, 1993) found that there were 4% fewer deliveries before thirty-three weeks in the cerclage group compared with the non-cerclage group. This is the equivalent of the prevention of one very preterm delivery for every twenty-five sutures inserted. This result was of only marginal statistical significance. It is currently recommended by the Royal College of Obstetricians and Gynaecologists that use of transvaginal cervical cerclage is only considered when there is a high likelihood of benefit, for example, women who have had three or more second-trimester miscarriages or preterm deliveries (MRC/RCOG, 1993).

A more recent study (Rust *et al*, 2000) found that on diagnosis of preterm dilatation of the internal os by ultrasound, there was no statistical difference between those patients who underwent cerclage and those who did not. By contrast, a pragmatic, prospective, randomised study from the Netherlands (Sietske *et al*, 2000) has recently shown that cervical cerclage is beneficial in those for whom it is indicated. Starting in early pregnancy, serial ultrasound measurements of cervical length may help to reduce the need for traditional prophylactic cerclage and can prevent unnecessary intervention. Reduction in cervical length has been shown to increase the risk for preterm delivery (Iams *et al*, 1996).

Transabdominal cervical cerclage

Transabdominal cervical cerclage was first described by Benson and Durfee in 1965 (Olka and Lesinski, 1967) Since then, it has become an increasingly established procedure and has been shown to be effective in a number of case groups.

Since 1965, a number of articles have been published in which case series are described and fetal survival rates included (*Table 16.1*). What is clear from these papers is that careful selection and monitoring of patients can lead to extremely good outcomes. Patients serve as controls and are compared against survival rates in the same patients before and after they had the transabdominal cervical cerclage operation. Although this is a historically impressive way of showing the success rate of a procedure, evidence-based practice demands that the efficacy of the procedure must be compared to no cerclage or transvaginal cerclage in a randomised controlled clinical trial. Understandably, there are ethical objections to this approach in terms of patient acceptability, unachievable power calculations and patient recruitment for a small defined group and the need for a multicentre collaboration.

Table 16.1: Published case series of transabdominal cervical cerclage operation with results and indications for cerclage included

Authors	Year	No. of patients	No. of pregnancies	Indications for cerclage	Fetal survival before cerclage	Fetal survival after cerclage
Benson and Durfee	1965	10	13	If transvaginal cerclage is impossible due to shape of cervix	11%	82%
Mahran M	1978	10	10	Shape of cervix and hx of failed transvaginal cerclage	10%	70%
Novy	1982	16	22	Shape of cervix	24%	95%
Olsen and Tobiassen	1982	17	17	Past obs hx and shape of cervix	12%	88%
Herron and Parer	1988	8	13	Shape of cervix and failed vaginal cerclage	15%	85%
Gibb and Salaria	1995	50	61	Shape of cervix, or previous failed vaginal cerclage	18%	93%
Cammarano, Herron and Parer	1995	23	29	Shape of cervix, or previous failed vaginal cerclage	18%	93%
Craig and Fliegner	1997	12 (8 preconcept)	14	History and failed Cx suture	17.8%	69%
Anthony *et al*	1997	13	13	Previous failed vaginal suture or impossible to insert trans-vaginal suture	16%	86.6%
Davis *et al*	2000	82	96	Prior failed trans-vaginal cerclage	N/A	>82%

Unlike transvaginal cerclage, transabdominal cerclage involves laparotomy at ten weeks' gestation using a transverse suprapubic incision under general anaesthesia. The bladder peritoneal fold is dissected off the anterior aspect of the cervix. A suture is placed at the level of the uterine isthmus, medial to the uterine vessels through the body of the cervix (*Figures 16.1a, b*). In the series of operations to be described, the suture material was double stranded, 2 gauge ethilon.

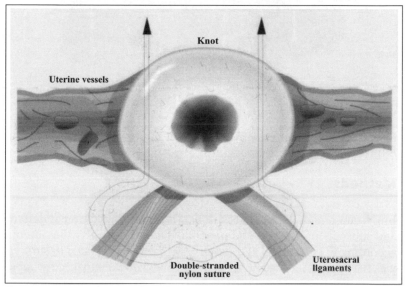

Figure16.1a: Pathway of suture insertion through cervical substance, avoiding blood vessels. Reproduced from Topping and Farquharson, 1995

The knot was tied anteriorly and covered by the loose peritoneal fold, from the initial dissection (Topping and Farquharson, 1995).

When first described, transabdominal cerclage was performed as an alternative to the transvaginal approach in those patients for whom this was not possible due to the shape and size of the cervix (Benson and Durfee, 1965; Novy, 1982). Such women included those with a history of operative intervention on the cervix, for example, a cone biopsy and those with a congenital absence or malformation of the cervix such as those with exposure to diethylstilbestrol in utero (Novy, 1982). Recently, as cone biopsies and diethylstilbestrol exposure history have become less common, obstetricians are concentrating far more on poor obstetric history and previous failed transvaginal cerclage as part of the decision-making process towards insertion of transabdominal suture.

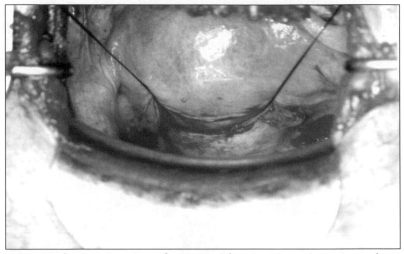

Figure16.1b: Anterior view of uterus with suture insertion prior to knot formation

Methods

Important outcome measures are live birth rate, gestation at delivery and subsequent survival and neonatal death. To stratify the outcome according to gestational age at delivery (intimately related to survival) was felt appropriate and hence was narrowed down into three groups:

- those delivered before thirty weeks
- those delivered at thirty to thirty-six weeks
- those delivered after thirty-six weeks.

The reasons for any preterm delivery were also examined.

Results

Of the twenty-four transabdominal cervical cerclage operations carried out, twenty-one (87%) resulted in a successful outcome, defined as a live birth with no ensuing neonatal death. However, not all these deliveries were at term.

The gestational age at delivery include five (21%) that took place below thirty weeks gestation ranging from twelve to twenty-nine weeks. Of these five deliveries, three ended with a poor outcome. One case suffered ruptured membranes and extreme preterm labour at twenty-four weeks and underwent an emergency Caesarean section. The infant died at three days of age from acute pulmonary haemorrhage and extreme prematurity. The second case underwent a spontaneous abortion at twelve weeks through a defect in the posterior fornix left as a result of previous transvaginal suture tear, preceeded by sudden onset of heavy fresh PV bleeding. The third case reported spontaneous rupture of membranes at seventeen weeks, followed by infection and chorioamnionitis. A hysterotomy was performed followed by control of infection, but the patient developed a tubo-ovarian abscess three months after hysterotomy, despite aggressive antibiotic administration. The other two deliveries before thirty weeks, progressed to twenty seven and twenty-nine weeks and both infants are doing well, although one suffers with Down's syndrome (*Table 16.2*).

Table 16.2: Outcome of pregnancies after transabdominal cervical cerclage

	Stillbirth/neo-natal death at gestation <30 weeks	Live birth at gestation <30 weeks	Live birth at gestation 30–36 weeks	Live birth at gestation >36 weeks	Total deliveries
No. of patients	3 (12%)	2 (8%)	7 (29%)	12 (50%)	24

Outcome after transabdominal cerclage

Between thirty and thirty-six weeks, seven women (29%) were delivered. This was for a variety of reasons including spontaneous rupture of membranes, preterm labour and intrauterine growth restriction. All infants subsequently did well. Twelve of the patients (50%) delivered at over thirty-six weeks, and all infants showed normal progress (*Figure 16.2*).

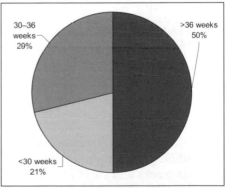

Figure 16.2: Proportion of deliveries at <30 weeks (n=5), 30–36 weeks (n=7) and >36 weeks (n=12) after 24 cases of insertion of transabdominal cervical cerclage

Pregnancy loss history

The patient group had suffered a combined loss of eighty-nine previous pregnancies that carried until the second trimester. Of those pregnancies, seventeen went on to live births. Only six of these infants lived until over one-year-old, two of whom died as a result of the chronic problems associated with prematurity. This gives a 7% live birth rate among the pregnancies that occurred before the transabdominal suture was inserted.

Associated pathology

Identification of known causes prior to conception had a direct impact on subsequent performance, especially preterm delivery (*Table 16.3*). Of the twenty-four patients, fifteen (60%) showed evidence of dual or greater pathology.

Table 16.3: Gestation at subsequent delivery according to identified cause and pathology

Pathology	Delivery at <30 weeks' gestation	Delivery at 30–36 weeks' gestation	Delivery at >36 weeks' gestation	Total
Cervical weakness alone	0	3	6	9
Cervical weakness and one other pathology	2	4	5	11
Two or more pathologies	3	0	1	4
Total	5	7	12	24

In the group of nine patients for which cervical weakness was the only pathology found on screening, three were delivered at thirty to thirty-six weeks and six (67%) were delivered over thirty-six weeks. Of those delivered in the thirty to thirty-six weeks group, one delivered at thirty-five weeks and two at thirty-six weeks.

In the eleven patients with cervical weakness in association with one other treated pathology, eg. bacterial vaginosis or antiphospholipid syndrome, two delivered before thirty weeks' gestation with one neonatal death in this group, four delivered between thirty and thirty-six weeks and five (45%) delivered after thirty-six weeks.

In the four patients with more than two pathologies, all had cervical weakness and antiphospholipid syndrome. Two were also positive for factor V Leiden mutation, one homozygous, one had a XXXY chromosomal abnormality and one also had bacterial vaginosis. Three of these patients delivered before thirty weeks' gestation, with two delivering at twelve and seventeen weeks due to spontaneous abortion. Only one of these patients (25%) delivered at over thirty-six weeks' gestation.

The presence of dual or greater pathology confirms higher risk status for preterm and extreme preterm delivery and poorer survival as a consequence. There was a 50% preterm delivery rate compared to a normative rate of 8% (LWH birth statistics, 1995–2000).

Growth restriction

Of the twenty-one deliveries, three neonates (12%) were below the third birth weight centile at delivery, with one requiring delivery at thirty-two weeks.

In total, six infants (25%) were delivered at or below the tenth centile. Of this group, two were delivered to mothers also positive for antiphospholipid syndrome. Of the fifteen delivered with no problems relating to weight, three (18%) were positive for antiphospholipid syndrome.

Discussion

These results show, as with other studies, that compared with past obstetric history, patients undergoing transabdominal cervical suture can have a much better chance of delivery at or near to term. By looking at the past histories of all the patients in this series, a live birth rate of 7% was calculated, excluding any first-trimester losses. By undergoing a transabdominal cerclage operation, this was increased to a live birth rate of 87%. However, only 50% of the deliveries occurred above thirty-six weeks. This indicates that 50% of the patients were delivered early, a much larger figure than that of the normal population. This was for a variety of reasons including the fetus being small for gestational age, antepartum fetal distress necessitating delivery, spontaneous rupture of membranes and premature labour.

Cervical weakness is a significant cause of mid-trimester miscarriage, but as discussed briefly earlier, other causal factors are involved. Reported studies looking at transabdominal cervical cerclage have concentrated on cervical weakness as the sole cause of miscarriage in these patients. It is likely that after insertion of a transabdominal cervical cerclage, cervical weakness is effectively treated and is therefore no longer a cause of premature delivery in these patients. Premature labour occurs in these cases despite the cerclage, indicating that there may be another cause for the recurrent miscarriage as well as the presence of cervical weakness. Five patients, delivered at less than thirty weeks' gestation, had been diagnosed with bacterial vaginosis and cervical weakness. The remaining three had cervical weakness and antiphospholipid syndrome as well as another pathology — bacterial vaginosis, factor V Leiden mutation and chromosome abnormality XXXY respectively.

Although mentioned earlier, there are other associations with recurrent miscarriage apart from those reported in this series. New and emerging causes such as activated protein C resistance may play a role in compounding pathology and contribute to increased morbidity. Further research needs to be carried out so that this effect on premature delivery can be elucidated.

Where cervical weakness was the only diagnosed cause of recurrent mid-trimester miscarriage, six of the nine patients delivered at over thirty-six weeks and three between thirty and thirty-six weeks. Despite falling into this category, this group all delivered at thirty-five weeks and above. Currently, infants delivered at these gestations are at a low risk of any major complications due to prematurity.

The presence of dual pathology should always be borne in mind when investigating cervical weakness. As 60% may have further pathology, the clinician must be ever vigilant, especially as antiphospholipid syndrome may arise de novo in pregnancy.

Although patients with both bacterial vaginosis and antiphospholipid syndrome were treated, there is some controversy surrounding treatments, especially for antiphospholipid syndrome (Bricker and Farquharson, 2000), and it is very likely that these conditions influence the pregnancy. It is known that the presence of antiphospholipid syndrome can increase the likelihood of infants that are small for gestational age (Bricker and Farquharson, 2000). This is observed in the present series although the numbers are too small for any conclusions to be made.

Transvaginal cervical cerclage remains controversial and some surgeons employ this approach more often than others (MRC/ RCOG, 1993). Results from the use of transabdominal cervical cerclage are so successful compared with those of the transvaginal approach that it may be that this procedure becomes more and more an acceptable alternative to transvaginal cerclage. The drawbacks are that this procedure necessitates two laparotomies; one for insertion of the stitch and one for the Caesarean section. However, the stitch can remain *in situ* in between pregnancies and there have been successful second and third pregnancies reported. It is possible to perform the procedure using laparoscopic techniques, which could reduce some of the risks involved (Scibetta *et al*, 1997; Lesser *et al*, 1998). There will be obvious reasons why this operation is not suitable for some patients, for example, hypercoagulable states, but in the main it is a viable alternative to the transvaginal approach.

As yet there have been no trials comparing the use of transabdominal cerclage with transvaginal. One highly selective study attempted to look retrospectively at women with a history of recurrent miscarriage and a failed transvaginal suture (Davis *et al*, 2000). All underwent either a further transvaginal suture insertion or insertion of a transabdominal suture. Assignment to either group was at the discretion of the authors. They found that delivery at <35 weeks occurred significantly less frequently in the transabdominal cerclage group compared with the transvaginal cerclage. No randomisation took place and there was no investigation into other causes of mid-trimester miscarriage.

A randomised study is required to look at the benefits of transabdominal cerclage over transvaginal. If it is shown that it is more effective, perhaps with the aid of cervical ultrasound to assess cervical length, it may be that in the future transabdominal cervical cerclage will be the first line of treatment for some patients with a history of mid-trimester loss.

In summary, this is an extremely useful operation when indicated. It is important that all patients are screened thoroughly before and after conception and treated appropriately as it is possible that cervical weakness could exist concurrently with one or more causes for mid-trimester loss.

The authors wish to thank Annie Ward for her diligence and valuable contribution to the production of the audit and chapter.

References

Anthony GS, Walker RG, Cameron AD, Price JL, Walker JJ, Calder AA (1997) Transabdominal cervico-isthmic cerclage in the management of cervical incompetence. *Eur J Obstet Gynaecol* **72**: 127–30

Benson RC, Durfee RB (1965) Transabdominal cervicouterine cerclage during pregnancy for the treatment of cervical incompetency. *Obstet Gynaecol* **25**: 145–55

Bricker L, Farquharson RG (2000) Recurring miscarriage. *The Obstetrician and Gynaecologist*, RCOG Press **2**(4): 17–23

Caruso A, Trivellini C, De Carolis S, Paradisi G, Mancuso S, Ferrazzani S (2000) Emergency cerclage in the presence of protruding membranes: Is pregnancy outcome predicable? *Acta Obstet Gynecol Scand* **79**: 265–8

Cammarano CL, Herron MA, Parer JT (1995) Validity for transabdominal cervicoisthmic cerclage for cervical incompetence. *Am J Obstet Gynaecol* **172**(6): 1871–5

Craig S, Fliegner JRH (1997) Treatment of cervical incompetence by trans-abdominal cervicoisthmic cerclage. *Aust NZ J Obstet Gynaecol* **37**(4): 407–11

Davis G, Berghella V, Talucci M, Wapner RJ (2000) Patients with a prior failed transvaginal cerclage: A comparison of obstetric outcomes with either transabdominal or transvaginal cerclage. *Am J Obstet Gynecol* **183**(4): 836–9

Drakeley AJ, Quenby S, Farquharson RG 1998 Mid-trimester loss — appraisal of a screening protocol. *Hum Reprod* **13**(7): 1975–80

Flint H, Gibb DMF (1996) Recurrent second trimester miscarriage. *Curr Opin Obstet Gynaecol* **8**: 449–53

Gibb DMF, Salaria DA (1995) Transabdominal cervicoisthmic cerclage in the management of recurrent second trimester miscarriage and preterm delivery. *Br J Obstet Gynaecol* **102**: 802–6

Herron MA, Parer JT (1988) Transabdominal cerclage for fetal wastage due to fetal incompetence. *Obstet Gynaecol* **71**(6,1): 865–7

Iams JD, Goldenberg RL, Meis PJ, Mercer BM, Moawad A, Das A *et al* (1996) The length of the cervix and the risk of spontaneous premature delivery. *New Engl J Med* **334**(9): 567–72

Lesser KB, Childers JM, Surwit EA (1998) Transabdominal cerclage: a laparoscopic approach. *Obstet Gynaecol* **91**(5, 2): 855–6

MacDonald IA (1957) Suture of the cervix for inevitable miscarriage. *J Obstet Gynaecol Br Emp* **64**: 346–53

Mahran M (1978) Transabdominal cervical cerclage during pregnancy. *Obstet Gynaecol* **52**(4): 502–6

MRC/RCOG Working party on cervical cerclage (1993) Final report of the Medical Research Council/Royal College of Obstetricians and Gynaecologists Multicentre Randomised Trial of Cervical Cerclage. *Br J Obstet Gynaecol* **100**: 516–23

Novy MJ (1982) Transabdominal cervicoisthmic cerclage for the management of repetitive abortion and premature delivery. *Am J Obstet Gynecol* **143**(1): 44–54

Olka J, Lesinski J (1967) Shirodkar's procedure in cervical incompetence. *Am J Obstet Gynecol* **97**: 13–16

Olsen S, Tobiassen T (1982) Transabdominal isthmic cerclage for the treatment of incompetent cervix. *Acta Obstet Gynaecol Scand* **61**: 473–5

Rust OA, Atlas RO, Jones KJ, Benham BN, Balducci J (2000) A randomised trial of cerclage versus no cerclage among patients with ultrasonographically detected second-trimester preterm dilatation of the internal os. *Am J Obstet Gynecol* **183**(4): 830–5

Scibetta JJ, Sanko SR, Phipps WR (1997) Laparoscopic transabdominal cervicoisthmic cerclage. *Fertil Steril* **69**(1): 161–3

Seppälä M, Vara P (1970) Cervical cerclage in the treatment of incompetent cervix. *Acta Obstet Gynecol Scand* **49**: 343–6

Sietske MA, Dekker GA, van Geijn HP, Bekedam DJ, Hummel P (2000) Cervical incompetence prevention randomized cerclage trial (CIPRACT): Study design and preliminary results. *Am J Obstet Gynecol* **183**(4): 823–9

Topping J, Farquharson RG (1995) Transabdominal cervical cerclage. *Br J Hosp Med* **54**(10): 510–12

17

Activated protein C resistance in pregnancy

Arvind K Arumainathan, Roy G Farquharson, Cheng Hok Toh

The term thrombophilia is used to define a group of disorders in which there is a predisposition to thrombosis due to abnormally enhanced coagulation (Simmons, 1997). Pregnancy induces a hyper-coagulable state, due to an increase in circulating procoagulants, venous damage, and venous stasis.

The coagulation system is a thrombin generator. Thrombin generation is a complex enzymatic biological amplification network. The process is dependent on the assembly of macromolecular enzymatic complexes assembled on negatively charged phospholipid surfaces with non-enzymatic co-factors forming the foundation stones. The negatively charged phospholipid surface is provided by activated platelets and the activated non-enzymatic cofactors (Factors Va and VIIIa) are the foundation stones. The cofactors are substrates for activated protein C (APC). Protein C is a natural anticoagulant by its inactivation of Factor Va and VIIIa by proteolysis. On activation by thrombin, a complex is formed between thrombin, thrombomodulin, protein C, and protein S (*Figure 17.1*). Protein C is the key component of the protein C system and is a vitamin K dependent, liver-produced protein.

The association of procoagulant conditions, such as anti-phospholipid syndrome (APS), and pregnancy loss is well established. More recently, activated protein C resistance (APCR) has been discovered to be associated with recurring pregnancy loss in a small number of cases. Consideration of other thrombophilias, such as protein C and protein S deficiency and hyperhomocysteinaemia has brought further attention to an emerging area of aetiology in the appearance of serious obstetric outcome including intrauterine death in pregnancy.

In 1993, Dahlback *et al* described a previously unknown thrombo-philia in which activated factor V is resistant to inactivation by APC. This condition is known as activated protein C resistance (APCR). Subsequently, a point mutation in the factor V gene was discovered (substitution of Arg with Gln at nucleotide 506) which codes for activated factor V resistant to APC-mediated inactivation (Bertina *et al*, 1994). This mutation is known as Factor V Leiden (FVL).

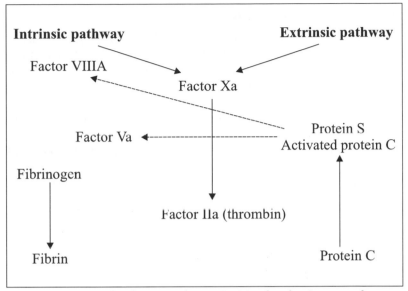

Figure 17.1: The role of activated protein C in the clotting cascade

The prevalence of FVL has been reported as varying between 3% and 7% among white Europeans, and significantly less in other ethnic groups (Rees *et al*, 1995). The UK prevalence has been reported as 3.5% (Beauchamp *et al*, 1994). Lindqvist *et al* (1999) suggested that the high prevalence of this mutation might in fact be an evolutionary mechanism to prevent excessive blood loss in child-birth, as they found that carriers of the mutation experienced significantly less blood loss postpartum than controls. However, APCR is also seen in non-carriers, and is commonly reported in patients on oral contraceptives and in pregnancy (Hellgren *et al*, 1995).

APCR carries an increased risk for venous thromboembolism. For carriers of FVL, the risk of venous thromboembolism (VTE) is reported as 5–10x in heterozygotes, and 100x in homozygotes (Rosendaal *et al*, 1995).

The link between APCR and adverse pregnancy outcome is currently a subject of interest. For this chapter, a Medline search using the keywords 'Activated protein C resistance AND pregnancy' and 'Factor V Leiden AND pregnancy' was carried out. This produced a total of 274 matches. A selection of these is reviewed here.

APCR during normal pregnancy

Functional APCR is diagnosed using the APTT based assay, and is expressed as a ratio. A significant decrease in APC activity in the second and third trimesters of pregnancy in a study of 128 normal patients (Walker *et al*, 1997) has been reported confirmed in a smaller group of twenty healthy women, screened during pregnancy and at eight weeks postpartum (Cumming *et al*, 1995). In addition, the ratios obtained postpartum were used as a baseline for non-pregnant levels, and were significantly higher than in the pregnant state.

In turn, this led to the conclusion that a certain degree of physiological APCR occurs in pregnancy, regardless of whether a Leiden mutation is present, and related this to the physiological increase in Factor VIII and decrease in protein S that is observed in pregnancy.

APCR and abnormal pregnancy outcome

Several adverse pregnancy outcomes have been sporadically associated with APCR, including recurrent miscarriage or fetal loss, pre-eclampsia, placental abruption, and prematurity.

Pregnancy loss

The relationship between APCR and miscarriage remains unclear. Case-control studies have suggested a strong link (Brenner *et al*, 1997; Younis *et al*, 2000a; *Table 17.1*). Of a total of 184 pregnancies, only thirty-four (18%) resulted in live births, of which eleven (32%) were premature deliveries. None of the controls had a pregnancy loss, which is in stark contrast to a prospective observational study of a similar idiopathic group with recurring miscarriage, where a 20% embryo loss and 5% fetal loss rate can be expected (Brigham *et al*, 1999).

Table 17.1: APCR in recurrent miscarriage				
Study	**APCR**		**FVL**	
	Cases	**Controls**	**Cases**	**Controls**
Brenner, 1997	28/39, 71%	?/40	19/39, 47%	?/40
Younis, 2000a	30/78, 38%	11/139, 8%	15/78, 19%	8/139, 6%
Rai, 1996 (2nd trimester only)	10/50, 20%	3/70, 4.3%		
Balasch, 1997	1/55, 1.8%	1/50, 2.0%	1/55, 1.8%	1/50, 2.0%

Further studies have shown that patients with APCR (either Leiden-positive or acquired) were significantly more likely than controls to suffer a pregnancy loss either in the first trimester (17/48 against 25/214) or in the second trimester (10/48 against 14/214) (Tal *et al*, 1999). A link between APCR and second-trimester miscarriage only has been reported where functional APCR was found in 20% (10/50) women with second-trimester miscarriage, 4.7% (4/70) women with first-trimester miscarriage, and 4.3% (3/70) in their controls (Rai *et al*, 1996; *Table 17.1*). Although these reports can be criticised for selection bias there is a reasonable platform to suggest that APCR is related to fetal loss after ten weeks' gestation. This makes mandatory testing for APCR essential in the investigation of intrauterine death, along with the commoner thrombophilia of antiphospholipid syndrome.

Failure to demonstrate any link between miscarriage and APCR has added further confusion. From their multi-centre, retrospective study of women with inherited thrombophilias, Preston *et al* (1996) reported that the odds ratio of miscarriage for women with the Leiden mutation was similar to that of their controls (odds ratio 0.9, 95% CI 0.5–1.5). Similarly, Balasch *et al* (1997; *Table 17.1*) undertook a case-control study of fifty-five women with first-trimester miscarriage and fifty controls. From each set of subjects, less than 2% of cases or controls tested positive for APCR, and both patients were subsequently shown to be heterozygous for FVL. Dizon-Townson *et al* (1997) investigated forty couples with a history of recurrent miscarriage and twenty-five couples with >7 live births. There were no differences in prevalence of APCR or the Leiden mutation in either group

It appears that APCR has a stronger link with mid-trimester loss. A prospective study involving thirty-eight subjects who had suffered recent intrauterine death, found that nineteen (50%) had functional (Leiden-negative) APCR in the non-pregnant state (personal communication). McColl *et al* (1999) suggested that while first-trimester miscarriage reflects a failure in implantation, second-trimester loss probably points to a thrombotic event within the placenta, involving impaired development and function due to a compromised vascular support system.

Adverse late pregnancy outcome.

Vascular wall damage occurs in pregnancy, and the presence of a thrombophilia exacerbates this phenomenon. Excessive vascular damage to the placental blood vessels impairs vascular support to the fetus. This mechanism has been put forward to explain the links that have been demonstrated between APCR and intrauterine growth restriction (IUGR), prematurity, pre-eclampsia, and stillbirth (*Table 17.2*).

Table 17.2: FVL prevalence in studies documenting pre-eclampsia, IUGR, and stillbirth and abruption		
Study	**FVL**	
	Cases	**Controls**
Erhardt, 2000 — prematurity	9/50, 18%	6.3% (population)
IUGR	4/56, 7.2%	6.3% (population)
Dizon-Townson, 1996	14/158, 8.9%	17/403, 4.2%
Kupferminc, 1999 — overall	22/110, 20%	7/110, 6%

Erhardt *et al* (2000; *Table 17.2*) reported associations between APCR and prematurity, and APCR and IUGR. They found FVL in 18% (9/50) mothers of premature infants, and 7.2% (4/56) of mothers with growth-retarded fetuses. The former is markedly higher than the prevalence of FVL in Hungary (6.3%), where the study was carried out.

Kupferminc *et al* (1999, see *Tables 17.2* and *17.3*) performed a case-control study of 110 women with a history of severe pre-eclampsia, abruption, IUGR, or stillbirth, selected from a tertiary referral centre for high risk obstetrics. They found FVL in 22% of the cases, and 6% of the controls. Not surprisingly, they found statistically significant odds ratios for FVL and stillbirth, IUGR, placental abruption, and severe pre-eclampsia.

Table 17.3: Summary of Kupferminc *et al*, 1999	
Complication	**N, Odds ratio (95% CI) of FVL in cases against controls**
Pre-eclampsia	9/34, 5.3 (1.8–15.6)
IUGR	5/44, 1.9 (0.6–6.3)
Stillbirth	3/12, 4.9 (1.1–22.3)
Placental abruption	5/20, 4.9 (1.4–17.4)

In addition, Preston *et al* (1996) found an odds ratio of 2:0 (95% CI 0.5–7.7) for FVL in women who experienced a stillbirth.

Dizon-Townson *et al* (1996; *Table 17.2*) found that 8.9% (14/158) of their sample of women with severe pre-eclampsia were Leiden-positive, as compared with 4.2% (17/403) of the controls.

Maternal thrombosis (*Table 17.4*)

Table 17.4: APCR and thrombosis in pregnancy				
Study	APCR		APCR	
	Cases	Controls	Cases	Controls
Gerhardt, 2000			52/119, 44%	18/233, 8%
Hellgren, 1995	20/34, 60%	6/57, 10%		
Kupferminc, 2000			4/12, 33%	1/24, 4%
Hallak, 1997			7/15, 46.6%	

An increased incidence of venous thrombotic events in pregnancy, such as pulmonary embolism, deep venous thrombosis, and transient ischaemic attacks, is also seen with APCR. Hallak *et al* (1997; *Table 17.4*) studied fifteen subjects with a venous thromboembolic event during pregnancy or the puerperium, and discovered that seven of the fifteen were Leiden-positive. Kupferminc *et al* (2000; *Table 17.4*) reported an increased incidence of FVL in women who had a transient neurological deficit in pregnancy. Hellgren *et al* (1995; *Table 17.4*) found that 60% (20/34) of women with a history of VTE in pregnancy had functional APCR, as opposed to 10% of the fifty-seven controls. Gerhardt *et al* (2000; *Table 17.4*) found an increased incidence of the Leiden mutation in women with histories of VTE.

Deep venous thrombosis is the most common clinical manifestation of the factor V mutation and APC resistance but with a lower risk of pulmonary embolism than with other thombophilias (Baglin *et al*, 1997; Manten *et al*, 1996).

Screening

There is general agreement that population based screening programmes for APCR and FVL are unnecessary at this time (Rouse *et al*, 1997; Spina *et al*, 2000). However, certain groups of women would certainly benefit from thrombophilia screens. Principal among these are women who have suffered a previous thrombotic event such as deep venous thrombosis or transient ischaemic attack, either in pregnancy or in the non-pregnant state. In addition, there are clear clinical indications to screen women who suffer from poor obstetric outcomes, especially with cases of stillbirth and fetal death.

Treatment

To date there have been no controlled trials of the treatment of APCR or FVL in pregnancy. Thromboprophylaxis with anticoagulant therapy in pregnancy may utilise unfractionated heparin 10000IU twice daily or, preferably with low-molecular-weight heparin, 5000IU dalteparin or 40mg enoxaparin SC daily. Doses may need to be adjusted to body weight (Greer, 1999). In a small study, Younis *et al* (2000) administered 100mg aspirin and 40mg enoxaparin daily to seven FVL carriers who suffered from recurrent miscarriage. Five of the seven progressed uneventfully to delivery at term, and two suffered missed abortions.

Further evaluation of treatment intervention during pregnancy remains to be done in terms of pregnancy outcome, maternal dose response to LMWH and appropriate evidence-based practice.

References

Baglin T, Brown K, Williamson D (1997) Relative risk of pulmonary embolism and deep venous thrombosis in association with factor V leiden in a UK population. *Thromb Haemost* **77**: 1219

Balasch H, Reverter JC, Fabregues F (1997) First-trimester repeated abortion is not associated with activated protein C resistance. *Hum Reprod* **12**: 1094–7

Bertina RM, Koelemans BP, Koster T *et al* (1994) Mutation in blood coagulation factor V associated with resistance to activated protein C. *Nature* **369**: 64–7

Beauchamp NJ, Daly ME, Hampton KK *et al* (1994) High prevalence of a mutation in the Factor V gene within the UK population: relationship to activated protein C resistance and familial thrombosis. *Br J Haematol* **88**: 219–22

Brenner B, Mandel H, Lanir N *et al* (1997) Activated protein C resistance can be associated with recurrent fetal loss. *Br J Haematol* **97**: 551–4

Brigham S, Conlon C, Farquharson RG (1999) A longitudinal study of pregnancy outcome following idiopathic recurring miscarriage. *Hum Reprod* **14**: 2868–71

Cumming AM, Tait RC, Fildes S *et al* (1995) Development of resistance to activated protein C during pregnancy. *Br J Haematol* **90**: 725–7

Dahlback B, Carlsson M, Svensson PJ (1993) Familia thrombophilia due to a previously unrecognised mechanism characterized by poor anticoagulant response to activated protein C: Prediction of a cofactor to activated protein C. *Proceedings of the National Academy of Sciences* **90**: 1004–8

Dizon-Townson DS, Nelson LM, Easton BS *et al* (1996) The factor V Leiden mutation may predispose women to sever pre-eclampsia. *Am J Obstet Gynecol* **175**: 902–5

Dizon-Townson DS, Kinney S, Branch DW *et al* (1997) The factor V Leiden mutation is not a common cause of recurrent miscarriage. *J Reprod Immunol* **34**: 217–23

Erhardt E, Stankovics J, Molnar D *et al* (2000) High prevalence of Factor V Leiden mutation in mothers of premature neonates. *Biol Neonate* **78**:145–6

Gerhardt A, Scharf RE, Beckmann MW *et al* (2000) Prothrombin and factor V mutations in women with a history of thrombosis during pregnancy and the puerperium. *New Engl J Med* **342**: 374 80

Greer IA (1999) Thrombosis in pregnancy: maternal and fetal issues. *Lancet* **353**: 1258–65

Hallak M, Senderowicz J, Cassel A *et al* (1997) Activated protein C resistance (factor V Leiden) associated with thrombosis in pregnancy. *Am J Obstet Gynecol* **176**: 889–93

Hellgren M, Svensson PJ, Dahlback B (1995) Resistance to activated protein C as a basis for venous thromboembolism associated with pregnancy and oral contraceptives. *Am J Obstet Gynecol* **175**: 210–13

Kupferminc MJ, Eldor A, Steinman N *et al* (1999) Increased frequency of genetic thrombophilia in women with complications of pregnancy. *New Engl J Med* **340**: 9–13

Kupferminc MJ, Yair D, Bornstein ND *et al* (2000) Transient focal neurological deficits during pregnancy in carriers of inherited thrombophilia. *Stroke* **31**: 892–5

Lindqvist PG, Svensson PJ, Marsaal K *et al* (1999) Activated protein C resistance (FV:Q506) and pregnancy. *Thromb Haemost* **81**: 532–7

Manten B, Westendorp R, Koster T (1996) Risk factor profiles in patients with different clinical manifestations of venous thromboembolism: a focus on the factor V leiden mutation. *Thromb Haemost* **76**: 510–13

McColl MD, Walker ID, Greer IA (1999) The role of inherited thrombophilia in venous thromboembolism associated with pregnancy. *Br J Obstet Gynaecol* **106**: 756–66

Preston FE, Rosendaal FR, Walker ID *et al* (1996) Increased fetal loss in women with heritable thrombophilia. *Lancet* **348**: 913–6

Rai R, Regan L, Hadley E *et al* (1996) Second-trimester pregnancy loss is associated with activated protein C resistance. *Br J Haematol* **92**: 489–90

Rees DC, Cox M, Clegg JB (1995) World distribution of Factor V Leiden. *Lancet* **346**: 1133–4

Rosendaal FR, Koster T, Vandenbroucke JP *et al* (1995) High risk of thrombosis in patients homozygous for factor V Leiden. *Blood* **85**: 1504–8

Rouse DJ, Goldberg RL, Wenstrom KD (1997) Antenatal screening for factor V Leiden mutation: a critical appraisal. *Obstet Gynecol* **90**: 848–51

Simmons A (1997) *Hematology: a combined theoretical and combined approach.* 2nd edn. Butterworth-Heineman, Massachusetts

Spina V, Aleandrini V, Morini F (2000) The impact of factor V Leiden on pregnancy. *Hum Reprod Update* **6**: 301–6

Tal J, Schliamser LM, Leibovitz Z *et al* (1999) A possible role for activated protein C resistance in patients with first and second trimester pregnancy failure. *Hum Reprod* **14**: 1624–7

Walker MC, Garner PR, Keely EJ *et al* (1997) Changes in activated protein C resistance during normal pregnancy. *Am J Obstet Gynecol* **177**: 162–9

Younis JS, Brenner B, Ohel G *et al* (2000a) Activated protein C resistance and Factor V Leiden mutation can be associated with first as well as second-trimester recurrent pregnancy loss. *Am J Reprod Immunol* **43**: 31–5

Younis JS, Ohel G, Brenner B *et al* (2000b) The effect of thromboprophylaxis on pregnancy outcome in patients with pregnancy loss associated with factor V Leiden mutation. *Br J Obstet Gynaecol* **107**: 415–19

18

Bone density changes with pregnancy and heparin

Andrew Carlin, Roy G Farquharson, William Fraser

The effect of pregnancy on bone structure and bone turnover has become a focus for recent research as bone thinning (osteoporosis) is such an important health issue later in women's lives. Osteoporosis is a systemic skeletal disease characterised by low bone mass and microarchitectural alterations associated with increased fragility and susceptibility to fractures. During pregnancy, bone remodelling is uncoupled with a marked increase in bone resorption (Black *et al*, 2000) as well as alteration of bone architecture (Shahtaheri *et al*, 1999). Osteoporotic fracture in pregnancy is an alarming condition, yet, fortunately, it is rare and sporadic in frequency. To understand the superimposed effect of bone losing therapy, such as corticosteroids and heparin, on maternal bone, we must first study the effect of pregnancy on maternal bone metabolism.

Osteoporosis and pregnancy

The diagnosis of osteoporosis of pregnancy has historically been made by a cluster of case reports, which draw attention to the typical patient presentation. As vertebral fracture, causing back pain and occasionally loss of height is the commonest case scenario, the maternal spine, containing trabecular bone, is the most frequent area affected. Presentation is seen in the third trimester and after delivery of the first child (Smith *et al*, 1995).

What happens to bone in pregnancy?

An interesting and vital clue to the understanding of bone metabolism in pregnancy came from a contemporaneous, but non-sequential, study of bone biopsy analysis in the first and third trimester of pregnancy (Purdie *et al*, 1988). These authors showed clear evidence that the bone response to pregnancy is biphasic with early bone resorption and later bone formation.

A larger prospective observational study starting pre-conceptually yielded further discriminatory changes in maternal bone metabolism (Black *et al*, 1996, 2000). These authors showed further proof of the biphasic uncoupling of bone resorption (starting early first trimester) with later bone formation (starting in third trimester) with subsequent reduction in bone mineral density of the maternal spine in normal untreated pregnancy (*Figure 18.1*). This study showed that bone resorption markers increased immediately in the first trimester and continued to rise until delivery. In contrast, bone formation markers remained at pre-pregnancy levels until twenty-two weeks' gestation, then increased until delivery. Prospective evaluation of maternal spine bone density showed a fall of 3.6% on average (range 0–12) between pre-conceptual and immediate postnatal measurements.

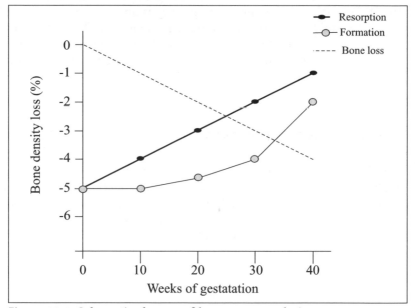

Figure 18.1: Schematic changes of bone turnover during pregnancy

The effect of pregnancy on bone density is seen to be divided into two separate areas, with regard to osteoporosis. Pregnancy causes bone demineralisation in women with a previous normal skeleton. In addition, for a small number of pregnant women with osteoporotic consequences, pregnancy is a stress that unmasks a defective maternal skeleton. This latter theory is supported by an epidemiological study, which showed that mothers of patients with idiopathic osteoporosis of pregnancy had a higher prevalence of fractures compared with controls (Dunne *et al*, 1993).

Heparin and pregnancy

Early case reports have led to the causal association of long-term heparin therapy and the development of osteoporosis. A study of heparin prophylaxis in a large population of 184 women found evidence of symptomatic vertebral fractures in 2.2% (Dahlman *et al*, 1993) where the minimum duration of exposure was seven weeks (range 7–27 weeks). This large retrospective study led in turn to a prospective study of thirty-nine patients and thirty-four controls, starting at twelve and sixteen weeks respectively, using forearm bone density measured by single photon absorptiometry, followed by a postnatal measurement (Dahlman *et al*, 1994). There were no significant changes or differences between the two groups in the assessment of cortical bone (one third from the distal end of the forearm). Assessment of trabecular bone (spine-like) at the ultra-distal end of the forearm showed a 4.9% reduction with heparin and a background physiological loss of 2.3% in the control group. Their conclusion was that trabecular (spine-like) bone was more affected by pregnancy and by heparin than cortical bone (hip-like), although the baseline measurement was taken after active bone resorption from the first trimester had already commenced.

Further evidence of a trabecular bone effect was shown by prospective study of seventeen heparin patients and eight controls during pregnancy (Shefras and Farquharson, 1996). These authors showed a lumbar spine loss of 5.2% in the heparin thrombo-prophylaxis group compared to a 3.1% reduction in the control group between preconceptual and immediate postnatal readings.

Studies of hip (cortical bone) bone density during pregnancy with heparin thromboprophylaxis showed significant loss in approximately 30% of patients (Barbour *et al*, 1994). This study used a shorter window of gestation for observation, starting at thirty weeks' gestation until a postnatal measurement. A greater than 10% decrease from baseline proximal femur measurement contrasted sharply with no loss recorded for the control group as, by this gestation, pregnancy-induced bone formation had caught up with constant bone resorption started in the first trimester. In addition, no dose-response relationship could be demonstrated, which is a consistent finding for many authors (Dahlman *et al*, 1994). A significant problem for clinicians is the use of hip measurement, which carries a precision of 3%, whereas the lumbar spine has a precision of measurement of 1%. When dealing with small changes in percentage, these values of precision assume significant meaning in data interpretation. Standardisation of reference values continue to improve with standard setting and consensus agreement (Kanis *et al*, 1994; Simmons *et al*, 1997)

At present, there has been no longitudinal prospective bone turnover marker study in pregnancy, comparing controls and heparin patients, but an ongoing study will hopefully report preliminary findings in the future.

Type of heparin

The development and use of low molecular weight heparin preparations (LMWH) (molecular weight less than 15,000 Daltons) has led to the possibility of a bone-sparing effect. An early study on a non-pregnant rat population suggested that the osteopenic effect of heparin was less with LMWH, compared to unfractionated heparin preparations (1,000–150,000 Daltons) (Monreal *et al*, 1990).

The use of LMWH in pregnancy has been shown to be effective and safe and without harm to the mother or fetus (Nelson-Piercy *et al*, 1997). Their advantage is that an equigravimetric dose is not required to produce an equivalent thromboprophylactic effect and such a reduced dose can be given less frequently, eg. one daily injection (Fejgin and Lourwood, 1994). Clinical experience and publication of LMWH studies are limited, but their safety and effectiveness in thromboprophylaxis and treatment during pregnancy seems equivalent (Shefras and Farquharson, 1996; Granger and Farquharson, 1997).

Studies with low molecular weight heparin in pregnancy provide reassurance that there seems to be no significant difference in bone density loss, effectiveness or safety over UFH, other than reduced dosage and improved patient acceptability with reduced frequency of administration (Rai *et al*, 1997, Dahlman *et al*, 1993, Backos *et al*, 1999).

Discussion

In conclusion, heparin thromboprophylaxis in pregnancy is effective and safe in a high risk population, whether LMWH or UFH is used. In large series, the reported incidence of venous thromboembolism is of the order of 3%–4% (Dahlman, 1993; Granger and Farquharson, 1997). Although not clearly assessed, patient compliance with LMWH is probably better, in view of a once daily injection.

The development of osteoporosis in pregnancy, associated with heparin use, is probably low, but, in a genetically disposed mother, heparin and pregnancy may both create an abnormal stress load in a susceptible individual. Pre-pregnancy bone density measurement and the detection of an existing low bone density reading would seem mandatory in a patient utilising heparin thromboprophylaxis during pregnancy. Further prospective studies are needed to target an at-risk population for osteoporosis and to assess the avoidance of osteoporosis by implementation of treatment modalities.

Key points

* Osteoporosis in pregnancy is a rare condition.
* Heparin therapy can cause osteoporosis when used long term.
* In a genetically susceptible population, the combination of pregnancy and heparin can unmask a defective maternal skeleton.
* A prospective physiological study of bone metabolism in pregnancy is needed.

References

Backos M, Rai R, Thomas E (1999) Bone density changes in pregnant women treated with heparin: a prospective, longitudinal study. *Hum Reprod* **14**: 2876–80

Barbour L, Kick S, Steiner J, Loverde ME *et al* (1994) A prospective study of heparin induced osteoporosis in pregnancy using bone densitometry. *Am J Obstet Gynaecol* **170**: 862–9

Black AJ, Topping J, Farquharson RG, Fraser WD (1996) Bone metabolism in pregnancy. *Contemp Rev Obstet Gynecol* **8**: 192–6

Black AJ, Topping J, Durham B, Farquharson RG, Fraser WD (2000) A detailed assessment of alterations in bone turnover, calcium homeostasis, and bone density in normal pregnancy. *J Bone Miner Res* **15**: 557–63

Dahlman TC (1993) Osteoparotic fractures and the recurrence of thromboembolism during pregnancy and puerperium in 184 women undergoing thromboprophylaxis with heparin. *Am J Obstet Gynecol* **168**: 1265–70

Dahlman TC *et al* (1994) Bone mineral density during long-term prophylaxis with heparin in pregnancy (prospective study). *Am J Obstet Gynecol* **170**: 1315–20

Dunne F, Walters B, Marshall T, Heath D (1993) Pregnancy-associated osteoporosis. *Clin Endocrinol* **39**: 487–90

Fejgin MD, Lourwood DL (1994) Low molecular weight heparins and their use in obstetrics and gynaecology. *Obstet Gynaecol Surg* **49**: 424–31

Granger K, Farquharson RG (1997) Obstetric outcome in antiphospholipid syndrome. *Lupus* **6**: 509–13

Kanis J, WHO study group (1994) Assessment of fracture risk and its application to screening for postmenopausal osteoporosis. *Osteoporosis Int* **4**: 368–81

Monreal M, Vimas L, Monreal L, Lavin S, Lafoz E, Angles AM (1990) Heparin-related osteoporosis in rats. *Haemostasis* **20**: 204–7

Nelson-Piercy C, Letsky E, de Swiet M (1997) Low molecular weight heparin for obstetric thromboprophylaxis: experience of sixty-nine pregnancies in sixty-one women at high risk. *Am J Obstet Gynecol* **176**: 1062–8

Purdie DW, Aaron JE, Selby PL (1988) Bone histology and mineral homeostasis in human pregnancy. *Br J Obstet Gynaecol* **95**: 849–54

Rai R, Cohen H, Regan L (1997) A randomised trial of aspirin versus aspirin and heparin during pregnancy in women with antiphospholipid antibodies. *Br Med J* **314**: 253–6

Shahtaheri SM, Aaron JE, Johnson DR, Purdie DW (1999) Changes in trabecular bone architecture in women during pregnancy. *Br J Obstet Gynaecol* **106**: 432–8

Simmons A, Simpson DE, Doherty MJ (1997) The effects of standardisation and reference values on patient classification for spine and femur DEXA. *Osteoporosis Int* **7**: 200–6

Shefras J, Farquharson RG (1996) Bone density studies in pregnant women receiving heparin. *Eur J Obstet Gynaecol* **65**: 171–4

Smith R, Athanasou NA, Ostlere SJM, Vipond SE (1995) Pregnancy-associated osteoporosis. *QJM* **88**: 865–78

Useful addresses

Miscarriage Association
c/o Clayton Hospital
Northgate
Wakefield WF1 3JS
Tel: 01924 200799
web site: www.the-ma.org.uk

Association of Early Pregnancy Units
Department of Obstetrics and Gynaecology
Llandough Hospital
Penlan Road
Penarth CF64 2XX
web site: www.earlypregnancy.org.uk

Ectopic Pregnancy Trust
Maternity Unit
Hillingdon Hospital
Pield Heath Road
Uxbridge
Middlesex B8 3NN
National help line: 01895 238025
web site: www.ectopic.org.uk